THE C[...]

Fiercely independent!

Each Avant✻Guide is created by independent experts who never accept discounts or payments in exchange for positive coverage.

Our visits to restaurants, clubs and other establishments are anonymous, and expenses are paid by Avant✻Guide.

Few Other Guidebooks Can Make This Claim.

AVANT GUIDE

New York City

EMPIRE PRESS

Empire ~ New York

EMPIRE PRESS MEDIA, INC.
New York

Email:	editor@avantguide.com
Web:	www.avantguide.com

Editor-in-Chief:	Dan Levine
Chief Writer:	Marilyn Wood
Photo Editor:	Liz Steger
Design:	>0< Mowshe = ßacosh + Gregorini + Klecek
Copy Editors:	Peter Metzenbaum, Andy Markowitz
Photography:	Liz Steger, Cali Alpert, NYCVB
Cover:	Bradley W. Whitmore/CVB
Back Cover:	Liz Steger
Digital Cartography:	Copyright © Empire Press Media, Inc.
Films:	Generace = 2H & Houmr

Very Special Thanks:
David Hershkovits, Peter Gatien, Cynthia Rowley,
Riad Nasr, Lee Hanson, Ondra Matya5,
Fran & Alan Levine, Petra Lustigová, Chronic,
Jonathan Pontell, Marilyn Wood, Mak Stehlik.

ISBN 1-891603-20-5
Third Edition

Printed in the Czech Republic
Distributed in North America by Publishers Group West

Also From Avant-Guide

Avant-Guide Orlando & Disney World
Avant-Guide Prague
Avant-Guide London
Avant-Guide San Francisco
Avant-Guide Paris
Avant-Guide New Orleans
Avant-Guide Amsterdam
Avant-Guide Las Vegas
Avant-Guide Toronto

Coming Soon

Avant-Guide Boston
Avant-Guide Washington, DC
Avant-Guide Barcelona
Avant-Guide Italy
Avant-Guide Cuba

Contents

Contents

#01 EnGaGinG

NEW YORK CiTY UNZiPPeD

The New York State of Mind

Avant-Guide New York City is designed to capture Manhattan as a snapshot does at a particular moment in time, including the good, the bad and the evil. It's a strange time to be a New Yorker. Confidence levels are shaken, services are being cut, the fiscally-minded Mayor is one of the least-popular in history and, even though it's unspoken, everyone harbors the fear of something else awful happening. At the same time, the city is stoic, going on because there is really no other choice. Everything is cyclical, right? And another upswing has to be right around the corner.

In a sense, everything has changed, while nothing has changed at all. This is still a fantastically rich city full with an obscene number of things to do. It's a city so big that no single person can take in the entire scene. The city is clean and relatively crime-free. There are tons of new restaurants and places in which to be entertained, and despite the drop on the NASDAQ, people are still building, spending, and partying hard.

Now, we suppose a lot of would-be clubbers and jay-walkers would disagree, but we're not worried about the long-term future of Manhattan or the "Disneyfication" of 42nd Street. It just 'aint that easy to tame Zoo York. (But, oh, how we pine for those heady days of yesterdecade when Times Square was full of pickpockets, porno parlors, and drop-outs pan handling for drug money!). So what if SoHo is now packed with celebutants, Mercer Street has become one of the priciest gutters in town and TriBeCa is full of Cab-Sauv swillers up from their Wall Street veal-fattening pens? There's still plenty New-Wave-A-York in which to roll around with the hygienically-challenged. New York remains real and is hardly in danger of slipping into ersatzery like a lot of other places we've seen. Safer, cleaner, kinder, gentler—yes. But, the "mallification of Manhattan?" We don't think so. As sure as Robbie Williams pounds his chest on the word "heart," the pornocrats will never be able to tame such a huge hodgepodge of millionaires, artists, belle boys, slackademics, breadlosers and born-against Christians.

We continue to embrace New York precisely because it's a big, demanding and neurotic place. Over abundance remains this city's strongest suit. London also has theater, LA also has film, Milan also has fashion, Tokyo also has finance, Paris also has art, Berlin also has clubs, but only New York has them all—in spades. This is not a city that honors bodies at rest. Unlike European cities, in which change and creativity are body-checked by the conventions of age, decorum, and tradition, New York is so gloriously unburdened by history that anything feels possible here. Raw competitiveness is the reason they say "if you can make it here..." well, you know the rest.

TAXI

011

The People

There are two kinds of natives in New York: the ones who were born here and the ones who were not. The ones who are native-born make up the majority of commuters; the millions of worker bees who flood in and out of Manhattan daily with the rising and the setting of the sun. They give the city roots and stability. But it's the energetic transplants, who give the city its dreams. The cream of the world's talent rises to the top and floats in from hometowns everywhere to this cultural kaleidoscope. New York is, as essayist EB White wrote, a magnet for "...the literary genius of Aurora High School, the most gifted actress in the Burlington dramatic club, a farm boy hoping to start for Wall Street." Even the panhandlers are talented. Step out your front door in the morning onto a busy Manhattan street and you feel like you've woken up in the middle of the world. In a sense, you have, because representatives from every nook and cranny of the globe are here.

The Personality

New York is not the biggest city in the world, it just feels like it. Standing on Sixth Avenue, in the middle of the skyscrapers lining the Corporate Canyon, it's easy to feel like the insignificant creature you are. The great European cities can make you feel unimportant by virtue of their age, but New York proclaims your irrelevance by virtue of its height. It's a strangely unnatural environment for human beings: There are few long vistas, the horizon is blocked, and the sun is often obscured so that much of the day is spent in the shadows–which is, perhaps, one of the reasons why Manhattan pulsates at night.

But it's also a difficult place to live for many marooned souls who have fallen through society's cracks and are at the butt end of all that is wrong with urban life. You frequently have to avert your eyes from the human misery that's played out on the city's streets. You have to thicken your skin so that you don't get too caught up emotionally by the homeless, the poor, the dispossessed, and the distraught.

The City Itself

The megalopolis is Manhattan-centric. That the East River is so named proves the point, since it is located west of the far more populous boroughs of Brooklyn and Queens. Manhattan is a 22-square mile (57-square km) protrusion of rock that rises just a few hundred feet above sea-level. The southern tip and the center of the island are solid granite, which is why Manhattan's tallest buildings are located in these two areas. Constrained by its geography, the island was forced to build up. Viewed from across the river, it looks like a single architectural entity—a stone, glass, and steel ship or a cathedral of stalactites.

Avant-New Yorker: David Hershkovits

David Hershkovits

is co-editor and publisher of *PAPER* magazine, New York's hippest monthly. He and partner Kim Hastreiter started the magazine 15 years ago and, together, have built it into the city's undisputed authority on the Downtown scene.

Avant*Guide_ Is the future of Downtown looking bright?

David Hershkovits_ The future has never looked better. Some people might say "it's over" because SoHo, for example, has been taken over by mega-stores and is turning into a huge upscale fashion mall. But commercially, it's vibrant. More than ever, Downtown is becoming its own little world.

A*G_ But, aren't you concerned about the "mallification" of SoHo?

D.H._ I am! The overall trend is not something I'd want, but I'm not going to go out and fight it. The worst thing that's happened is that it's become so expensive that young people are discouraged from coming here. Now the person who moves in is a little more advanced in their career; someone who can afford it more.

A*G_ Is New York better, now that it's "kinder and gentler" than it used to be?

D.H._ Well, New York's not as hard as it used to be. If you used to live on the Lower East Side, you put on your armor when you went out the door—and that created punk rock and a lot of art forms in reaction to it. It's really a much softer city now, and I don't think that it nurtures young talent as much as it used to. On the other hand, for people with jobs, [local employers] are paying a lot of money right now and you can go to restaurants and bars and have a really good time.

A*G_ If you were "King of Downtown" for a day, what would you do?

D.H._ I'd have a big street party where all the restricted cultures—rave music, drag queens, S&M, all of the worlds that are a very big part of New York living that people come here for, but that official New York pretends doesn't exist or doesn't really pay any attention to—let them all come out and have a big party and show everybody what New York's really made of. It's not Times Square or Disneyland, it's the people who come here with all these crazy ideas from all over the place looking for a community that will support them in the pursuit of their crazy ideas.

A*G_ What is *PAPER's* secret editorial mission?

D.H._ To cut through all the bullshit of what's going on out there. Multiculturalism is a big part of what we're trying to do: I think of the magazine as my utopia, where all people and ideas can live in harmony. You'd have a hard time getting those same people in the same room but, in the magazine at least, they can all come together.

N.Y.C By Numbers

Population

New York City	7,300,000
Manhattan	1,500,000
Bronx	1,200,000
Brooklyn	2,300,000
Queens	2,000,000
Staten Island	379,000
Tri-State Area	18,000,000

Area

New York City	301 sq. miles (485 sq. km)
Manhattan	22.7 sq. miles (36.5 sq. km)
Length	13.4 miles (21.5 km)
Width	2.3 miles (3.7 km) at widest point; .8 miles (1.3 km) at narrowest point

Religion

Catholic	43.4%
Jewish	10.9%
Baptist	10.7%
Agnostic	7.4%
Other Protestants	6.8%
Methodist	2.9%
Pentecostal	2.3%
Episcopalian	2.2%
Muslim	1.5%
Lutheran	1.3%
Presbyterian	1.2%
Other	9.4%

Ethicity

Caucasian	3,827,088
African-American	2,102,512
Hispanic	1,783,511
Asian	478,925
Native American	27,531
Pacific Islands	2,764
Other	852,714

Sources: NYCVB, PKF Consulting

History In a Hurry

1524 - First European explorer, Giovanni da Verrazzano, reaches New York Harbor.

1624 - First shipload of Dutch settlers arrives.

1625 - Settlement founded and named New Amsterdam.

1626 - Dutch Governor Peter Minuit "buys" Manhattan Island from the Indians for $24.

1664 - The Dutch surrender New Amsterdam to British troops without bloodshed; city is renamed New York.

1725 - The city's first newspaper, the *New York Gazette*, is founded

1754 - Founding of King's College, later renamed Columbia University.

1775 - Patriots take over city government, setting the stage for the Revolutionary War.

1776-81 - New York is the site of numerous battles and skirmishes during the War of Independence.

1783 - The British evacuate the city.

1784-96 - New York City serves as the state capital (later moved to Albany).

1812 - Construction of City Hall completed.

1834 - Brooklyn becomes a city.

1840-60 - Major wave of immigrants, especially Irish and Germans, nearly triple city's size to 800,000.

1844 - First city police force organized.

1846 - Telegraph service opens between NYC and Philadelphia.

1847 - City College of New York opens.

1856 - Land purchased for Central Park.

1861 - New York joins the Union cause under President Lincoln during the Civil War.

1865 - NYC Fire Department is founded.

1869 - Construction of Grand Central Station begins.

1870 - First subway opens on Broadway.

1877 - Alexander Graham Bell makes first interstate phone call from Fifth Avenue and 18th Street; President Rutherford B. Hayes opens Museum of Natural History.

1879	First telephone installed at the New York Stock Exchange.
1880	Metropolitan Museum of Art opens.
1883	Brooklyn Bridge links Brooklyn and Manhattan.
1886	Statue of Liberty dedicated in New York Harbor.
1891	Carnegie Hall opens.
1892	First immigrants arrive at Ellis Island.
1896	NY's first automobile accident.
1897	First cab company opens in New York City.
1898	Manhattan, Brooklyn, the Bronx, Queens and Staten Island join to become boroughs of NYC.
1902	Construction begins on the main branch of the New York Public Library.
1908	First New Year's Eve celebration held in Times Square.
1911	Fire at the Triangle Waist Company factory kills 141 people.
1927	Holland Tunnel opens.
1913	The 60-story Woolworth Building becomes the tallest in the country.
1931	Empire State Building completed; George Washington Bridge connects Manhattan with New Jersey.
1933	RCA Building (Rockefeller Center) opens; Fiorello LaGuardia elected mayor.
1936	Triboro Bridge opens.
1937	Lincoln Tunnel connects Manhattan to Queens.
1946	United Nations begins meeting in New York. UN headquarters completed six years later.
1973	World Trade Center (WTC) completed.
1976	Roosevelt Island Tramway begins operations.
1977	Edward Koch becomes mayor.
1993	Rudolph Giuliani elected mayor.
1998	New York City celebrates 100th birthday.
2000	New York Yankees win the World Series in a subway series
2001	Hillary Clinton becomes junior senator from New York; Former President Bill Clinton sets up offices in Harlem; WTC destroyed by Islamic radicals.
2003	Grammy Music Awards returns to Madison Square Garden.

TAXI

019

#02 Navigating
The Lay Of the Land

Streetwise: Know Thy Neighborhoods

Like every city, New York is a conglomeration of neighborhoods, each with its own unique history and characteristics. See Chapter 5/Exploring for in-depth information on all of Manhattan's neighborhoods.

The Financial District, at the southern tip of the island, is the site of the first European settlement in New York. Now America's financial center, these narrow, historical streets are home to the New York Stock Exchange, the World Trade Center site, Battery Park City, and hundreds of other office buildings. Ferries to the Statue of Liberty, Ellis Island, and Staten Island leave from here.

Chinatown is home to about 100,000 Chinese, as well as tens of thousands of immigrants from Malaysia, Thailand, Vietnam and other Asian nations, making it one of the largest Asian settlements in the West (see Chapter 4/Top Sights).

Little Italy, the 19th-century locus of new immigrants from Europe's boot, is only a shadow of it's former self and is quickly being swallowed up by a burgeoning Chinatown. What's left—primarily along Mulberry Street—has become something of a cannelloni Disneyland.

Nolita, North Of Little ITAly, is Manhattan's funkiest new neighborhood, and the one to watch for fresh, youth-oriented restaurants and boutiques.

The Lower East Side, the famous former home of Jewish immigrants from the turn-of-the-century until the 1950s, is now largely Hispanic in character. Lots of cool bars and clubs have opened along Ludlow and Orchard streets, making it a happening late-night scene.

Tribeca, the TRIangle BElow CAnal street, is a former warehouse district turned industrial-chic by wealthy Wall Streeters and creative types. Some of the city's best restaurants are lurking in these shadows.

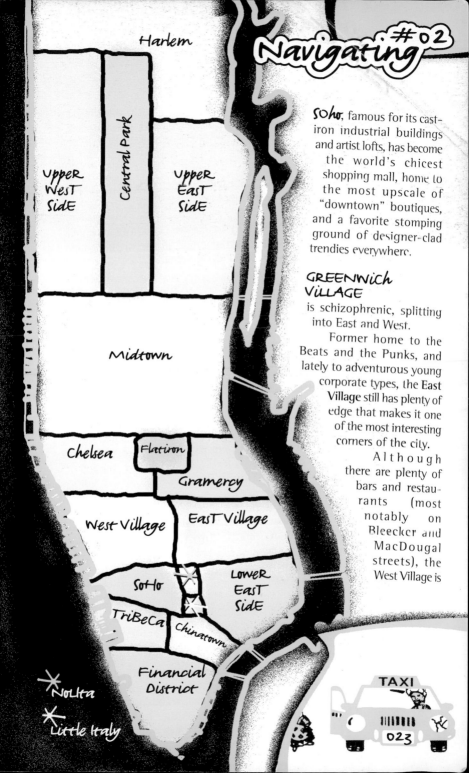

Harlem

Central Park

Upper West Side

Upper East Side

Midtown

Chelsea

Flatiron

Gramercy

West Village

East Village

SoHo

Lower East Side

TriBeCa

Chinatown

Financial District

NoLIta

Little Italy

SoHo, famous for its cast-iron industrial buildings and artist lofts, has become the world's chicest shopping mall, home to the most upscale of "downtown" boutiques, and a favorite stomping ground of designer-clad trendies everywhere.

GREENWICH VILLAGE

is schizophrenic, splitting into East and West.

Former home to the Beats and the Punks, and lately to adventurous young corporate types, the **East Village** still has plenty of edge that makes it one of the most interesting corners of the city.

Although there are plenty of bars and restaurants (most notably on Bleecker and MacDougal streets), the West Village is

TAXI

023

far more sedate. It's known for the historic traces of the bohemian-literary community that lived here in the 1920s and 1930s, for its beautiful 19th-century townhouses on tree-lined streets, and for its large gay community.

Gramercy, for the most part, is a quiet residential district, studded with some excellent bars and restaurants.

The Flatiron District, directly west, is the city's fashion center, home to model agencies, photographers' studios and film labs. Fashionable restaurants and clubs abound here too.

Chelsea, rivaling San Francisco's Castro district as the gay capital of America, is one of the hottest neighborhoods of the moment. Streets here are lined with elegant brownstones, while the avenues are packed with bustling restaurants, cafes, bars and shops. The city's best art galleries continue to relocate here too.

Midtown is where most of the city's landmark office buildings, hotels and top restaurants are. It's also home to Times Square, Broadway theaters, the Museum of Modern Art, and Fifth Avenue shops.

Central Park, that giant green rectangle in the center of the city, covers an area larger than the principality of Monaco. Most New Yorkers are fiercely proud and protective of their urban Garden of Eden (*see* Chapter 4/Top Sights).

The Upper West Side possesses Lincoln Center, the Museum of Natural History, and Columbia University, but it's primarily a residential neighborhood, popular with Jewish families and others who appreciate the abundance of services that are so close at hand.

The Upper East Side, home to some of the city's wealthiest residents, feels more luxurious and sedate than the bustling West Side. Many of Manhattan's most famous museums, including the Met, Guggenheim, and Whitney, are up here, as are plenty of good restaurants.

Harlem remains the heart of African-American Manhattan. Most of the area still looks pretty dilapidated, although there are pockets of great beauty and the community is fast becoming a real-estate magnet for creative types and gay males. A tour of Harlem makes for some fascinating cultural tripping.

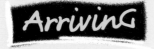

Arriving

New York City is one of the least-welcoming places to land in the entire world. Whether at LaGuardia, Newark, or JFK, deplaning passengers are routinely ushered through narrow, dingy halls or massive construction sites to antiquated baggage-claim areas where long waits for luggage are fraught with "baggravation." If you are arriving on a domestic flight, keep your baggage-claim tickets handy for inspection by security guards. The terminals are filthy and the ride into the city is far from scenic and invariably includes plenty of car exhaust and traffic jams. Welcome to New York.

The fastest and easiest way to Manhattan is by taxi. **Yellow cabs** line up in front of each terminal. At JFK taxis charge a flat fee to Manhattan; fares are metered from the other airports. If two or more are traveling together in a yellow cab, so much the better—in New York City, there are no extra charges for additional passengers (up to a limit of 4 in most cabs) or for baggage placed in the trunk. A minimum 15% tip is customary.

Private Car Services are usually a bit cheaper than yellow cabs, and they might only be slightly more inconvenient. Here's the routine: When you arrive at the airport, telephone the car service. They probably already have a car at the airport and will send it around to your terminal to pick you up. Among the services offering 24-hour airport pick-up are **Carmel** (tel. 1-212/666-6666 or 1-800/922-

7635), **Tel Aviv** (tel. 1-212/777-7777) and **Sabra** (tel. 1-212/777-7171).

You can arrive in style by calling the operators at Grand Limousine (tel. 1-212/344-8999 or 1-800/995-1200). They will pick you up in a stretch limousine and transport you from Kennedy or Newark to downtown for $120, and from LaGuardia for $90. A regular town car costs $45 and $40 respectively.

The **New York Airport Service Express Bus** (tel. 1-800/247-7433) goes from LaGuardia and JFK to Grand Central Station (Park Ave/42nd St), the Port Authority (Eighth Ave/42nd St.) and Penn Station (Seventh Avenue/34th St). Express in name only, it's hard to imagine a worse welcome to the city than a journey aboard one of these smog-belching old avenue tanks. But they're cheap for single travelers. Look for "New York Airport Service Bus" signs outside baggage claim areas. They operate every half-hour from 7am til midnight.

See individual airports, below, for complete transportation options.

#02 Arriving

John F. Kennedy International (JFK)

Queens, NY. Tel. 1-718/244-4444

Miles from Midtown
About 15

Average Car Travel Time
About one hour

Yellow Taxi (flat fare from airport)
$35 + tolls ($5) and tip (15%)

Private Car Service
$37 + tolls ($5) and tip (15%)

Limousine
$120 + tolls ($5) and tip (20%)

Bus
$13

Light-Rail (MTA)
$2

A new light-rail system connects the airport to the subway in Queens, from where you can continue your trip into Manhattan. Because a transfer is required, this is a good option only for travelers with light luggage. Otherwise, taxi is still your best bet for getting from JFK into the city. It's a flat fare from the airport, but the meter runs normally in the other direction and will cost about $35 from the East Side and $40 from the West Side, plus tolls and tip.

La Guardia (LGA)

Queens, NY. Tel. 1-718/533-3400

Miles from Midtown
About 8

Average Car Travel Time
About 40 minutes

Yellow Taxi (metered)
$18-$26 + tolls ($5) and tip (15%)

Private Car Service
$27 + tolls ($5) and tip (15%)

Limousine
$90 + tolls ($5) and tip (20%)

Bus
$12

Theoretically, the Metropolitan Transit Authority (MTA) can get you to Manhattan for the price of subway ride, starting from the airport with the Q-10 city bus (use a Metrocard), then transferring to the E or F trains at the Union Turnpike Station in Queens. Frankly, we don't know anyone who has ever braved this service, but the MTA claims it should take less than two hours to get to Midtown.

Newark International (EWR)

Tel. 1-973/961-6000

Miles to Midtown
About 16

Average Car Travel Time
45-60 minutes

Taxi
$34-$44 + tolls ($7.20) and tip (15%)

Private Car Service
$37 + tolls ($7.20) and tip (15%)

Limousine
$120 + tolls ($7.20) and tip (20%)

Olympia Trails Bus
$11

Taxis line up for passengers at each terminal and charge fixed-price fares to Manhattan ranging from $30-$40, depending on how far into the Apple you go—West Side destinations are cheaper then those on the East Side.

Olympia Trails (1-212/964-6233 or 1-908/354-3330) buses depart to Grand Central, Port Authority, and Penn Station every 20 to 30 minutes between 5am and 11pm. It's not a terrible schlep and the fare is only $12.

ARRIVING BY TRAIN

Amtrak (tel. 1-800/872-7245, www. amtrak.com) trains roll into Manhattan from about 500 American cities. Big Apple-bound trains from Los Angeles depart daily and pass through Denver and Chicago. The journey takes about three and a half days and seats fill up quickly. The lowest round-trip fare costs about $420 from L.A. and $180 to $320 from Chicago. The Explore America fare is the most flexible, allowing you to complete the journey in 45 days with up to three stops along the way. The New York City terminus is Penn Station (Seventh Ave, btw 31st/33rd Sts).

ARRIVING BY Bus

You may have to travel for days squeezed between Charles Manson and the Elephant Man but **Greyhound** (tel. 1-800/231-2222) is relatively cheap and can get you here from almost anywhere. Round-trip fares vary depending on your point of origin, but few, if any, ever exceed $200. Several money-saving advance purchase tickets, multi-day passes, and companion fares are also on offer. The main New York City bus station is Port Authority (Eighth Ave/42nd St), in the seedy heart of Midtown. There are other Greyhound stations around New York too, but not all of them are serviced by interstate buses.

ARRIVING BY WATER

If you're cruising to the Big Apple, chances are you'll walk down the gangplank at the Passenger Ship Terminal, on the Hudson River between 48th and 55th streets (tel. 1-212/246-5451). After claiming your baggage and clearing customs you can easily find a cab or hop onto subways A, C, or E.

...'s buses and subways are run by the
...olitan Transit Authority (MTA; ...30-1234).

...bways) and buses cost $1.50 per ride, no matter how far you go. If you're staying in the city for a few days, it makes sense to buy a Metrocard, an electronic fare card. The cards are sold at all subway stations in amounts from $3 to $80, and allow for free transfers (within two hours) between buses and subways. Metrocard offers a ten-percent bonus for purchases of $15 or more—that's 11 rides for the price of 10. You can also buy a 7-Day Unlimited Ride card. It costs $17 and lets you travel as much as you want in any 7-day period—a good deal if you take 13 rides or more.

Getting Around By Subway

A Japanese guidebook tells tourists about New York's "famous filthy subways" that have to be seen to be believed. Although they now appear to be practically crime- and graffiti-free, most stations remain noisy to the level of being hazardous to your hearing and are often distinctly grubby-looking. The first subway line opened in 1904. Today, more than 6000 cars stopping at 469 stations on 23 lines make the NYC subway system one of the largest in the world. It's also the most complicated, and can feel like the Disorient Express.

Each line is marked by a letter or number and station entrances are signed to show which lines stop there. Platforms are also marked with the lines that service them, though re-routing and frequent track work often renders these signs a little out of whack.

Local trains stop at every station along the particular line in Manhattan while express trains stop only at major stations—marked with a white circle on subway maps. "Bronx-bound" and "Queens-bound" trains are heading uptown and "Brooklyn bound" trains are heading downtown.

The subway operates 24 hours a day, seven days a week. Although the subway is pretty safe these days (we've never had a problem—even at 3am), single

travelers and women in short skirts should think about splurging on a taxi late at night. If you do travel post-midnight, keep alert, wait in the "off-hours" waiting areas and ride in the busiest cars. At any hour it's a good idea to hide rings and chains and to know the whereabouts of your valuables.

Subway turnstiles accept subway tokens and Metrocards, both of which are available from station booths, which also dispense free route maps. Note that subway tokens (as opposed to Metrocards) do not allow you to transfer from subway to bus or vice versa.

Getting Around By Bus

The world's largest fleet of municipal buses criss-crosses the city 24 hours a day, seven days a week. Some locals prefer riding buses on the avenues to taking the subways below them. But these lumbering giants stop every couple of blocks and idle in their own fumes through endless miles of traffic.

Buses are identified by a letter representing the borough it serves, followed by the number of its route. Most run every 10 minutes from 7am to 10pm, and on a reduced schedule throughout the night.

Two routes we do recommend are scenic city bus rides: The M5 from Greenwich Village to Riverside Drive passes Chelsea, Rockefeller Center, Lincoln Center and Central Park South. The M4 is also a great ride, from Madison Avenue through Harlem to the Cloisters.

Buses require exact change, a subway token or a swipe of a Metrocard. Dollar bills are not accepted.

Getting Around By Foot

New York is not for windshield tourists. Walking is the best way to get around and you'll quickly learn how to play chicken with cars like a native. There are about 20 blocks to a mile (1.6 km) and, depending on how many slow-moving "Meanderthals" are in your way, walkers average about one minute per block.

...g Taxi

...vrolet Caprices and Ford ... along Manhattan's streets ... like blood through the city ... il a cab and tell the Punjabi driver where you want to go (when the center of the rooflight is lit, the cab is available for hire). The flag drops at $2, and then the meter clocks 30 ... each additional 1/5-mile or 90 seconds ...ow traffic. There's a 50-cent surcharge on rides from 8pm-6am. In moving traffic on Manhattan streets, the meter should "click" approximately every four blocks, or one avenue going cross-town. The average taxi fare in M...attan is $6 and cabbies expect a 15% tip. There is a limit of four passengers per cab. One fare covers all passengers, and cabs don't have to be shared. Drivers will print receipts when asked.

Taxis are strictly regulated by the New York City Taxi and Limousine Commission (tel. 1-212/221-8294). Threaten to call them if you run into any problems.

Finding an Address

Every listing in this guide includes the nearest cross street.

Fifth Avenue runs from the "top" of Manhattan to Washington Square in Greenwich Village and divides Manhattan into East and West sides. Almost all street addresses north of Washington Square are prefaced "East" or "West." Street numbering begins at Fifth Avenue. Thus, 345 East 59th Street is about three and a half blocks east of Fifth Avenue—and quite far from 345 West 59th Street, which is three and a half blocks west of Fifth Avenue. South of Washington Square streets are named rather than numbered and, with few exceptions, the east-west policy is substituted with sequential numbering.

Avenues run north-south and buildings are numbered serially, starting from the south. Addresses on most avenues have no direct relation to the nearest cross street.

TAXI

031

Manhattan Street Finder

This chart has been devised to help locate any address on an avenue: Cancel the last number of the address, divide by two, and add or subtract the applicable number below. For example, to find the nearest cross street to 350 Fifth Avenue (the Empire State Building), lop off the last number (0), divide 35 in half (17), and add 17. The result is 34th Street.

Avenue A	add 3
Avenue B	add 3
Avenue C	add 3
Avenue D	add 3
First Avenue	add 3
Second Avenue	add 3
Third Avenue	add 10
Fourth Avenue	add 8
Fifth Avenue (below 200)	add 13
Fifth Avenue (above 200)	add 17
Sixth Avenue	subtract 12
Seventh Avenue	add 12
Eighth Avenue	add 9
Ninth Avenue	add 13
Tenth Avenue	add 14
Eleventh Avenue	add 15
Madison Avenue	add 26
Park Avenue	add 35
Lexington Avenue	add 22
Columbus Avenue	add 60
Amsterdam Avenue	add 60
Broadway	subtract 30

There is absolutely no need to carry a bundle of cash when traveling to New York, or any other major American city for that matter. In fact, you can travel to New York without a penny in your pocket and obtain all the dough you need from hundreds of ATMs that work seamlessly with banks around the globe. Your bank will charge between $1 and $3 for each withdrawal.

Credit cards are widely accepted in New York's restaurants, hotels and shops. Cash advances from Visa and MasterCard can be obtained from most banks. Most of the city's ATMs also accept Visa or MasterCard, as long as you have a Personal Identification Number (PIN). You are better off using a bank debit card or similar because you will avoid the enormous interest charges levied by credit-card companies on cash advances.

Travelers Cheques

Travelers cheques are obsolete. You don't use them at home, so why embarrass yourself with these clumsy dinosaurs when you're away? Any company that claims their travelers cheques are as good as cash is lying. Even the tellers at American Express may refuse to exchange *their own* cheques without your picture ID in tow. Stick to ATMs and debit or credit cards.

Infomedia

The www.avantguide.com Cyber-Supplement is the best source for happenings in New York during your stay. Once in the city, head to the nearest newsstand, stock up on the city's listings magazines and check out the metropolis' mediascape. *Time Out New York* is an excellent weekly entertainment guide with art, theater, film, music and club listings. *PAPER*, a very cool monthly magazine, is the best publication in the city for nightlife and downtown happenings. It's a great read too. *New York* magazine is a great glossy weekly with good listings and updates on the newest clubs and restaurants. *The New Yorker* magazine has extensive listings of highbrow events. Other sources of entertainment news and listings include the *Village Voice* and *New York Press*, both of which are published on Wednesdays and are available free from sidewalk boxes. *The New York Times* has a good Weekend section on Fridays that's particularly strong on movies, theater, and special events. *H/X* magazine and *HX for Her* have good listings of gay and lesbian happenings. Both are available free at many downtown clubs, restaurants and clothing stores.

New York Convention & Visitors Bureau, (tel. 1-212/484-1200 or 1-212/397-8299, www.nycvisit.com) operates a visitor information center at 810 Seventh Avenue (at 53rd Street) where you can pick up maps, and the Official New York City Visitor Guide.

TAXI

033

CREDIT CARDS

American Express/Optima (tel. 1-800/528-4800); MasterCard/EuroCard (tel. 1-800/307-7309); Visa (tel. 1-800/336-8472).

EMERGENCIES

Police/Fire/Ambulance (tel. 911)

EYEWEAR/CONTACT LENSES

Disrespectacles, 82 Christopher St (tel. 1-212/741-9550) is one of the coolest places in the city for Oliver Peoples, Matsuda, Kisura, and other dandy frames. Replacement contacts in a hurry? Go to **Optical Express**, 122 East 42nd St (tel. 1-212/856-0636) for immediate, inexpensive replacements.

FILM PROCESSING/PHOTOGRAPHY

Fromex is the city's largest chain of one-hour developing spots. Midtown locations at 1156 Sixth Ave (btw 44th/45th Sts; tel. 1-212/398-3579) and 678 Lexington Ave (at 56th St; tel. 1-212/644-3394). For professional developing, head to **B&H**, 420 Ninth Ave (btw 33rd/34th Sts; tel. 1-212/444-6606). See Chapter 7/Shopping for info on buying camera equipment.

INTERNET

If you have trouble jacking in, visit EasyEverything, 234 West 42nd St (btw Seventh/Eighth Aves) a cyber spot with 648 PCs that's the choice of NYs digerati.

LAUNDRY/DRY CLEANING

In some neighborhoods you'll find launderers and dry cleaners on most every block. Ask at your hotel or check the yellow pages under "Cleaners."

LOST PROPERTY

If you lost it in New York it's probably gone forever. Try calling the police precinct closest to where you think you left it. To find the nearest precinct dial 1-646/610-5000; if you lost it on a subway or bus call 1-212/712-4500.

LUGGAGE STORAGE

All three New York area airports have luggage-storage facilities that are open nonstop. You can also leave luggage at almost any hotel. At an average cost of $2 per item, your bags can stay at the Palace, even if you can't.

PHARMACIES

Duane Reade fills prescriptions round the clock at the following locations: 224 West 57th St (at Broadway; tel. 1-212/541-9708); 485 Lexington Ave (at 47th St; tel. 1-212/682-5338); 661 Eighth Ave (at Port Authority; tel. 1-212/977-1562); 2465 Broadway (at 91st St; tel. 1-212/799-3172); 1279 Third Ave (at 74th St; tel. 1-212/744-2668) and 378 Sixth Ave (at Waverly Pl; tel. 1-212/674-5357).

POSTAL SERVICES/ EXPRESS MAIL

The Main Post Office, on Eighth Avenue between 31st and 33rd streets (tel. 1-800/222-1811) is open 24/seven. DHL (tel. 1-800/225-5345), FedEx (tel. 1-800/463-3339), and UPS (tel. 1-800/742-5877) are all well represented in NYC.

TAXES

In New York, the combined city and state sales taxes amount to 8.25%. Local hotel-occupancy taxes are 13.25% plus $2 per room, per night.

TELECOMMUNICATIONS

Directory assistance (tel. 411) is free from pay phones. Examine the handset for crud before putting it anywhere near your face. Only about 50% of sidewalk payphones seem to be working at any given time so listen for a dial tone before depositing money. You may still lose your quarter.

VIDEO

NTSC is the video standard. DVDs and multi-format machines can be rented from any one of almost a dozen Blockbuster Video stores. Check the phonebook for the nearest location.

Hotels

#03 Sleeping

#03 Sleeping

If there was ever a time to own a hotel in New York, this is it. Business is booming and occupancy rates are higher than a D-student on angel dust. And, according to the law of supply and demand, so are prices.

Not surprisingly, at least a dozen new hotels have opened in the last couple of years, and more are scheduled to have their ribbons cut soon. Happily for us, many of these newbies are of the avant-design variety. Once again, Ian Schrager is making the biggest splash with the 1000-room Hudson, followed by remakes of the Barbizon, the Empire and the St. Moritz. Boutique hotels continue to open apace in Midtown and the West Village, while chains are expanding their presence downtown with the Regent, Embassy Suites, Holiday Inn and the Ritz Carlton.

Finding an expensive hotel in the city doesn't take much effort and our favorites are listed here, including The Four Seasons, The Mercer Hotel, The Lowell and The Carlyle. Finding something decent for not too much money is decidedly less easy, as budget accommodations in Manhattan is something of an oxymoron: Even "inexpensive" hotels top $100 per night for a double. Quality ranges from Spartan to spectacular and is usually—but not always—reflected by price. All the hotels listed below share one thing in common: they have enviable locations and are within walking distance to major sights. Hotels that are far from the action, or difficult to reach by public transportation,

are not listed below—we wouldn't want to stay in them.

The hotels in this book represent the very best in each price category that New York City has to offer. All present something special in the way of local color and character. And we have gone to great lengths to flush out the very best of the city's budget hotels. Every establishment listed here meets our strict criteria for service, facilities and value. Hotels get extra points for shower power, room-service reaction time, a sound system when you want it, and silence when you don't. Then, of course, there's the cool factor....

The Truth About Pricing

The average price of a hotel room in New York City is currently $210.54. The prices quoted below are "rack" rates; that is, the highest rate that a hotel charges for its rooms—13.25% tax not included. These are the prices printed on the hotel's rate card, and the rate that's usually quoted if you phone and simply ask "how much do you charge?" Increasingly, hotels will refuse to provide you with a rate unless you provide them with a definite date. This is because, like airlines, hotels are applying yield-management techniques to their businesses, raising and dropping prices based on supply and demand. Remember, hotel rooms are a perishable commodity. That's why it's possible to get great deals in most of the hotels listed in this book just by asking if they have anything cheaper. It's always a good idea to ask for a package rate on the basis of an AAA membership, student status, an AARP

membership, or virtually anything else that seems valid. Hotel reservation clerks may not volunteer deals if they aren't asked.

New York does not have a seasonal rate drop, although some hoteliers will tell you that business falls off in January/February. Your best bet to secure a room at as low a price as possible is to phone, fax, or email a hotel and ask for its best "corporate rate." Then ask if there are any special promotions or if there is a time period when room prices drop to a lower price. To compare prices and save time, contact several hotels at once.

Discount Reservations Services

These companies negotiate bulk rates with specific hotels to offer discounted hotel rooms and act as a kind of clearinghouse for last-minute reservations. The result is often steep discounts on quality lodgings, including many options for under $100.

Hotels.com (tel. 1-800/964-6835; www.hotels.com) offers rates as low as $80 per night for economy-class accommodations and features discounts at many New York hotel chains (including Marriott, Sheraton, and Hyatt) and independent properties.

Apartment Rentals

Several companies rent apartments to short-term visitors when their owners are away. These range from corporate-owned flats to highly personalized places belonging to vacationing locals. Amenities vary, but every apartment is carefully pre-screened and priced far below a comparable hotel room. Expect to pay between $150 to $450 per night. Recommended companies include **City Lights** (tel. 1-212/737-7049) and **At Home in New York** (tel. 1-212/956-3125, www.athomeny.com).

TAXI

04

The cost ($) reflects the average price of a double room

$ = Under $125 $$$ = $200-$300
$$ = $125-$200 $$$$ = $300-$500
$$$$$ = Over $500

Downtown, The Village, SoHo & TriBeCa

TAXI

The Carlyle

35 East 76th St (btw Madison/Park Aves). Tel. 1–212/744–1600 or 1–800/227–5737. Fax 1–212/717–4682. www.rosenwoodhotels.com. Rates: $550–$825 single/double; suites from $825. AE, MC, V.

Members of the New Guard looking for privacy and those from the Establishment who don't want to encroach on friends hole up at the Carlyle, long the bastion of privilege and the lap of luxury. This is where POTUS (President of the US) stays, along with A-list celebs looking for opulent anonymity. Built with Old World style in 1930, the stunning Art Deco building rises 38 stories, dwarfing most of the luxury Upper East Side apartment buildings that surround it. Each room is like a mini apartment, fitted with European furnishings and fully loaded with all the requisite top-hotel trimmings. Bathrooms are particularly impressive—each is larger than most New York apartments and contains a telephone, TV and Jacuzzi tub. Bemelmans Bar, downstairs, features murals by Ludwig Bemelman, author of the *Madeleine* series of children's books. Bobby Short has been cabareting in the adjacent Café Carlyle since time immemorial, and others play there, too (see Chapter 9/Bars & Clubs). In 2001 the hotel was sold to a private investment group and, ever since, both residents and repeat visitors have been praying that the Carlyle's traditions will continue.

180 Rooms: Air-conditioning, cable TV, VCR, telephone, modular jacks, fax, hair dryer, minibar, radio, CD player, room service (nonstop), concierge, restaurant, bar, fitness center, swimming pool.

The Four Seasons

57 East 57th St (btw Madison/Park Aves). Tel. 1–212/758–5700. Fax 1–212/758–5711. www.fourseasons.com. Rates: $625–$970 single/double; suites from $1475. AE, MC, V.

The most expensive hotel in the city is a flashy IM Pei-designed showstopper built for visiting celebs, "globo-bosses" and entertainment-

industry arrivistes. The 53-story limestone tower became an instant NYC landmark when it opened in 1993, and is nothing if not dramatic. The huge hotel happily flaunts its wealth of space, which is, of course, Manhattan's most precious commodity. Guestrooms are some of the largest in the city, averaging 600 square feet apiece. They are also über-luxurious, designed in Art Deco style with contemporary prints, top-quality custom furnishings and unusual extras that include power-operated silk drapes opened via bedside switch, and turbo bathtubs that fill in just 60 seconds. The marble-clad bathrooms are also huge and connected to separate dressing areas paneled with sycamore. Suites include walk-in closets with tie racks large enough to accommodate 50 ties, and private balconies on higher floors that open onto unobstructed city views. Superb service catering to any type of neurotic need, plus a famously well-connected concierge round out the attributes that keep the Four Seasons on lots of guests' "best hotel" lists.

370 Rooms: Air-conditioning, cable TV, VCR, telephone, modular jacks, fax, hair dryer, minibar, radio, CD player, room service (nonstop), concierge, restaurant, bar, business center, large fitness center (with full spa), wheelchair access.

The Mark

25 East 77th St (at Madison Ave). Tel. 1–212/744–4300 or 1–800/843–6275. Fax 1–212/472–5714. www.themarkhotel.com. Rates: $550–$675 single/double; suites from $750. AE, MC, V.

When money is no object and pampering is a priority, The Mark is sure to hit the... well, you know. The consummate model of understated luxe, the hotel attracts unpretentious old-money guests, who themselves are not necessarily old. This is a beautiful hotel that is at once elegant and upbeat; refined, yet lively; cultivated and cool. It lives up to its motto, which is "no jacket, no tie, no attitude." An entrance lined with potted palms leads to a marble lobby decorated with Piranesi prints. Every ample room upstairs is built with fantastic Whirlpool bathrooms and separate dressing areas. Two-line phones, Frette linens, heated towel racks, down pillows and umbrellas are par for the course. Suites come with wet bars, pantries, and French doors that open onto balconies with views of Central Park. There is an excellent gym and top-notch services.

180 Rooms: Air-conditioning, cable TV, VCR, telephone, modular jacks, fax, hair dryer, minibar, radio, room service (nonstop), concierge, restaurant, bar, fitness center, wheelchair access.

The New York Palace

455 Madison Ave (btw 50th/51st Sts). Tel. 1-212/888-7000 or 1-800/697-2522. Fax 1-212/303-6000. www.NewYorkPalace.com. Rates: $525-$675 single/double; suites from $1000. AE, MC, V.

The Sultan of Brunei has poured a good chunk of his pocket change into this landmark hotel that unites a contemporary 55-story tower with the 1882 Villard Houses—a group of six historical brownstone mansions designed by McKim Mead and White assisted by Auguste Saint-Gaudens and Louis Comfort Tiffany. The result is a beautiful, well-run hotel that is geared for serious business but allows for plenty of pleasures. The courtyard entrance and lavish public areas exude an elegance that seems to make guests walk a little taller and feel a little swankier. Upstairs rooms are as luxe as the downstairs lobby is plush. Each accommodation is outfitted in one of two schemes—classic European or Art Deco—both of which are exceedingly comfortable and perfectly designed. Each has a large, firm bed, executive-size desk, good lighting, three phones, voice mail and a fax machine. Good views make rooms on higher floors more expensive than those below. Rooms on executive floors include access to a private lounge with complimentary continental breakfast, and hors d'oeuvres and beverages in the evening. The well-stocked fitness center includes a roller blade-training machine. Le Cirque 2000, the hotel restaurant, is one of New York's best for both food and people-watching (*see* Chapter 8/Top End). Istana, a Mediterranean restaurant, features an olive bar with more than 30 types of olives, a sherry menu and a "tapas" afternoon tea.

963 Rooms: Air-conditioning, cable TV, telephone, fax, hair dryer, minibar, radio, room service (nonstop), concierge, restaurant, bar, business center, fitness center, wheelchair access.

The Plaza

768 Fifth Ave (btw 58th/59th Sts). Tel. 1–212/759-3000 or 1–800/759-3000. Fax 1–212/546-5324. www.fairmont.com. Rates: $550-$900 single/double; suites from $1325. AE, MC, V.

A New York institution if ever there was one, this Edwardian masterpiece (1907) speaks of romance and Old-World opulence. It's also a Middle American's dream of a fine New York hotel. The luxury extends to most guestrooms, some of which are extensive multi-room affairs with marble fireplaces, gilded ceilings and perfect Central Park views. To be fair, other accommodations can be quite small, and all you might see out your window is a dingy airshaft. This is one place where you get what you pay for, and the Plaza is large enough to cater to a wide range of budgets. But ask for a park view and you're unlikely to be disappointed. The Plaza's faultless location and unimpeachable design makes it the grand dame of Manhattan hotels and an important historical landmark. Architect Frank Lloyd Wright long occupied a sprawling suite here while designing the Guggenheim Museum. Once the exclusive province of society that included the Vanderbilts, Whitneys, Harrimans and Goulds, the public areas are now overrun with candy-ass tourists drawn by the allure of such locally shot films as *Crocodile Dundee* and *Home Alone 2*. Locals also come here in droves, for afternoon tea in the Palm Court or a drink in the classic Oak Bar, which is adorned with evocative Shinn murals.

805 Rooms: Air-conditioning, cable TV, telephone, hair dryer, minibar, radio, room service (nonstop), concierge, restaurant, bar, business center, fitness center (with full spa), wheelchair access.

RIHGA Royal

151 West 54th St (btw Sixth/Seventh Aves). Tel. 1–212/307-5000 or 1–800/937-5454. Fax 1–212/765-6530. www.rihga.com. Rates: $545-$695 single/double. AE, MC, V.

This luxurious Midtowner is a flamboyant, all-suite hotel with huge rooms and huge prices. Its 54 stories cater to successful Japanese

biznizmen (it's owned by an Osaka-based company), well-to-do Italian tourists, and a wide spectrum of rich and famous from Emperor Akihito to the rock band Oasis. In addition to great Central Park views, the hotel offers in-room ice-makers, free limos to Wall Street and 24-hour in-suite dining with china, crystal and silver. The top-of the line Pinnacle suites have state-of-the-art techno features like videophones, cell phones, and electronic bidet-toilets... what?

500 Suites: Air-conditioning, cable TV, VCR, telephone, modular jacks, fax, hair dryer, minibar, radio, room service (nonstop), concierge, restaurant, bar, business center, fitness center, wheelchair access.

Trump International Hotel & Tower

1 Central Park West (at Columbus Circle). Tel. 1–212/299-1000. Fax 1–212/299-1058. www.trumintl.com. Rates: $525–$575 single/double; suites from $825. AE, MC, V.
Despite our prejudices against the Versace of real estate, even we have to admit that The Donald gives great hotel. Trump International transformed one of the nation's 10 worst buildings into a neighborhood beacon and helped tidy an entire district in the process. The hotel's black-and-gold exterior is designed to attract the kind of nouveau riche European that thinks the Trump trademark is one of sophistication. But the interior really is all class. Guestrooms are designed with rich textures and tasteful colors, and fitted with sensuously stained wood furnishings and elegant marble baths. On the higher floors the hotel's floor-to-ceiling windows offer amazing, unobstructed views over Central Park. Suites include telescopes amongst the furnishings, as well as good-sized Jacuzzi tubs. Other amenities include in-room faxes, computers and entertainment systems, a terrific on-premises fitness center (with lap pool and spa), and a personal concierge assigned to each guest. Of course, all this finery isn't cheap, but for those lucky enough to occupy a corner room facing northeast and holding dinner reservations at Jean-Georges downstairs (*see* Chapter 8/Celebrity Chefs) it's easy to identify with the owner and feel like you're King of the World.

167 Rooms: Air-conditioning, cable TV, VCR, telephone, modular jacks, fax, hair dryer, minibar, radio, CD player, room service (nonstop), concierge, restaurant, bar, fitness center, swimming pool, wheelchair access.

Sleeping #03

TAXI

051

The Lowell

28 East 63rd St (btw Madison/Park Aves). Tel. 1-212/838-1400. Fax 1-212/605-6808. www.lhw.com. Rates: $435-$535 single/double; suites from $675.AE, MC, V.

The Lowell is the best New York hotel you've never heard of, and that's one of the reasons for its success. Queen of the boutique hotels, this very personal property is the choice of Hollywood players, in-the-know Euros and stars so famous they are recognizable by their first names. It's a stunningly fine hotel; a discrete townhouse on a tranquil tree-lined street, built in 1925-26. Inside, it's furnished with ultra-fine antiques and offers perfect personal service. Most of the guestrooms are like small apartments, with super deluxe *House & Garden* details like stocked bookshelves, potted plants, Chinese porcelains, Italian marble baths, tufted ottomans, and glass coffee tables. Extra-special amenities include Frette bathrobes and Bulgari toiletries. Most of the suites have working fireplaces and kitchens, and 10 have private terraces. The Garden Suite has twin terraces, one with a fountain and rose garden, the other with a vine-trellised dining area furnished with elegant wrought-iron pieces. The Gym Suite, supposedly created for Madonna, has a room for free weights, a Nautilus system, stationary bike and a treadmill.

68 Rooms: Air-conditioning, cable TV, VCR, telephone, modular jacks, fax, hair dryer, minibar, radio, room service (nonstop), concierge, restaurant, bar, fitness center, wheelchair access.

The Inn at Irving Place

56 Irving Place (btw 17th/18th Sts). Tel. 1-212/533-4600 or 1-800/685-1447. Fax 1-212/533-4611. www.InnAtIrving.com. Rates: $325-$455 single/double; suites from $525. AE, MC, V.

A little bit country and a little bit rock and roll, The Inn at Irving Place is among the prettiest little properties anywhere. Its country-in-the-city atmosphere is part romance and part sophistication, swathed with faux Victorian charm but equipped with all the necessary contemporary conveniences. Inside these two attractive townhouses, built in 1834, are a dozen rooms of varying sizes, each fitted with antique furnishings, a fireplace and a four-poster bed dressed with Frette linens. No two rooms are alike but all have two-line phones and CD players and are so well designed they're even a bit trendy. Guests check-in in a wonderful parlor-lounge and are invited to sip tea each afternoon in Lady Mendl's Tea Room, which is plushly furnished with tufted sofas and armchairs. At Cibar women are even encouraged to indulge in the pleasure of a good cigar. A more charming and wonderful place in Manhattan we can not find. Note that the hotel is not a good place for babies, dogs and other ankle-nippers.

12 Rooms: Air-conditioning, cable TV, VCR, telephone, modular jacks, fax, hair dryer, minibar, radio, CD player, room service (7am-11pm), concierge, restaurant, bar, access to local gym.

The Mercer Hotel

147 Mercer St (btw Prince/Spring Sts). Tel. 1-212/966-6060. Fax 1-212/965-3838. www.themercer.com. Rates: $425-$590 single/double; suites from $1100. AE, MC, V.

An ultra-trendy hot spot since 1998, The Mercer will remain one of Manhattan's toughest reservations well into this millennium. Its tranquil atmosphere and low-key homey design is meant to contrast with Schrager-Starck's dazzling party palaces. And its fantastic SoHo location is bolstered by an impressive pedigree: The hotel's owner is Andre Balazs of Chateau Marmont in Los Angeles, who attracts a star-studded Euro and American crowd (Cher, Alexander McQueen, Leonardo di Caprio...). The Mercer offers spacious, loft-like studios that are expensive, roomy, minimalist and just oh-so-SoHo. Their Zen-like serenity, conceived by designer Christian Liaigre, includes luxurious woods—African wenge and ipe—for much of the custom-made furniture. Closets, shelving and minibar are concealed behind glass doors, which are backed with starched colored linen. The marble bathrooms are extra-large (some with two-person tubs) and offer bath products by FACE Stockholm. Room features include a table large enough for dining or working and a suite of chairs, plus loads of extra amenities both hi-tech and indulgent—three telephones including a portable, and a minibar stocked by Dean & DeLuca. Word is that the staff is as capable as it is good-looking, making for excellent service. To top it all off, the bamboo and brick Mercer Kitchen, downstairs is under the control of Manhattan mega-chef Jean-Georges Vongerichten, and SubMercer, below, remains one of the neighborhood's white-hottest bars.

75 Rooms: Air-conditioning, cable/Web TV, VCR, telephone, modular jacks, hair dryer, minibar, CD player, radio, room service (nonstop), concierge, restaurant, bar, access to nearby fitness center, wheelchair access.

TAXI

053

#03
just Expensive

Morgans Hotel

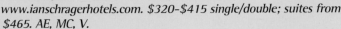

237 Madison Ave (btw 37th/38th Sts).
Tel. 1–212/686-0300. Fax 1–212/779-8352.
www.ianschragerhotels.com. $320-$415 single/double; suites from
$465. AE, MC, V.

Despite its slightly offbeat Murray Hill location and Armani-clad staff (yawn), Morgans is one of our favorite Manhattan hotels. Opened in 1985 by former Studio 54 men Ian Schrager and the late Steve Rubell, Morgans is a sophisticated place with just a small brass namplate by the door. It attracts high-level creatives and B-list celebs, who aren't in desperate need of an audience. The first designer boutique hotel in NYC remains subdued and well-run, not frenetic and crazy like the Paramount farther uptown or the Tribeca Grand farther down. Taupe-colored glass walls, French leather club chairs, and a cubist-inspired wall rug give the small lobby the ambience of a living room. Asian-minimal guest rooms— which have been called sterile by some—include such unique characteristics as suede headboards, corduroy ottomans and club chairs, bronze floor lamps, and built-in maple cabinets and window seats. The striking bathrooms are lined with matte black and white tiles and granite floors, and feature stainless-steel hospital-style bathroom fixtures and Jacuzzi baths. The penthouse, one of the premiere places to stay in New York, sprawls out with two terraces, a multimedia room and a private greenhouse. Downstairs you'll find Asia de Cuba Restaurant (see Chapter 8/The Restaurant Scene) and Morgans Bar (see Chapter 9/Nightlife), two of the most chi-chi spots in Manhattan.

154 Rooms: Air-conditioning, cable TV, VCR, telephone, modular jacks, fax, hair dryer, minibar, radio, room service (nonstop), concierge, restaurant, bar, access to nearby fitness center, wheelchair access.

Royalton

44 West 44th St (btw Fifth/Sixth Aves). Tel. 1–212/869-4400. Fax 1–212/575-0012. www.ianschragerhotels.com. Rates: $345-$570 single/double; suites from $570. AE, MC, V.

In 1988, when disco kings Ian Schrager and Steve Rubell hired Philippe Starck to create this new hostelry, the idea was to design an entertaining and provocative frolic pad. Starck took a historic hotel and rendered it unrecognizable, with a playroom lobby full of oversized furniture, showplace guestrooms and a "modelicious," black-clad staff. The result is an international fashion center, catering to visiting mannequins and oodles of entertainment-industry personnel. Sleek modish beds, serene neutral-tone furnishings and steel, slate, and glass bathrooms with round tubs feel very 1990s. And low lighting and small desks are the epitome of form over function: The Royalton is not great for suits on business, but bathrooms are large and bedrooms are comfortable, equipped with VCRs and stereos. Some even have working fireplaces. "44," the hotel's lobby restaurant, is well known as the unofficial commissary for editors at Condé Nast. The lobby-level Vodka Bar, almost literally a watering hole, is one of the coziest places in the city for a drink (see Chapter 9/Bars & Lounges).

168 Rooms: Air-conditioning, cable TV, telephone, modular jacks, fax, hair dryer, minibar, radio, room service (nonstop), concierge, restaurant, bar, fitness center, wheelchair access.

SoHo Grand

*310 West Broadway (btw Canal/Grand Sts).
Tel. 1-212/965-3000 or 1-800/965-3000.
Fax 1-212/965-3244. www.sohogrand.com. Rates:
$390–$600 single/double; suites from $1399. AE,
MC, V.*

Almost too cybersexy for its own shirt, the SoHo
Grand is an over-the-top, self-consciously stylish spot
that's best approached with tongue firmly in cheek.
Its location is both perfect and unique—within walking
distance of Soho's art galleries and shops, plus
Greenwich Village, Tribeca, Little Italy, Chinatown and
Wall Street. Contrary to the horrible, pile-of-bricks
exterior (inspired, perhaps, by the NYU gymnasium),
the wonderful, post-modern interior is clearly influenced
by the neighborhood's commercial roots. Guests enter
past bouncer-like doormen into a dramatic dance-
club interior that grooves with high-volume chill-out
music. A glowing staircase of translucent Coke-bottle
glass and cast iron leads to the main lobby-salon,
a trendy showplace of colossal art where great-looking
people in black gather in front of enormous windows
treated with muslin and velvet. The drama continues
with cool gray and beige guestrooms, each of which
is small and minimalist, designed with overscale
furniture, original photographs from a local gallery
and heavy velvet drapes. Pampering comes in the form
of Frette linens and velour bathrobes, fleece throws,
Kiehl toiletries, and non-fat-munchie-stocked
minibars. As might be expected, the hotel attracts
all manner of jet-lagged waifs, advertising urchins,
design brats and other hip folk. It also caters (thanks
to the Hartz Mountain owners) to quadrupeds and
other animals. Bring your feather boa and your pet
boa; both are welcome here.

369 Rooms: Air-conditioning,
cable TV, VCR, telephone,
modular jacks, hair dryer,
minibar, radio, CD player, room
service (nonstop), concierge,
restaurant, bar, business
center, fitness center,
wheelchair access.

TAXI

057

Tribeca Grand Hotel

*2 Sixth Ave (at Church St). Tel. 1–212/519-6600
or 1–877/519-6600. Fax 1–212/519-6700.
www.TribecaGrand.com. Rates: $439–$599
single/double; suites from $700. AE, MC, V.*

The first hotel to open in this cool neighborhood south
of Canal Street has quickly become a hotspot for local
film execs, venture capitalists and the e-types who love
them. The hotel occupies a triangular lot, which defines
the striking interior and determines its layout. The entire
first floor is taken up by a vast lounge-restaurant, which
sweeps down from the lobby past a dramatic blue light
sculpture. The windows stretch one whole block and are covered
with sheer copper colored curtains that cast a bronze glow over
the entire soaring eight-story atrium, giving it a sexy-sensual
ambience at night. The drama continues in the rooms which are
contemporary in design and equipped with up-to-the-minute tech
toys, including wireless keyboards, ergonomic chairs, and built-in
bathroom TVs with water-proof remotes(!). Additional luxuries include
Frette bathrobes and linens, toiletries from Kiehl's, and a luxurious,
private 98-seat screening room. Equipped with workstations with
flat panel screens, even the business center is cool.

203 Rooms: Air conditioning, Web TV/VCR, two-line cordless
telephone, high-speed internet access, fax/printer/copier/scanner,
Bose Wave radio/CD player, room service (nonstop), concierge,
restaurant, bar, business center, fitness center, wheelchair
access.

The Waldorf-Astoria Hotel & Towers

*301 Park Ave (btw 49th/50th Sts). Tel. 1–212/355-
3000 or 1–800/925-3673. Fax 1–212/872-7272.
www.hilton.com. Rates: $325–$660 single/double;
suites from $550. AE, MC, V.*

Associated in most minds with high society (and
a delicious salad), the Waldorf opened in 1931 as
one of New York's swankiest hotels. It was the
world's largest too, and perhaps the very first
anywhere to offer room service. Now Hilton-
owned and catering to corporate-types and
conventions, this toast of the Jazz Age feels
a bit soggy, but there's still plenty to coo
about, including a spectacular mahogany-

paneled lobby and surrounding Cocktail Terrace—both of which have been meticulously restored to their Art Deco heyday—and the clubby Sir Harry's Bar, which seems purpose-built for sipping rare cognacs and liqueurs. Upstairs, you'll find well-sized rooms with good accouterments, bad plumbing and plenty of quiet. The staff is pleasant, but the hotel is just too large to provide speedy or personal service. The adjacent Waldorf Towers has a separate entrance and check-in area, and is operated as if it were a completely separate property. Newer, sleeker and in much better shape than their venerable old partner, the Towers offer luxe accommodations with CEO rooms.

1380 Rooms: Air-conditioning, cable TV, telephone, modular jacks, fax, minibar, radio, room service (nonstop), concierge, restaurants, bars, business center, fitness center, wheelchair access.

W-Union Square

201 Park Avenue South (at 17th St). Tel. 1–212/253-9119. Fax 1–212/253-9229. www.whotels.com. Rates: $399-$549 single/double; suites from $849. AE, MC, V.

The Starwood chain's fourth foray into New York's burgeoning hip hotel market is a relentlessly stylish hotspot that's so right it feels like it was designed by a focus group. It's located on the northeast corner of Union Square in the handsome Beaux-Arts Guardian Life building. Guests enter to a double story lobby lounge furnished with clusters of plush velvet sofas. Each W hotel has a signature object, and here it's boardgame tables that are dotted throughout. Rooms are done in serene grays and whites and are luxe comfortable, furnished with down comforters, a chaise lounge and a decent sized desk. Olives, the New York debut restaurant of Boston's famous Todd English, turns out exciting Med cuisine and remains a hot reservation. In the Underbar (another Rande Gerber creation) guests vie for one of the sexy curtained booths.

270 Rooms: Air conditioning, Web TV, telephone (cordless with data ports), high speed internet access, room service (nonstop), restaurant, bar, business center (nonstop), fitness center (nonstop).

TAXI

059

Moderately Expensive

The Ameritania

230 West 54th St (btw Broadway/Eighth Ave). Tel. 1–212/247-5000 or 1–800/922-0330. Fax 1–212/247-3316. www.ameritaniahotel.com. Rates: $225–$395 single/double; suites from $350. AE, MC, V.

The Ameritania's close proximity to the Hard Rock Cafe is reflected by the nature of its guests—American tour bussers and "Euro-peons" for whom *American Idol* seems exotic and *Phantom* is a hot ticket. On the plus side, this hotel is well-located and offers plenty of clean, cookie-cutter rooms with firm beds and marble-clad baths. Non-smoking rooms are available. The staff is understandably harried but the price is relatively light, making the Ameritania thoroughly recommendable for anyone on a moderate budget.

250 Rooms: Air-conditioning, cable TV, telephone, hair dryer, radio, room service (1130am-10pm), concierge, restaurant, bar, fitness center.

The Beekman Tower Hotel

3 Mitchell Place (49th St at First Ave). Tel. 1–212/355-7300 or 1–800/637-8483. Fax 1–212/753-9366. www.mesuite.com. Rates: $210-$329 single/double. AE, MC, V.

A deco masterpiece built in 1928 near the United Nations, this refined Jazz Age hotel is one of the finest places to stay on the East Side. Situated close to the UN and popular with diplomats' friends, business people and a wide assortment of wealthy visitors, this is an all-suite hotel with large rooms at reasonable (for New York) rates. In addition to an oversized bedroom or two, each recently refurbished suite contains a sitting and dining area and a fully-equipped kitchen (for which there is a grocery shopping service). The hotel is well known among locals for its dramatic 26th-floor Top of the Tower bar/restaurant, a contemporary, theatrical masterpiece with an absolutely stunning view.

174 Suites: Air-conditioning, cable TV, telephone, modular jacks, hair dryer, radio, room service (7am-1am), concierge, restaurant, bar, fitness center, wheelchair access.

Casablanca Hotel

*147 West 43rd St (btw Sixth/Seventh Aves).
Tel. 1-212/869-1212 or 1-888/922-7225. Fax
1-212/391-7585. www.casablancahotel.com. $290-
$375 single/double; suites from $395 AE, MC, V.*

An intimate boutique hotel in the heart of Theaterland,
The Casablanca pleases with a luxurious Moroccan style
that indulges each guest like a pasha with beautifully
appointed rooms and a plethora of amenities including
VCRs, two-line speaker phones, terry bathrobes,
complimentary soft drinks and fresh flowers in every
room. Breakfast is served in the lobby-level Rick's Cafe,
along with snacks throughout the day and wine and
cheese in the evening. Guests also have carte blanche
to the New York Sports Club, a few blocks away.

48 Rooms: Air-conditioning, cable TV, telephone,
modular jacks, hair dryer, minibar, radio, access to
nearby fitness center, wheelchair access.

The Chambers

*15 West 56th St (btw Fifth/Sixth Aves).
Tel. 1-212/974-5656. Fax 1-212/974-5657.
www.chambershotel.com. Rates $275-$350
single/double; suites from $500.*

One of the latest offerings from über-hotelier Ian
Schrager, The Chambers is a hot hotel packed with
sophistication and sleek touches. All the hallmarks
of hip hoteling are here, including public areas that
double as party venues and beautifully-decorated
rooms swanked out with special touches that include
etched-glass bathroom doors and a roll of butcher
paper you can pull over the glass writing desk for
notes or cleanliness. This place is a winner.

77 Rooms: Air-conditioning, cable TV, VCR,
telephone, hairdryer, minibar, clock radio, shoe shine
& laundry service, restaurant, bar, business
center, florist, wheelchair access.

Chelsea Hotel

222 West 23rd St (btw Seventh/Eighth Aves). Tel. 1-212/243-3700. Fax 1-212/675-5531. www.chelseahotel.com. Rates: $200-$325 double; suites from $330. AE, MC, V.

Completed in 1884 and seemingly little changed since, the historic Chelsea is one part hotel, two parts mysterious phenomenon. Throughout the 20th century, the building has been the shabbiest of chic flophouses for a roster of bohemian transients, from Mark Twain, O. Henry and Sarah Bernhardt to Vladimir Nabokov, Thomas Wolfe, Jefferson Airplane and Ethan Hawke. Titanic survivors with second-class tickets were lodged here for a few days, and in 1953, at age 39, the hard-drinking poet Dylan Thomas collapsed in his room here, later dying in nearby St Vincent's Hospital. Andy Warhol made a film here, and Sid killed Nancy in room 100, which has since been enlarged and renumbered. Wide hallways with windows at each end open into guestrooms that run the gamut from decent to horrible. Like the proverbial box of chocolates, you never know what you're going to get. Some rooms are tiny, some are huge. Some are renovated and some are not. Some are fitted with huge, carved 19th-century furnishings, and some contain 1950s-era tubular steel dinettes. Suites, for the most part, are the best bets, as many retain their Victorian layouts and have spectacular carved-marble fireplaces that still work. Suite 822 includes a living room, bedroom, small kitchen and expansive southern views. The only way to ensure acceptable accommodations is to show up in person with your bags in tow and ask to see a room before committing.

400 rooms: Air-conditioning, cable TV, computer ports.

TAXI

063

The Franklin

164 East 87th St (btw Lexington/Third Aves). Tel. 1–212/369-1000 or 1–800/600-8787. Fax 1–212/369-8000. www.franklinhotel.com. Rates: $209-$249 single/double. AE, MC, V.

If you're young and avant and want to stay on the Upper East Side, then The Franklin is your hotel. "Affordable, chic, boutique" should be the motto of this slightly eccentric fashion-industry charmer that was transformed from a former crack house into a proverbial house of style. Minimalist design emphasizes a few important pieces in otherwise clutter-free rooms. Look for brushed steel furnishings, canopy beds, cedar closets, fresh flowers and VCRs. A sleek place at plain prices, The Franklin represents good value in one of the city's toniest neighborhoods. Rates include breakfast, in-room movies, parking, and tea each afternoon in the lobby.

51 Rooms: Air-conditioning, cable TV, telephone, modular jacks, hair dryer, radio.

The Gorham

136 West 55th St (btw Sixth/Seventh Aves).
Tel. 1-212/245-1800.
Fax 1-212/582-8332. www.gorhamhotel.com. Rates: $225-$480 single/double; suites from $260. AE, MC, V.
Old-fashioned in spirit, up-to-date in substance, the Gorham is a decent mid-priced Midtowner featuring oversized rooms and an enviable location. A fine wood and marble lobby leads to less-intensively designed bedrooms containing Whirlpool baths, VCRs, two-line phones, and espresso machines on request. Suites have kitchenettes.

115 Rooms: Air-conditioning, cable TV, telephone, modular jacks, fax, hair dryer, radio, room service (11am-1030pm), concierge, bar, fitness center, wheelchair access.

Hudson

356 West 58th St (btw Eighth/Ninth Aves).
Tel. 1-212/554-6000 or 1-800/444-4786.
Fax 1-212/554-6001. www.ianschragerhotels.com.
Rates: $105 single, $200-$465 double.
AE, MC, V.
Ian Schrager and Philippe Starck do it again in NYC with this enormous community for guests that doubles as as pseudo house party. The whole hotel is designed for fun, with whimsical gathering places arranged around a captivating ivy-covered conservatory/reception area. Typically, guest rooms are small, but still manage to contain a suite of sleek Starke-designed objects—stainless steel table and aluminum chair, gold-leaf stools, upholstered headboards, and brass studded leatherette loveseat. The most dramatic room features are the bedside light boxes designed by Francesco Clemente.

The Hudson Bar is the most happening space in the complex. Its glass bottom, lit from below, doubles as a dance floor. Playful furniture sculptures (a log punctuated with several chairbacks) add zing to the space, and so does the kaleidoscopic drip-painted ceiling by Francesco Clemente.

The Hudson Cafeteria, which looks like an Ivy League college dining hall, serves classic American comfort food—meat loaf, beef stew, chicken and mushroom pot pie, plus lighter dishes like chicken paillard and roasted red snapper in carrot orange glaze.

Even the fitness facilities are top-notch and fun, including a David Barton gym, a bowling alley, and basketball, volleyball, and archery courts.

1000 Rooms: Air-conditioning, cable TV, two-line telephones with fast internet access, CD/DVD player, radio, room service (nonstop), concierge, restaurant, bar, business center.

Sleeping #03

TAXI

065

The Mansfield

12 West 44th St (btw Fifth/Sixth Aves). Tel. 1–212/944-6050 or 1–800/255-5167. Fax 1–212/764-4477. www.mansfieldhotel.com, Rates: $225-$325 single/double; suites from $300. AE, MC, V.

This bright boutique hotel is filled with seductive Beaux Arts charm. The lovely 1904 building features the original terrazzo floors, a handsome oval staircase with mahogany railings and iron balustrade, and an iron-and-glass elevator. A magnificent copper dome is the centerpiece of the hotel's salon where guests gather for cappuccino (which is available nonstop) and desserts (between 10 and 11pm). Rooms are not large but they are thoroughly contemporary, in an Ian Schrager kind of way. The sleigh beds have steel mesh headboards and swingline bedside tables. The armoires too have been ingeniously crafted from metal and fabric. Each room possesses high-quality extras including Belgian linens, designer bath soaps and the collected stories of Sherlock Holmes. Suites have etched glass doors, wooden blinds and plush sofas. Evening desserts and morning breakfasts are complimentary.

123 Rooms: Air-conditioning, cable TV, VCR, telephone, radio, CD player, restaurant, access to local health club, wheelchair access.

The Mayflower Hotel on the Park

15 Central Park West (at 61st St). Tel. 1–212/265-0060 or 1–800/223-4164. Fax 1–212/265-0227. www.mayflowerhotel. com. Rates: $210-$275 single/double; suites from $285. AE, MC, V.

Overlooking Central Park, this reasonably priced Upper West Sider offers spacious rooms with high ceilings, walk-in closets and terrific views for the lucky guests in front rooms. Many of the rooms also have pantries with a sink and refrigerator. Located steps from Lincoln Center, the hotel attracts lots of musicians—the "serious" kind who travel with oboes and violins stay here when they are in town for a recital. The rooms' American reproduction furniture and décor are old-fashioned and there is certainly evidence of wear throughout the hotel, but regulars shrug it off as "charm." As with most properties, the higher floors are best and brightest. Here, the accommodations culminate with terraced penthouses offering breathtaking views over the park and all of Manhattan.

365 Rooms: Air-conditioning, cable TV, telephone, modular jacks, hair dryer, minibar, radio, room service (7am-1130pm), concierge, restaurant, bar, business center, fitness center, wheelchair access.

TAXI

067

The Muse

130 West 46th St (btw Sixth/Seventh Aves).
Tel. 1–212/485-2400 or 1–877/692-6873.
Fax 1–212/485-2900. www.TheMuseHotel.com. Rates:
$300-$550 single/double; suites from $495. AE, MC, V.
The best attributes of this fast-forward hotel are: 1) Its location in
the heart of the theater district and 2) the extra-large size of its
guestrooms (at least by New York standards). Some are even large
enough to accommodate two double beds and a pullout couch. The
Muse is way stylish, starting with the lobby, where guests are invited
to sit down as they check in at individual desks. Rooms are attractively
furnished with contemporary light cherry furnishings. Beds are dressed
with abstract patterned duvets, and windows have sleek Roman blinds.
There's also a full raft of luxuries, including in-room coffeemakers, and
toiletries by Philosophy (cardamom soap, real loofah) in the bathrooms.
  200 Rooms: Air-conditioning, cable TV, VCR, CD player, multi-line phone
with dataport and high speed internet access, hairdryer, minibar, radio, room
service (6am-midnight) concierge, restaurant, bar, fitness center.

The Roger Williams

131 Madison Ave (at 31st St). Tel. 1–212/448-7000. Fax 1–212/448-7007.
www.rogerwilliamshotel.com. Rates: $285-$600 single/double; suites from
$425. AE, MC, V.
The Roger Williams is another member of the design-conscious Unique Hotels
group, owner of several stylish Manhattan properties known for good décor,
service and value. The charm is clear right from the lobby, with its warm maple
paneling and fluted zinc columns. Upstairs, sleek, contemporary rooms are
designed with minimalist style and maximum tech. Each has a VCR and CD
player, and comes with Unique's signature array of freebies: continental
breakfast, dessert buffet, all-day cappuccino and espresso, and even free parking.
  185 Rooms: Air-conditioning, cable TV, telephone, modular jacks, radio,
access to nearby health club, wheelchair access.

The Shoreham

33 West 55th St (btw Fifth/Sixth Aves). Tel. 1–212/247-6700 or
1–800/553-3347. Fax 1–212/765-9741.www.shorehamhotel.com.
Rates: $300-$425 single/double; suites from $450. AE, MC, V.
As stylish as the Royalton but at frumpier prices, the
Shoreham is an ultra-modern designer hotel
attracting in-the-know guests (actors, models,
fashion buyers) with fresh contemporary rooms,
personal service and a good Midtown location. The
hotel's perfect mix of contemporary and classical
fashions includes retro 1930s décor combined
with metal-mesh headboards, aluminum
furnishings, VCRs and CD players. The terrific

TAXI

069

result is an upscale, creative atmosphere that's appropriate to the hotel's close proximity to the Museum of Modern Art. Ask for one of the newer rooms and note too that the quietest ones are in the rear. Continental breakfast is included.

174 Rooms: Air-conditioning, cable TV, VCR, telephone, modular jacks, hair dryer, radio, CD player, room service (nonstop), restaurants, bar, business center.

The Time

224 West 49th St (btw Broadway/Eighth Ave). Tel. 1–212/320-2900 or 1–877/846-3692. Fax 1–212/245-2305. www.TheTimeNY.com. Rates: $300-$400 single/double. AE, MC, V.

If we didn't warn you to look out for it, you'd miss the tiny unprepossessing entrance to this Midtown style spot. Once inside, a large glass elevator lifts you to a candle-lit lounge/reception area with wall holograms and low-rider leather seating that has become a stellar gathering place for a theater/media crowd. Designed by Adam Tihany, the hotel's guest rooms are fun and colorful, but universally snug. Each is decorated in one of three primary colors, and the red motif is our favorite. Windows are covered with a spotlighted mesh scrim and each room includes color-inspired soaps and shampoos and an edible color accent (red apple, blueberries, and the like).

200 Rooms: Air-conditioning, Web TV, dual-line telephone with data port, fax/photocopier/printer, hair dryer, minibar, Bose wave radio, room service (18 hrs), concierge, bar, fitness center.

The Warwick

65 West 54th St (btw Fifth/Sixth Aves). Tel. 1–212/247-2700 or 1–800/223-4099. Fax 1–212/713-1751. www.warwickintl.com. Rates: $285-$350 single/double; suites from $500. AE, MC, V.

Built by William Randolph Hearst to accommodate his Hollywood friends, the Warwick once attracted everyone from Elvis Presley to Cary Grant, who lived in the top-floor suite. The heydays are history and Hollywood has moved elsewhere, but these renovated rooms remain top-of-the-line, unmatched in size and just as big on comfort. Each accommodation is a generously proportioned suite containing walk-in closets and a large marble bathroom. The conservative décor is less memorable, but that's like complaining that the caviar is too cold. The Warwick is located close to Radio City Music Hall.

424 Rooms: Air-conditioning, cable TV, telephone, modular jacks, fax, hair dryer, radio, room service (nonstop), concierge, restaurant, bar, fitness center, wheelchair access.

W-New York

541 Lexington Ave (btw 49th/50th Sts). Tel. 1-212/755-1200. Fax 1-212/832-9673. www.whotels.com. Rates: $229-$540 single/double; suites from $439. AE, MC, V.

W opened this, their first New York hotel, in 1998, debuting their trademark design-driven attitude that rides the fence between corporate and cool. It's the perfect vibe for fashionable Midtowners who love lounging in the lobby, hanging at Whiskey Blue (the province of LA Skybar's Rande Gerber), dining in Drew Nieporent's Heartbeat restaurant, and pampering themselves at the large spa. Like other links in this chain, the hotel features lots of fashion-forward elements, including walls of running water, a juice bar in the lobby, organic cuisine in the restaurant, and even pots of wheatgrass in the rooms. Organic elements define the décor (kota stone floors, schist counters) and the comfort (down quilts, Aveda products). And there's always terrific music—that's the key to all the W hotels.

722 Rooms: Air-conditioning, Web TV, VCR, CD player, two-line telephone, modular jacks, hair dryer, minibar, radio, room service (nonstop), concierge, business center, fitness center, wheelchair access.

Wyndham

42 West 58th St (btw Fifth/Sixth Aves). Tel. 1-212/753-3500. Fax 1-212/754-5638. Rates: $185-$210 single/double; suites from $210. AE, MC, V.

It should say a lot that no Manhattan hotel has a more fanatically loyal clientele than this slightly cranky Midtowner with no website. Perfectly located, steps from Fifth Avenue and just one block south of Central Park, the Wyndham is an extremely detailed Old World charmer, featuring shabby chic rooms packed with eccentricities. First and foremost, this place is extremely comfortable: Chintz-draped rooms are large and quiet, and imbued with the privacy of home. There are no tour groups and few business types, except for those who appear to be on vacation. Suites contain cold pantries, refrigerators and walk-in closets. The Wyndham is owner-occupied and unusually well priced. The fact that there is nothing modern about it is an integral part of this dame's charm. People love this place because it's beautiful, warts and all.

200 Rooms: Air-conditioning, cable TV, telephone, radio.

Moderate

Abingdon Guest House

13 Eighth Ave (at 12th St). Tel. 1-212/243-5384. www. AbingdonGuesthouse.com. Rates: $147-$212 single/ double AE, MC, V.

Precisely because it is one, Abingdon feels just like a high-quality home. All nine crisply decorated, smoke-free units are swathed with appealing vibrant palettes. They contain good beds, (some four-posters), covered with country quilts, and are furnished in a warm, personal way with characterful pieces. They also feature such extras as good lighting, telephones with answering machines, and VCRs. All of the rooms have private bath, though a few are situated off the hall. Located above a coffeehouse directly on Eighth Avenue, this is not the quietest place in the city, but the absence of street-level signage, your own key to the front door and complimentary breakfast downstairs will make you feel like a native.

9 Rooms: Air-conditioning, cable TV, telephone, hair dryer, minibar, radio, restaurant.

Beacon Hotel

2130 Broadway (btw 74th/75th Sts). Tel. 1-212/787-1100. Fax 1-212/724-0839. www. beaconhotel.com. Rates: $195-$235 single/double; suites from $275. AE, MC, V.

With a great Upper West Side location—close to Lincoln Center, good shopping and Central Park—the Beacon is a value-packed standby offering decent-sized, renovated rooms with firm beds, standard furnishings, and great views, for those lucky enough to be on the upper stories. Extras include kitchenettes (with two-burner stove, microwave, and refrigerator), voice mail, hair dryers, coffee makers and a nonstop coffee shop on the ground floor.

230 Rooms: Air-conditioning, cable TV, telephone, hair dryer, radio, room service (nonstop). wheelchair access.

Best Western Manhattan

17 West 32nd St (Btw Fifth Ave/Broadway). Tel. 1-212/736-1600 or 1-800/551-2303. Fax 1-212/790-2760. www.applecorehotels.com. Rates: $149-$359 single/double; suites from $229. AE, MC, V.

Typical of the properties run by Apple Core Hotels, this Best Western is a former fleabag, that was turned into a serviceable place to stay for a modest amount of money. The hotel is one block from the Empire State Building in a neighborhood that's awful quiet at night and on weekends. A black marble lobby leads up to small rooms designed in several different motifs, from floral to contemporary. Choose the former, fitted with a TV and coffeemaker.

176 Rooms: Air-conditioning, cable TV, telephone, modular jacks, hair dryer, radio, wheelchair access.

Edison Hotel

228 West 47th St (btw Broadway/Eighth Ave). Tel. 1-212/840-5000. www.edisonhotelnyc.com. Rates: $190 single/double; suites from $250. AE, MC, V.

This huge hotel with an Art Deco lobby offers plenty of small and clean plain-Jane rooms that are perfect for budget-oriented groups. Outside, the Edison is nondescript. Inside, it's descript to a fault, overly decorated and in perpetual disarray. The location is perfect for theatergoers.

1000 Rooms: Air-conditioning, cable TV, telephone, radio, concierge, restaurant, bar, wheelchair access.

Excelsior

45 West 81st St (btw Columbus Ave/Central Park West). Tel. 1-212/362-9200 or 1-800/368-4575. Fax 1-212/580-3972. www.excelsiorhotelny.com. Rates: $179-$279 single/double; suites from $239. AE, MC, V.

A decent value on the Upper West Side, this recommendable hotel is clearly showing its age, but at the often-discounted prices, nobody seems to mind. Close to the Museum of Natural History and Central Park, the location gets two enthusiastic thumbs up. Lots of repeat guests convince us that this place is worth writing home about.

190 Rooms: Air-conditioning, cable TV, telephone, modular jacks, hair dryer, radio, wheelchair access.

Gramercy Park Hotel

2 Lexington Ave (at 21st St). Tel. 1-212/475-4320. Fax 1-212/505-0535. www.thegramercyparkhotel.com. Rates: $200-$220 single/double; suites from $240. AE, MC, V.

Once well on its way to seed, the Gramercy Park Hotel has been rejuvenated by West Coast artists, traveling models, slumming celebrities and second-rate rockers who have turned it into one of the best places to stay in the city. Despite it's enviable ground-zero Gramercy location this charming hotel keeps rates reasonable, making it one of our top choices in the price range. There's not much to the frumpy rooms, except that they are exceedingly large and still have a remote whiff of elegance. The entire hotel is tattered enough to keep the high-rollerboys away but elegant and comfortable enough to make it a wonderful place to stay. A key to the lovely and exclusive Gramercy Park, next door, is provided to all guests. The hotel bar, an ancient, mirrored club lounge with heavy red drapes and candelabra sconces, is a great place to drink even if you're not staying upstairs.

509 Rooms: Air-conditioning, telephone, radio, room service (730am-1030pm), restaurant, bar, wheelchair access.

TAXI

073

Millenium Hilton

55 Church St (btw Fulton/Dey Sts). Tel. 1–212/693-2001 or 1–800/752-0014. Fax 1–212/571-2316. www.hilton.com. Rates: $175-$500 single/double; suites from $380. AE, MC, V.

Staying in the Financial District will give you a very different perspective on Manhattan than the one experienced by most visitors. Here you feel the historical city, experience the sea, and are within easy walking distance of both TriBeCa and Chinatown. It's especially great on weekends when the surrounding streets are almost empty and hotel rates are drastically slashed. The Millenium is a quality hotel, finer than most properties in the world with the Hilton brand, offering relatively small rooms filled with essential business gadgets: two-line phones, fax machines, hair dryers, lighted makeup mirrors, irons, safes, minibars, bathrobes and the like. And few workout spaces are more enjoyable than the hotel's glass-enclosed pool. Secure accommodations high up in this 5-story black tower and you'll be treated to incredible vistas over Lower Manhattan—and the World Trade Center site, which is located right across the street. Those facing south get lots of sun and also enjoy clear views to the Statue of Liberty and beyond.

561 Rooms: Air-conditioning, cable TV, telephone, modular jacks, fax, hair dryer, minibar, radio, room service (nonstop), concierge, restaurants, bar, business center, fitness center, swimming pool, wheelchair access.

The Paramount

235 West 46th St (btw Broadway/Eighth Ave). Tel. 1–212/764-5500 or 1–800/225-7474. Fax 1–212/575-4892. www.lanschragerhotels.com. Rates: $150-$395 single/double; suites from $410. AE, MC, V.

Ian Schrager, whose name is now synonymous with stylish boutique hotels, opened this modish youth magnet in 1990 before the word "trendy" ever preceded "hotel." The hook is excessive design, high-quality service, and moderate prices. The hotel wows, if not inspires. Philippe Starck's mind-altering design crams lots of over-the-top elements into painfully undersized rooms, where giant Vermeer reproductions double as headboards set against a pristine all-white décor. Bathrooms, fashioned from stainless steel, can be somewhat austere. Amenities include in-room VCRs and telephones with call-waiting. There's great people-watching from the Mezzanine restaurant over-looking a theatrically lit lobby that's furnished in eye-popping Starck style with custom made sofas and furnishings. Black-clad AMWs (actress/model/whatevers) staff the adjacent Whiskey Bar, which is as dark as it is loud. For quiet, plush comfort, head up to the Library Bar on the mezzanine, or find a different hotel altogether.

610 Rooms: Air-conditioning, cable TV, VCR, telephone, modular jacks, hair dryer, minibar, radio, room service (nonstop), concierge, restaurants, bar, nightclub, business center, fitness center, wheelchair access.

sleeping #03

TAXI
075

Roger Smith Hotel

501 Lexington Ave (at 47th St). Tel. 1–212/755-1400 or 1–800/445-0277. Fax 1–212/758-4061. www.rogersmith.com. Rates: $189–$285 single/double; suites from $350. AE, MC, V.

James Knowles, the Roger Smith's owner and resident sculptor, likes to think of his hotel as a place for artists and art-lovers. The lobby is something of a gallery for contemporary paintings and statues, and free passes to MoMA are offered to weekend guests. Indeed, pop groups and other creatives seem to like this hotel's well-sized rooms, each of which is uniquely furnished and full of character.

There's a generosity of spirit in this cozy inn, nestled amongst the skyscrapers of Midtown. Rooms come with refrigerators and coffee-makers, there's a video lending library, and breakfast is free to all guests.

130 Rooms: Air-conditioning, cable TV, telephone, modular jacks, hair dryer, radio, restaurant, bar, access to nearby health club, wheelchair access.

Roosevelt Hotel

45 East 45th St (at Madison Ave). Tel 1–212/661-9600 or 1–888/833-3969. Fax 1–212/885-6168. www.therooseveltel.com. Rates: $199–$339 single/double; suites from $500. AE, MC, V.

Reopened after a two-year, $65 million bout of cosmetic surgery, this charming circa-1924 hotel has been restored to its former splendor as an excellent workaday hostelry for both business and leisure travelers. A walk past the lobby's grand 27-foot-tall fluted columns and around the crystal-chandeliered public areas is a good alternative to time travel, especially if you're old enough to recognize the lounge from which Guy Lombardo broadcasted on so many New Year's Eves. Built above the tracks of Grand Central Station in the heyday of rail travel, this huge Midtown hotel contains just over 1000 rooms. Today, these conservatively styled guest quarters contain all the necessary fittings for first-class travel, but are relatively small and far less memorable than the public areas downstairs. All in all, this hotel is a good standby when others in the neighborhood are full. Even if you're not staying here you might want to step in for tea in the Palm Room or savor a cigar in the mahogany-paneled Madison Club Lounge.

1040 Rooms: Air-conditioning, cable TV, telephone, modular jacks, fax, hair dryer, radio, room service (6am–11pm), concierge, restaurant, bar, business center, fitness center, wheelchair access.

Thirty Thirty

30 East 30th St (btw Madison/Park Aves). Tel. 1–212/689–1900. Fax 1–212/689–0023. www.thirty-hirty-nyc.com. Rates: $135 single, $195 double. AE, MC, V.

Citylife Hotel Group has chosen the northern edge of the Flatiron District for this, their third and most value-conscious hotel in Manhattan. The hotel is a hit with Silicon Alley types and those who want to be near FIT and the Garment District. Located in a former residential hotel for women, the rooms are clean and comfortable and have a modern, minimalist look. Beds have padded bedheads and black side tables. But space is limited so that TVs are suspended from the walls, and the single chair is likely tucked into a corner. Still, the location and good amenities make 30/30 a good value in this town.

240 Rooms: Air-conditioning, cable TV, telephone, modular jacks, hair dryer, radio.

Washington Square Hotel

103 Waverly Pl (btw Fifth/Sixth Aves). Tel. 1–212/777-9515 or 1–800/222-0418. Fax 1–212/979-8373. www.washingtonsquarehotel.com. Rates: $150-$200 single/double. AE, MC, V.

If this hotel were in a lesser neighborhood it's unlikely we'd recommend its frumpy and cramped rooms and unremarkable public areas. As it happens, however, Washington Square Hotel is in the heart of Greenwich Village, and the price is relatively light. Bob Dylan stayed here and Joan Baez sang of it, but that shouldn't mean much to guests who have to be practically shoehorned into the rooms. If you do choose to stay here, remember, this hotel is trading on its location; the best rooms overlook Washington Square Park.

170 Rooms: Air-conditioning, cable TV, telephone, modular jacks, radio, restaurant, bar, fitness center.

Westpark Hotel

308 West 58th St (btw 8th/9th Aves). Tel. 1–212/246-6440. Fax 1–212/246-3131. www.westparkhotel.com. Rates: $150-$220 single/double; suites from $220. AE, MC, V.

Unremarkable, except for good prices and a great location two blocks from Central Park, Westpark Hotel is a well-managed small hotel with basic rooms and friendly service. There are few extras to coo about. Ask for one of the few rooms with park views.

90 Rooms: Air-conditioning, cable TV, telephone, modular jacks, radio.

TAXI

077

Inexpensive

Aladdin Hotel

317 West 45th St (btw Eighth/Ninth Aves). Tel. 1–212/977-5700. Fax 1–212/246-6036. www.aladdinhotel.com. Rates: $20–$27 per dorm bed; $80–$90 single/double. AE, MC, V.
Straddling the fence between hostel and hotel, the Aladdin is a colorful place in an energetic Times Square location. The theme at this appropriately named hotel is both whimsical and clownish, driven by primary colors and the carnival atmosphere that pervades the Theater District. And after a park bench, their dorm beds are the cheapest sleeps in the city.

Broadway Inn

264 West 46th St (btw Broadway/Eighth Ave). Tel. 1–212/997-9200. Fax 1–212/768-2807. www.BroadwayInn.com. Rates: $109-$195 single/double; suites from $195. AE, MC V.
Despite being right in the center of the Theater District, this small and comfortable hotel has a country-inn ambience. The tone is set in the second-floor lobby with its book-filled cases, brick hearth, comfy sofas and café tables at which continental breakfast is served. Rooms vary in size, and some are so small you'd think they were built for hobbits. Make sure your minimum space requirements are known. Each accommodation is furnished in metropolitan style and suites have refrigerator and microwave. There is no elevator. And if you're a light sleeper, ask for a room in the rear. The staff is super-helpful—a bonus for what is certainly one of the city's best deals... if you can manage to secure a room.
40 Rooms: Air-conditioning, cable TV, telephone, hair dryer.

The Chelsea Inn

46 West 17th St (btw Fifth/Sixth Aves). Tel. 1–212/645-8989 or 1–800/640-6469. Fax 1–212/645-1903. www.chelseainn.com. Rates: $110-$130 double with shared bath, $140-$160 studio, suites from $220. AE, MC, V.
The vibe at the Chelsea Inn is something akin to having you're own downscale apartment in the neighborhood. Although it's devoid of luxury, this 19th-century townhouse offers generously-sized rooms and suites fitted with stray furniture, flea-market foundlings and student-art bathroom murals. The cheapest have shared baths, but all have kitchenettes with a refrigerator, coffee maker and hot plate.
Air conditioning, cable TV, safe.

Chelsea Star Hotel

300 West 30th St (at Eighth Ave). Tel. 1–212/244-7827 or 1–877/827-6969. Fax 1–212/279-9018. www.starhotelny.com. Rates: $35 per dorm bed, $85 single, $105 double; apartments from $175. AE, MC, V.

This Jekyll and Hyde hotel/hostel extends its multiple personality disorder to its guestrooms, each of which is decorated according to a different fantasy. From Cleopatra to *Star Trek*, themes range across millennia. And their Madonna Room is something of a shrine to the star who stayed here before fame visited her. Decorations are more subdued in the dormitory rooms, each of which contains a sitting area and internet kiosk. On the other end of the spectrum are private apartments containing data ports and fax machines. Note that towels are not supplied for dormitory rooms.

Comfort Inn

129 West 46th St (btw Sixth Ave/Broadway). Tel. 1–212/221-2600 or 1–800/755-3194. Fax 1–212/790-2760. www.applecorehotels.com. Rates: $99-$329 single/double. AE, MC, V.

Apple Core Hotels has a knack for creating serviceable tourist hotels with both eyes on the bottom line. Guests receive minimum treatment at prices you can't complain too much about. The Comfort Inn is cheap, safe, clean and, um, comfortable. It's also conveniently located in the heart of the Theater District. When looking for an inexpensive place to rest your head, keep this basic budget standby in mind.

79 Rooms: Air-conditioning, cable TV, telephone, modular jacks, hair dryer, radio, business center, fitness room.

The Cosmopolitan

95 West Broadway (at Chambers St). Tel. 1–212/566-1900 or 1–888/895-9400. Fax 1–212/566-6909. www.cosmohotel.com. Rates: $125 double, $150 twin. AE, MC, V.

Situated in the heart of Tribeca, and five blocks north of the World Trade Center site, The Cosmopolitan is a clean, well-lighted place with simple furnishings and muted colors. The atmosphere is welcoming and modern as well as relatively quiet and laid-back. This is a very good place to stay in a happening neighborhood that has few hotels.

105 Rooms: TV, telephone.

The Gershwin

*7 East 27th St (btw Fifth/Madison Aves).
Tel. 1-212/545-8000. Fax 1-212/684-5546.
www.gershwinhotel.com. Rates: $40 per dorm bed;
$109-$229 single/double; suites from $300. AE, MC, V.*

The rest stop of choice for traveling alternateens and boho Europeans, The Gershwin offers funky, inexpensive lodgings, a great location and interestingly "decorated" rooms. A fun, Pop Art-painted lobby gives way to guest quarters so Spartan that ceiling cracks become decoration. Very clean and exceedingly bohemian, the hotel has the feeling of an upscale youth hostel that was opened in a week. Inexpensive doubles are augmented by super-cheap, eight-bed multi-shares—each a global village in microcosm. Closet space is nonexistent and the harried staff is of little help. Messages? Fugetaboutit. The Red Room, a dark and cheap bar, is the hotel's *piece de resistance*, reeling in guests and locals with live music seven nights a week.

147 Rooms: Air-conditioning, cable TV, telephone, modular jacks, radio, concierge, restaurant, bar.

Habitat

*130 East 57th St (at Lexington Ave). Tel.
1-212/753-8841 or 1-800/255-0482. Fax
1-212/829-9605. www.habitatny.com. Rates: $90-$119 si*
with shared bath; $115-$175 single/double; suites fi
AE,MC, V.

Catering to traveling tightwads and visiting students since 199
is that rarest of commodities: a hotel in which "conscious" fol....both
"style" and "budget." The lobby is bright and uncluttered and the rooms
are modern and comfortable. The cheapest have shared baths. Neutral
décor means beds covered in corduroy, then accented with cushions for
a homey feel. The amenities are great for the price, and the abfab location
is close to Midtown shopping and attractions.

200 Rooms: Air-conditioning, cable TV, telephone,
modular jacks, radio.

Hostelling International - New York

*891 Amsterdam Ave (at 104th St). Tel. 1-212/932-
2300. Fax 1-212/932-2574. www.hinewyork.org.
Rates: $25-$28 per dorm bed. MC, V.*

The largest hostel in the United States is housed in a century-
old landmark building on Manhattan's Upper West Side.
Configurations range from four to 12 beds per room, each air
conditioned in summer and heated in the winter. The
hostel's back garden, one of the largest private spaces in New
York City, is a great place to hang out. Plentiful facilities
include a lounge, gameroom, shop, coin-op laundry, lobby
coffee bar, cafeteria, and self-service kitchen. Linen and
towels are included, and reservations are necessary.

624 Beds.

Hotel 17

*225 East 17th St (btw Second/Third Aves).
Tel. 1-212/475-2845. Fax 1-212/677-8178.
www.hotel17.citysearch.com. Rates: $85-$139
single/double. No cards.*

Nothing attests to the power of public
relations more than this downtown
dive, packed with impoverished
young trendies
who read about it in *Details*.
A former welfare hotel, 17 has
a heroin-chic allure that has
landed almost as many

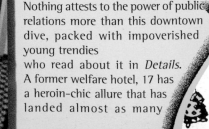

TAXI

081

fashion shoots as it has guests. Close to the East Village without actually being in it, the hotel thrives on its edgy image to the extent that carpet stains and bathroom rot remain unchallenged by the house cleaners. That said, Hotel 17 is not life-threatening, is great for late-nighters and has a unique atmosphere that is authentically hip.

120 Rooms: Air-conditioning, cable TV, telephone.

The Larchmont

27 West 11th St (btw Fifth/Sixth Aves). Tel. 1–212/989-9333. Fax 1-212/989-9496. www.larchmonthotel.com. Rates: $80-$119 single/double. AE, MC, V.
A haven for debt-ridden aristocrats and other well-heeled budget travelers, The Larchmont is an alluring little inn on a perfect Greenwich Village street. The antithesis of a corporate hotel, this place is homey and unique. Rooms are small, and none comes with private bath. But each is well decorated in muted earth tones, very clean, and equipped with good lighting, a writing desk, ceiling fan, bathrobe and slippers. It's a charming place that's pretty, not pricey. Breakfast, included, is served in an attractive basement cafe.

58 Rooms: Air-conditioning, cable TV, telephone, hair dryer (on request) , radio.

Malibu Studio Hotel

2688 Broadway (btw 102nd/103rd Sts). Tel. 1–212/222-2954 or 1-800/647-2227. Fax 1-212/678-6842. www. malibuhotelnyc.com. Rates: $55-$89 single/double with shared bath, $109-$149 single/double with private bath. No cards.
Low-rent parents, prospective students, and others who want great rates close to Columbia University can do no better than this comfortable budget hotel. *Miami Vice* colors and telephone-free rooms keep out the nobility. Shared baths are available for the truly underprivileged. CD players and hairdryers are available on request.

100 Rooms: Air-conditioning, TV (not cable), telephone.

Off-SoHo Suites

11 Rivington St (btw Christie/Bowery Sts). Tel. 1–212/979-9815 or 1-800/633-7646. Fax 1-212/979-9801. www.offsoho.com. Rates: $107-$145 single/double. AE, MC, V.
"Off-Bowery" is a little more like it: This budget inn is in a more-than-slightly-seedy neighborhood populated by some scary late-night street

workers. Despite the cachet-chasing name, this all-suite inn offers underpriced, oversized rooms and is one of the best accommodation deals in the city. Each suite includes a bedroom and living/dining area. But, since suites are built in pairs, each shares a kitchen and bath with the one next door. That's not such a bad thing, considering that this place is extremely clean and private, and each accommodation comes with plenty of extras, including a phone, TV, VCR and minibar. Despite surly management, Off-SoHo Suites is a great value in a dodgy location, perfect for Lower East Side clubbers but not, perhaps, for first-timers.

36 Suites: Air-conditioning, cable TV, telephone, modular jacks, radio, fitness center.

Pickwick Arms

230 East 51st St (btw Second/Third Aves). Tel. 1–212/355-0300 or 1–800/742-5945. Fax 1–212/755-5029. www.pickwickarms.com. Rates: $75-$120 single, $125-$180 double. AE, MC, V.

Single travelers, especially, should take notice of the Pickwick's great rates, fine location and surprisingly good staff. Except that it's quiet, clean and thoroughly acceptable, there's not much to say about this rather plain property, which feels somewhat devoid of soul. We can't imagine eating in the ground-floor restaurant or hanging out on the roof-top terrace. But, in a city where $100 doesn't go very far, the Pickwick feels like one of Manhattan's best buys.

350 Rooms: Air-conditioning, cable TV, telephone, restaurant.

Quality Hotel & Suites

59 West 46th St (btw Fifth/Sixth Aves). Tel. 1–212/719-2300 or 1–800/848-0020. Fax 1–212/790-2760. www.applecorehotels.com. Rates: $109-$239 single/double; suites from $189. AE, MC, V.

This is just your basic dive hotel, a place to rest your head. But if you're not planning to spend much time in your room, these recently renovated accommodations are perfectly acceptable places to stay. It's clean and safe, and the Theater District location is terrific.

193 Rooms: Air-conditioning, cable TV, telephone, modular jacks, hair dryer, radio, restaurant, business center, fitness center, wheelchair access.

#04 Sightseeing
The Top Sights

TAXI

#04
Sightseeing

Times Square

What the hell happened to Times Square? Once synonymous with prostitution and street crime, the deodorized intersection of Broadway and Seventh Avenue now seems like one of the cleanest in the city. Forty-Second Street in particular is so spic-and-span it almost feels like a film set. Bustling crime and grime is hardly a bad thing, but lots of locals are griping about the Disneyfication of the city's most distinctive district. Right before our eyes 42nd Street has been transformed into a milquetoasty suburban-style shopping mall— two malls, actually, on the north and south sides of the street. E-Walk, the larger of the two, includes dozens of shops, a SONY multiplex, "Vegas" theme restaurant, and a 47-story hotel that appears to be slashed from top to bottom by an arc of light. The tourist-oriented shopping center opposite contains a 25-screen megaplex —the largest in New York history—plus Madame Tussaud's Wax Museum and a variety of entertainment-related retail stores and theme restaurants.

The square got its name when *The New York Times* moved in at the turn of the century. When the subways opened, Times Square became an important commuter crossing, which in turn prompted theaters to relocate here from downtown. The district's golden years ended with the Great Depression, and the Great White Way became the grimy, porn-infected, dangerous place that we came to know and love from the 60s to the early 90s. Mercifully, some things

TAXI

087

haven't changed. The district is still a 24-hour circus plastered with wheatpasted posters. It's still Theaterland, home to the Broadway musical and the half-price TKTS booth. And the U.S. Army still maintains a recruiting station right in the heart of the hustle, cleverly positioned to prey on runaways who slip past chicken-hawking pimps at the nearby Port Authority Bus Terminal. The New Year's Eve balldrop, Times Square's most notable tradition, has survived too. It began at the end of 1906, when the *Times* lowered an illuminated ball down a pole atop its new headquarters. Now a half-million people turn up (and 300 million tune in) each December 31st to watch the dropping of a refurbished ball, glittering with thousands of rhinestones and flickering strobes.

While we hesitatingly approve of this kinder, gentler Times Square, we also openly hope that it will never be completely rid of pickpockets, prostitutes, porno parlors and psychodramatic panhandlers. The "new" Times Square may indeed be "safer, cleaner and brighter"—we're just wondering what we're going to do with all our extra Peepland tokens.

Statue of Liberty

Liberty Island. Tel. 1–212/363-3200; ferry information 1–212/269-5755. In summer ferries operate daily, every 20 minutes from about 830am-430pm with the last ferry returning at 630pm; in winter ferries operate daily, every 30 minutes from about 9am-330pm with last ferry returning 530pm. Admission $10 adults, $8 seniors, $4 children 3-17, includes round-trip transportation and admission to Ellis Island. No cards.

The colossal bronze *Liberty Enlightening the World*, as she was originally called, was the life work of 19th-century French sculptor Frederic-Auguste Bartholdi. The artist toiled tirelessly not only to create it, but also to sell it to the French and American people who had to pay for it. Motivated in part by a desire to embarrass their own repressive government, the French citizenry financed the statue's construction through public subscription. For their part, the Americans were required to pay for Liberty's enormous pedestal, a difficult fund-raiser that required repeated prodding by Joseph

Pulitzer's *New York World* newspaper. After Liberty's massive arm toured America to help the cash flow, enough money was raised and the rest of the body was shipped over from France in crates.

The statue was dedicated on October 28, 1886, but it wasn't until 1903, when Emma Lazarus' poem "The New Colossus" was inscribed on Liberty's base, that the statue became a symbol of American immigration. For the 12 million new Americans who sailed into New York Harbor in the late 19th and early 20th centuries, the "lady with the lamp" confirmed that they had arrived.

These days "Your tired, your poor, your huddled masses yearning to breathe free" seems to refer to the throng of tourists jostling for position in lines, on boats and up the cramped spiraling steps to the statue's crown. (Note: During the summer, only people arriving on the first ferry are allowed to climb into the crown.) Woody Allen once joked that the last time he was inside a woman was when he took a tour of the Statue of Liberty. It couldn't have been a great experience. The statue is best observed from the outside and, after 354 steps to the top, the summit is anti-climactic. From Liberty Island, views of both the statue and Lower Manhattan are breathtaking. Inside the statue's base you'll find good exhibits on the history and building of the statue, and a brief display on US immigration since 1600. Note that for security reasons no large bags or backpacks are permitted on the ferry.

The New Colossus

Give me your tired, your poor,
Your huddled masses yearning to breathe free,
The wretched refuse of your teeming shore.
Send these, the homeless, tempest-tossed to me,
I lift my lamp beside the golden door.
- Emma Lazarus

Tickets & Times

Circle Line ferries depart from Battery Park approximately every 30 minutes and stop at both Liberty Island and Ellis Island. Weekday mornings are the best times to go, as the tourist crush can be unbearable later in the day and on Saturdays and Sundays, especially during July and August. The ticket booth is located in Battery Park's Castle Clinton.

TAXI

089

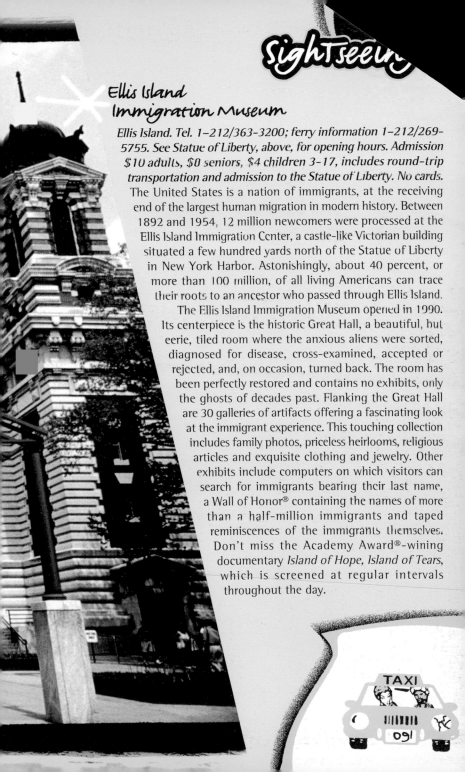

Ellis Island Immigration Museum

Ellis Island. Tel. 1–212/363-3200; ferry information 1–212/269-5755. See Statue of Liberty, above, for opening hours. Admission $10 adults, $0 seniors, $4 children 3–17, includes round-trip transportation and admission to the Statue of Liberty. No cards.

The United States is a nation of immigrants, at the receiving end of the largest human migration in modern history. Between 1892 and 1954, 12 million newcomers were processed at the Ellis Island Immigration Center, a castle-like Victorian building situated a few hundred yards north of the Statue of Liberty in New York Harbor. Astonishingly, about 40 percent, or more than 100 million, of all living Americans can trace their roots to an ancestor who passed through Ellis Island.

The Ellis Island Immigration Museum opened in 1990. Its centerpiece is the historic Great Hall, a beautiful, but eerie, tiled room where the anxious aliens were sorted, diagnosed for disease, cross-examined, accepted or rejected, and, on occasion, turned back. The room has been perfectly restored and contains no exhibits, only the ghosts of decades past. Flanking the Great Hall are 30 galleries of artifacts offering a fascinating look at the immigrant experience. This touching collection includes family photos, priceless heirlooms, religious articles and exquisite clothing and jewelry. Other exhibits include computers on which visitors can search for immigrants bearing their last name, a Wall of Honor® containing the names of more than a half-million immigrants and taped reminiscences of the immigrants themselves. Don't miss the Academy Award®-wining documentary *Island of Hope, Island of Tears*, which is screened at regular intervals throughout the day.

TAXI

091

The Brooklyn Bridge

Center Street and Park Row, Lower Manhattan.
Walking across the Brooklyn Bridge is one of the classic
New York experiences. The main point is the incredible
view of Manhattan. As you walk closer to—or farther
from—the city, the buildings appear to move in relationship
to one another, as in a slow waltz. Best time to go is on
a long summer evening around sunset.

This stone-and-steel bridge, constructed between 1868
and 1883, was built with a pedestrian promenade
that's perpetually awash with strollers and cyclists. A marvel
of 19th-century engineering, the Brooklyn Bridge was
designed by John Roebling, the man who invented wire
cable.

Once on the other side you can explore Brooklyn Heights
(*see* Chapter 5/The Best of Brooklyn), or simply turn around
and walk back.

To reach the footbridge, go through the Municipal Building
at the Brooklyn Bridge-City Hall subway stop and follow the
signs to the entrance at the traffic median.

Rockefeller Center

48th/51st Sts (btw Fifth/Sixth Aves). Tel. 1–212/632-3975.
Open nonstop. Admission free.
A masterpiece of modern design, Rockefeller Center is a limestone
complex of 19 buildings on 22 acres in the heart of Midtown. Mostly
completed between 1932 to 1940, the Center is basically just
a collection of Art Deco office buildings. But its unique design and
intricate styling create a compelling attraction. The best way to
approach the complex is through the Channel Gardens that run from
Fifth Avenue to the Sunken Plaza in the Center's middle. Lorded over
by the fabulous and famous *Prometheus* statue, the Plaza is best in
winter when ice skaters glide in the shadows of Manhattan's most

magnificent skyscrapers (see Chapter 6/ Recreation & Exercise). Each Christmas a giant tree is set up here, decorated with more than 25,000 multicolored lights which are lit the week following Thanksgiving.

The centerpiece and tallest building in Rockefeller Center is the 65-floor skyscraper known as "30 Rock." It's worth seeing the lobby, with its vast murals, gleaming black granite floors and lots of inlaid elements outlined in brass. Upstairs is the East Coast headquarters of NBC television, and the studios where *Saturday Night Live* and other major shows are taped. The building is topped by the magnificent Rainbow Room (see Chapter 9/Nightlife). Pick up a free map and self-guided tour of the Center in the main lobby.

The United Nations

First Avenue (at 46th St). Tel. 1-212/963-8687 . Open daily 930am-445pm. Closed Sat-Sun in Jan-Feb. Admission free; tours $10 adults, $7.50 seniors, $6.50 students/youth, $5.50 children grades 1-8. Under 5s not permitted.

One of the most striking things about the United Nations is that the ethnic mixture inside looks very much like a microcosm of New York City in general. But in here the hacks are not driving taxis—they're diplomats, which means they can park their cars anywhere they please with impunity. A UN tour may not be the most exciting event on the planet, but it's worth seeing how the countries of the world attempt to communicate and associate with each other. Guided tours swing through the General Assembly Hall and the Council Chambers before being pointed in the direction of the gift shop, the restaurant and the UN post office's stamp counter. Tours depart every 30 minutes, but be warned: Weekdays between 8am and 3pm the building is school-group hell.

TAXI

093

Empire State Building

350 Fifth Ave (at 34th St). Tel. 1–212/736-3100.
Open daily 9am–11pm. Admission $10 adults,
$9 seniors, $5 children 5–11.

Visiting the top of the Empire State Building may
sound like a tourist trap, but it's actually one of
New York's most thrilling attractions. At night,
when the lights of New York are twinkling
before you, the view is as wonderful and
awesome as any we've ever experienced. One
can't help being swept away by the enormity
of it all.

The Empire State Building is an icon of
American modernism and an Art Deco
masterpiece that's the architectural cousin
of the Chrysler Building and Rockefeller
Center. The 102-story office building
opened in 1931, right after the Great
Depression—unfortunate timing that would
have bankrupted the skyscraper had not
its observation terrace been such an
immediate hit. The view was completely
unobstructed until 1947 when a series
of jumpers led to the erection of a suicide
fence.

Because it's quite small and
completely enclosed, the view from
the 102nd floor is inferior to the one
on the 86th, and not worth the wait
for the elevator. Lines are longest
between 3 and 9pm. But generous
opening hours mean you can show
up late and have Manhattan almost
all to yourself.

When it comes to television production, New York's got nothing on LA. But a few top shows have yet to move to the Left Coast. Tours of NBC Studios, 30 Rockefeller Plaza (49th St. btw Fifth/Sixth Aves, tel. 1–212/664-3700), depart Monday through Saturday, every 15 minutes from 830am to 530pm, Sun 930am-430pm. You've got to show up early, though, as tickets sell out quickly. It costs about $17.50 adults, $15 seniors/students 6-16 (under 6 not admitted) for the 70-minute excursion into TV land, which is worth it only if you've never done anything like it before.

Tickets for all network TV tapings are free, but they must usually be requested in advance by postcard. Some programs release a few tickets on the day of the taping, and most offer same-day standby tickets (first come, first served—one per person), which do not guarantee admission. They are handed out at the 49th Street entrance. Audience members must be 16 or older. Here's what's happening:

Saturday Night Live (NBC)

A ticket lottery is held each year at the end of August and only postcards sent in August are entered. Standby tickets are distributed Saturday at 915am at NBC, on the mezzanine level of the 49th Street side of 30 Rockefeller Plaza. Shows are on Saturday from 1130pm to 1am. for information call 1–212/664-3056.

The Today Show (NBC)

Anyone can watch—Just show up and peer through the window at 30 Rockefeller Plaza (49th St, btw Fifth/Sixth Aves). Tapings are Monday through Friday from 7 to 9am.

Late Show with David Letterman (CBS)

Tickets must be requested six months in advance by postcard. Send your name, address, and telephone number to *Late Show with David Letterman*, c/o Ed Sullivan Theater, 1697 Broadway, New York, NY 10019. Same-day tickets go on sale at 11am and can be obtained by calling 1-212/247-6497. If there are any standby tickets left these are given out at the box office. Tapings are Monday through Thursday at 530pm, with a later show at 830pm on Thursday. Call 1-212/975-1003 for information.

Last Call with Carson Daly (NBC)

Reserve tickets by calling 1-212/664-3056. Standby tickets distributed on day of the show on a first-come first-served basis.

Late Night with Conan O'Brian (NBC)

Conan is one of the easiest seats in town. A small number of day-of and standby tickets are distributed Tuesday to Friday at 9am at the 49th Street entrance of 30 Rockefeller Plaza. Call 1-212/664-3056 for information.

Good Morning America (ABC)

A similar set-up to *The Today Show*: Anyone can stop by these Times Square windows, weekdays from 7 to 9am, and look into the street-front studios at 1500 Broadway (at 44th St).

The Best Museums

New York is a fabulous town for culture sluts because you can find something sensational from every civilization the world has ever seen. Artists, and their enlightened benefactors, turned New York into the postwar master of the art universe. And as they grow the city's museums just keep getting better.

Although it's actually closer to two miles, the 35-block stretch of Fifth Avenue from 70th Street to 105th Street is known as "Museum Mile" because of its incredible concentration of museums that include (from south to north) the Frick, the Met, the Guggenheim, the National Academy of Design, the Cooper-Hewitt, the Jewish Museum, the Museum of the City of New York, and El Museo del Barrio.

Take advantage of free or "pay what you wish" nights at the city's finest museums, including the Whitney (Fridays 6-8pm), the Guggenheim (Fridays 6-8pm), and the Cooper-Hewitt (Tuesdays 5-9pm). And don't overlook the museums' gift shops, as they are some of the best and most original stores in town.

American Museum of Natural History

Central Park West (btw 77th/81st Sts). Tel. 1-212/769-5100. Open Sat-Thurs 10am-545pm, Fri 10am-845pm. Suggested Contribution $12 adults, $9 students/seniors, $7 children.

An astounding 30 million artifacts are stashed on four floors at the Museum of Natural History, including 1 million species of spiders, 1.6 million kinds of beetles and 2 million types of butterflies. The sparklingly rich gems and minerals department glows with thousands of colorful geodes in glass cases and includes the huge Star of India sapphire. There's a 10-ton fiberglass-and-steel blue whale in the Hall of Ocean Life, and a new Biodiversity wing exploring the interconnectedness of nature. But, no matter how big this museum grows, dinosaurs will forever remain the star attractions. One of the world's largest collections of dino bones is augmented with ginormous animatronic models, constructed in part with money donated by *Jurassic Park* director Steven Spielberg.

The stunning architecture of the **Rose Center for Earth and Space** is becoming a global icon. From the outside, it looks as though the cosmos has been suspended in a clear glass cube. The sphere at the center contains the new planetarium, which is currently the city's hottest rubbernecking ticket. Here in the Space Theater you can see hyper-realistic visions of the planets, galaxies, and star clusters and then take a trip back to Earth through a black hole. The Hall of Planet Earth galleries are the only ones that we know of that make rocks and geology really rock and roll.

The museum is ridiculously crowded on weekends. It's best during the week after 3pm, when school groups are not clogging the buildings' arteries. Guided tours usually depart from the African Mammals Hall at 1015am, 1115am, 115pm, 215pm and 315pm. An additional tour is added at 1215pm on Saturdays and Sundays.

Guggenheim Museum

1071 Fifth Ave (btw 88th/89th Sts). Tel. 1-212/423-3500. Open Sat-Wed 9am-6pm, Fri 10am-8pm. Closed Thurs. Admission $15 adults, $10 students/seniors; free (contribution requested) Fri 6-8pm.

The Frank Lloyd Wright-designed museum itself is what makes the Guggenheim so special. That's not to say that the art isn't world-class. It is. But the landmark "chambered nautilus" seems capable of making almost anything seem like a masterpiece. The Guggenheim is great just because it's different, relatively small, quick and fun. The "proper" way to visit is to take the elevator to the top, then walk down the spiral ramp towards the exit. The majority of the main building is usually given over to one blockbuster temporary exhibition or another, often devoted to the work of a single significant modern artist. Side rooms are hung with the museum's own masterpieces of 20th-century art.

The permanent collection began with Old Masters collected by mining magnate Solomon Guggenheim that hung in his rooms at the Plaza Hotel. Encouraged by his mistress, the eccentric artist Baroness Hilla Rebay von Ehrenwiesen, Guggenheim turned his sights towards the non-figurative art of Klee, Chagall, Kandinsky and others. In 1943, Rebay convinced Guggenheim to hire Frank Lloyd Wright—who was 74 at the time—to design a "Museum of Non-Objective Painting." By the time these doors finally opened 16 years later, in 1969, both Lloyd Wright and Solomon Guggenheim were dead.

Many of the paintings from the original collection now hang in the museum's tower annex, a 1992 addition that some purists say "wronged Wright," and makes the museum resemble a giant toilet bowl. But the galleries inside are bright and spacious, and allow visitors to step away from the art, which is impossible on the narrow ramp of the main building. The other paintings here are from a post-Impressionist collection donated to the museum in the 1960s by art dealer Justin Thannhauser.

Whitney Museum of American Art

945 Madison Ave (at 75th St.). Tel. 1-212/570-3676. Open Tues-Thurs and Sat-Sun 11am-6pm, Fri 1-9pm. Closed Mon. Admission $12 adults, $9.50 students/seniors; free for children under 12; free Fri 6-9pm.

Gertrude Vanderbilt Whitney founded her own museum in 1929 after the Met rejected her collection of art by American realist painters. The museum was chartered to exhibit modern American artists exclusively, at a time when American art was overshadowed by European art.

The Whitney has been controversial from the get-go: It's risky business when your mission is to unsettle, challenge and provide a major venue for unproven and unfamiliar art. Despite frequent popular successes, critics are routinely dismissive of the quality of the museum's exhibitions, a matter that's not helped by the building itself—a postmodern fortress (complete with a concrete moat and bridge) that's often referred to as one of the city's worst pieces of important architecture. But, by all accounts, the Whitney is improving. The caliber of art is on the rise and their last Biennial (an every-other-year signature exhibition of contemporary American art, held in Spring in odd years) was the most intelligent in memory. Recent events included a retrospective of video-art pioneer Bill Viola, a major Warhol show, and the unveiling of the permanent collection in new galleries.

The Permanent Collection Galleries include works by Jasper Johns, Claes Oldenburg, and Ad Reinhardt, and dedicates entire rooms to Edward Hopper, Georgia O'Keeffe and Alexander Calder. Few post-1945 holdings make it onto the walls (and floors, and ceilings...). Calder's newly restored *Circus* (1926-31) is spotlighted in a separate gallery, where whimsical circus performers and creatures made from tin, paper clips, springs, rags and clock movements are displayed along with a film of the artist as ringmaster, performing a show.

Sarabeth's Kitchen, an outpost of Sarabeth Levine's well-known mini-empire (*see* Chapter 8/Breakfast & Brunch) is on the museum's lower level.

TAXI

101

Metropolitan Museum of Art

1000 Fifth Ave (at 82nd St). Tel. 1–212/535-7710. Open Tues-Thurs and Sun 930am-530pm, Fri-Sat 930am-9pm. Closed Mon. Suggested contribution $12 adults, $7 students/seniors, free for children 12 and under; includes entrance to the Cloisters.

The largest museum in the Western Hemisphere is jam-packed with some of the finest examples of 5000 years of art. The Met's collections are encyclopedic, spanning the entire history of humanity. From teacups to temples, the museum's vast collections are some of the world's most complete—a one-stop shop for Egyptian tombs, ancient Roman coins, meditating bronze Buddhas, Renaissance paintings, African ceremonial masks, muscular Greek torsos, Asian ceramics, Tiffany windows, European arms and armor... the list seems endless. The collections move from strength to strength, from Dutch masters like Vermeer and Rembrandt to Italian Renaissance works by Botticelli and Raphael to Impressionist paintings by Renoir, Gauguin, Cèzanne, Manet and Monet. The riches are repeated with equally broad collections of Asian, Egyptian, African and Islamic art. Only the 20th-century galleries lag, with a relatively small collection riddled with plenty of holes.

Most visitors head straight up the main stairs to the European galleries, or to the second-floor Annenberg Collection with its impressive Impressionist paintings. The Temple of Dendur, an entire 15 BC building saved from the rising waters of the Nile when the Aswan Dam was built, is theatrical and fun. Floating in a fake Nile, the dislocated Egyptian temple would be the centerpiece of almost any other museum. Here it's in a side wing.

Needless to say, the Met is way too big to see it all in one go. The best strategy is to pickup a floor plan and target specific collections. Better yet, latch on to one of the frequent, free docent tours, led by some of the most erudite and articulate volunteers anywhere. (Tours are scheduled mid-September through May from 1015am to 315pm. They depart every 15 minutes or so on weekdays, less frequently on Saturdays and Sundays. From June to mid-August tours are led by apprentice docents, and no tours are scheduled from mid-August to mid-September.)

Wherever you go, finish up on the small rooftop sculpture garden where you can enjoy an espresso or wine as you watch the sunset over Central Park (during warm months only). And pop into the enormous gift shop, a favorite of New Yorkers, boasting one of the best catalogs in town.

The Museum of Modern Art

11 West 53rd St (btw Fifth/Sixth Aves). Tel. 1–212/708-9400; films 1–212/708-9490. Open Sat-Tues & Thurs 1030am-545pm, Fri 1030am-815pm. Closed Wed. Admission $10 adults, $6.50 students/seniors; free Fri 430-815pm.

The greatest collection of modern art in the world reads like a summary of the creative hits from the 1880s to the present day. Pollock, de Kooning, Rothko, Rauschenberg, Twombly and most every other well-known 20th-century artist is represented, often by his or her very best work. While other museums thrill to have single canvases by masters like Monet, Matisse or Mondrian, MoMA's embarrassment of riches offers entire rooms filled with masterpieces and the chance to follow an artist's career in its entirety. Many icons of modern and contemporary art are always on display, including Pablo Picasso's *Les Demoiselles d'Avignon*, Vincent van Gogh's *The Starry Night*, Henri Matisse's *Dance*, Claude Monet's *Water Lilies*, Salvador Dali's *The Persistence of Memory*, Andy Warhol's *Gold Marilyn Monroe* and Andrew Wyeth's *Christina's World*. And frequent blockbuster exhibitions means that there is always something new to look at.

The collection goes far beyond paintings and sculpture to encompass drawings, prints, architecture, photography, film and industrial and graphic design. The museum has one of the most comprehensive collections of 20th-century drawings anywhere, and boasts a design collection that comprises objects ranging from appliances, furniture and tableware to tools, textiles, sports cars and even a helicopter. Established in 1940, the enormous photography department includes works by artists, journalists, scientists and entrepreneurs and features many examples by Alfred Stieglitz, Man Ray, Edward Weston, Lee Friedlander, Cindy Sherman and Nicholas Nixon.

MoMA is also the nation's preeminent cinematheque, with an archive of over 13,000 films. They show more than 30 films a week in two state-of-the-art theaters; screenings are included with museum admission.

Merciless crowds are our only gripe: Mondays, Fridays and Saturdays are cruelest.

MoMA reopens in 2005 after a multi-year renovation and expansion.

Other Collections

The Cloisters

In Fort Tryon Park, upper Manhattan. Tel. 1–212/923-3700. Open Mar–Oct, Tues–Sun 930am–515pm; Nov–Feb, Tues–Sun 930am–445pm. Closed Mon. Suggested contribution $12 adults, ▮ students/seniors; includes entrance to the Metropolitan Museum of Art.

The Cloisters, which incorporates architectural fragments from four European Gothic and Romanesque abbeys, occupies a beautiful perch at the northern tip of Manhattan. The entire stone Fuentidueña Chapel was brought to Fort Tryon Park from the church of San Martin, north of Madrid. And its landmark turret is a replica of one at St. Michel de Cuxa in France. This re-creation of an arcaded monastery of the Middle Ages was purchased in the 1930s by John D. Rockefeller, Jr. for the Metropolitan Museum of Art, then filled with JP Morgan's priceless medieval art collection. The result is a peaceful, even meditative, spot that seems a world away from the skyscrapers to the south. To protect its character, Rockefeller even bought land in New Jersey, on the opposite side of the Hudson River, so that views from here would never be spoiled.

Inside the chapels and stone exhibition halls are art and artifacts from the 11th through 16th centuries, arranged chronologically from Romanesque to late Gothic. The most important holdings are the famed 16th-century Unicorn Tapestries, which, when discovered on the La Rochefoucauld estate in Verteuil, were being used to keep vegetables fresh. Other exhibits include the only complete set of playing cards to survive from the 15th century and a single rosary bead incorporating an intricately carved Passion scene. The gardens are wonderful too, planted with shrubs and flowers that were cultivated during the Middle Ages.

Asia Society

725 Park Ave (btw 70th/71st Sts). Tel. 1–212/288-6400. Open Tues–Thurs and Sat–Sun 11am–6pm, Fri 11am–5pm. Closed Mon. Admission $7 adults, $5 students/seniors.

Pakistani devotional music, Tibetan sand mandalas, the shooting death of a Japanese exchange student—no cultural subject is out of bounds for this wonderful non-profit museum and cultural center that began as a pet project of John D. Rockefeller III. Frequently changing exhibitions are displayed on two floors. Guided talks are usually offered Tuesday to Saturday at 1230pm, Thursday at 630pm, and Sunday at 230pm. Phone for information on lectures, concerts and special programs.

American Museum of the Moving Image

35th Avenue at 36th St, Astoria, Queens. Tel. 718/784-4520. Open Mon-Fri noon-5pm, Sat-Sun 11am-6pm. Admission $8.50 adults, $5.50 seniors/children.

One of the few museums outside Manhattan that is worth the trip, AMMI is an unusually fun place devoted to film and television. Lots of the exhibits are interactive experiences related to motion picture sound and editing. You can create a short digital animation, layer sound effects into movies like *Terminator 2*, and loop your own voice onto De Niro's image ("You talkin' to me?"). There are also regular demonstrations of digital imaging and morphing. Costumes, cameras, props, pictures and frequent film screenings round out the offerings

Take the G or R subway to Steinway Street.

Cooper-Hewitt National Design Museum

2 East 91st St (btw fifth/Madison Aves). Tel. 1-212/849-8400. Open Tues-Thurs 10am-5pm, Fri 10am-9pm, Sat 10am-6pm, Sun noon-6pm. Closed Mondays hols. Admission $8 adults, $5 students/seniors.

The Cooper Union Museum for the Arts of Decoration, as it was originally called, was founded a century ago by three sisters named Hewitt, who were granddaughters of industrialist Peter Cooper. The museum was absorbed by the Smithsonian Institution in 1967 and, in 1976, moved to a Fifth Avenue mansion once owned by Andrew Carnegie. Inside you'll find particularly strong collections of textiles and wall coverings, along with what is said to be the world's largest assortment of architectural drawings. There is also jewelry, prints, and, so we're told, a major hoard of antique pornography. The 64-room Georgian mansion, which underwent a $20 million renovation in 1998, is spectacular for its pomposity. It is said that the organ in the dramatic Great Hall was played each morning at 8am to wake the household. It's an interesting contrast to the far more refined Frick, another millionaire's house at the other end of Museum Mile.

TAXI

107

Intrepid
Sea-Air-Space Museum

Pier 86, at West 46th St and Twelfth Ave. Tel. 1–212/245-0072. Open Apr-Sept, Mon-Sat 10am-5pm, Sun 10am-6pm; Oct-Mar, Tues-Sun 10am-5pm. Closed Mon in Winter. Admission $14 adults, $10 students/seniors.

This WWII-era aircraft carrier has been converted into a large naval museum. More than 40 aircraft on the flattop include a Stealth bomber, an F-14 Super Tomcat, and an F-16 Falcon. There's an Iraqi tank too, captured in the Gulf War. The carrier suffered numerous kamikaze attacks and these are dramatically described by the veterans who experienced them on the self-guided acousti-tour. The *USS Intrepid* is flanked by the *USS Edson*, a destroyer from the Vietnam war, and the *USS Growler*, a guided-missile submarine built in 1958. Get there by taxi, foot, or the M42 cross-town bus to the west end of West 42nd Street.

Forbes Magazine Galleries

62 Fifth Ave (btw 12th/13th Sts). Tel. 1-212/206-5548. Open Tues-Sat 10am-4pm. Closed Sun-Mon. Admission free.

The late Malcolm Forbes created a small museum on the ground floor of his magazine's headquarters to display the things he loved to collect: toy soldiers, model yachts, presidential papers and Faberge Imperial Eggs. The soldiers, which "march" around on moving platforms while toy trains tool about in the background, are worth the price of admission (it's free). The fabulously crafted and jeweled Easter eggs, on the other hand, are worthy of a museum all their own. Czar Nicholas commissioned the famous jeweler Faberge to create these amazing holiday gifts. Forbes has about a dozen of them, a collection that's second only to the Hermitage in St. Petersburg. There are guided tours on Thursdays (reservation is required).

Frick Collection

1 East 70th St (btw Fifth/Madison Aves). Tel. 1-212/288-0700. Open Tues-Sat 10am-6pm, Sun 1-6pm. Closed Mon. Admission $7 adults, $5 students/ seniors; children under 10 not admitted.

The former home of steel tycoon Henry Clay Frick is one of the most enjoyable spaces in the city. It's a warm and wonderful place filled with the millionaire's extraordinary sculptures, paintings, rugs, furniture, porcelain and other possessions. The Frick is a great place to be alone with art. Here you can stroll from room to room filled with paintings by European masters hung with casual elegance: a Titian here, two Goyas there, as well as Van Dykes, Vermeers, Rembrandts and others. Constructed in 1914, the block-long mansion itself is a masterpiece featuring intricate floors, crown moldings, carved ceilings, and spectacular light fixtures (don't overlook the Riccio lamp in the East Room). Henry's wife, Adelaid, lived here until 1931 and the house's temperature is still kept at a constant 70 degrees Fahrenheit, just the way she liked it.

TAXI

109

Guggenheim Museum Soho

575 Broadway (at Prince St). Tel. 1–212/423-3500. Open Thurs-Mon 11am-6pm. Closed Tues-Wed. Admission free.

The Guggenheim's southern annex puts the museum closer to the downtown neighborhoods frequented by contemporary New York artists—Soho, NoLlta, the East Village, the Lower East Side, and Brooooklyn. Exhibitions include works from the permanent collection as well temporary shows that often feature experimental electronic and video art.

Museum of the City of New York

1220 Fifth Ave (at 103rd St). Tel. 1–212/534-1672. Open Wed-Sat 10am-5pm, Sun noon-5pm. Closed Mon-Tues. Admission $7 adults, $4 students/seniors.

New York City's history museum is an upbeat, even irreverent place, with both permanent and temporary exhibitions from historical times to the present day. Much of the floor space is given over to tremendous collections—silver, model ships, toys—which, for us, is a yawn. But other exhibits are phenomenal, like the luxuriously appointed Stettheimer Dollhouse, fitted with y furnishings, a teensy-weensy sculpture by Gaston Lachaise and a Lilliputian version of Marcel Duchamp's *Nude Descending a Staircase.*

Other exhibits include a section of the plane that crashed into the Empire State Building in 1945, and the News Zipper that wrapped around the old New York Times Building On the top floor you can peek into John D. Rockefeller's antique-filled Japanese-style bedroom, which was moved here in its entirety when the Rockefeller townhouse was torn down to make way for MoMA.

International Center of Photography

1133 Sixth Ave (at 43rd St). Tel. 1–212/860-1777. Open Tues-Thurs 10am-5pm, Fri 10am-8pm, Sat-Sun 10am-6pm, Closed Mon. Admission $8 adults, $6 students/seniors; Fri 5-8pm by donation.

ICP is one of the most prestigious galleries of photography in the world and the refurbished center on 43rd Street makes this plain. The galleries here display temporary exhibitions, many of which are drawn from the center's vast original-print photo archives that include works by such greats as Robert Capa, gee, Cartier-Bresson, Berenice Abb, ndy Sherman, and Roman Vishniac. A brand-new school lies underneath the plaza.

The Jewish Museum

1109 Fifth Ave (at 92nd St). Tel. 1–212/423-3200. Open Sun-Wed 11am-545pm, Thurs 1am-8pm, Fri 11am-3pm. C d Sat. Admission $10 adults, $7.50 students/seniors; free children under 12 and Thurs 5-8pm.

One of the city's best-curated specialist museums contains the largest collection of Jewish art and Judaica in the US—thousands of artifacts and artworks spanning 4000 years of Jewish history. It's situated in the elegant Gothic-style Warburg Mans hich was donated to the Jewish Theological

Seminary of America in 1944. Temporary exhibitions, which are unusually intelligent and imaginative, have recently included Shows on modernism in art; literature, film and publishing in pre-World War 1 Berlin; and on Sigmund Freud's influence on 20th-century culture.

displayed alongside changing exhibits of American and European art that often lean toward outlandish or whimsical.

Museum of Television & Radio

25 West 52nd St (btw Fifth/Sixth Aves). Tel. 1–212/621-6600. Open Tues-Wed & Sat-Sun noon-6pm, Thurs noon-8pm, Fri non-9pm Closed Mon. Suggested contribution $10 adults, $8 seniors/students, $5 children under 14.
There are several galleries here with changing exhibits, but the museum's main draw is its archive of tens of thousands of TV and radio shows all of which are available for viewing or listening on demand. For media mavens this place is absolutely fabulous. Take a seat at one of 96 private consoles and a computer will serve up your choice of up to four selections in two hours.

National Academy of Design

1083 Fifth Ave (at 89th St). Tel. 1–212/369-4880. Open Wed-Thurs noon-5pm, Fri -Sun 11am-6pm. Closed Mon-Tues. Suggested admission $8 adults, $4.50 students/seniors.
Begun 1825 and modeled after the Royal Academy in London, NAD is a school for artists run by artists. It was founded by Samuel Morse, who was a painter in addition to being the inventor of the telegraph. In this elegant Upper East Side townhouse, worksfrom the Academy's permanent collection of paintings and sculpture are

National Museum of the American Indian

1 Bowling Green. Tel. 1–212/668-6624. Open Fri-Wed 10am-5pm, Thurs 10am-8pm. Admission free.
It's surprising to find such an enormous trove of Native American art and artifacts stashed in an old federal building in Lower Manhattan, but that's exactly where it is. This huge cache, impeccably curated by the Smithsonian Institute, includes more than a million objects—dolls, canoes, moccasins, masks, baskets, painted hides, jewelry and headdresses—from native communities all over the continent. The museum's best permanent exhibit features artifacts chosen for display by Native American scholars, artists, elders and others who disclose why they chose these particular pieces. The bulk of the collection was acquired early last century by the renowned pack-rat George Heye. It was purchased by the Feds in 1989, and will stay in this landmark, Beaux Arts former US Customs house for another few years, until a new home for the collection is completed in Washington, DC. Don't forget to check out the unusual gift shop.

Bowling Green.
Tel. 1-2... 40. Open Tues-Sat 10am-5pm. Closed Sun-Mon. Admission free.

This horde of law-enforcement memorabilia includes a huge cache of contraband weapons, from zip guns to machine guns, plus displays on ballistics and counterfeiting. We like the collection of solid ivory nightsticks and early wooden fire alarms, and are enthralled by the exhibits relating to gangs, drugs and New York's Mafia families. ID is required for entry.

Neue Galerie

1048 Fifth Ave (at 86th St). Tel. 1-212/628-6200. Open Sat-Mon 11am-6pm, Fri 11am-9pm. Closed Tues-Thurs. Admission $10 adults, $7 students.

Ronald Lauder's lifelong passion for collecting and exhibiting has culminated in this unique blending of early 20th-century German and Austrian fine and decorative arts, in the Beaux Arts Vanderbilt Mansion. Lauder is the chairman of Estee Lauder International, a noted philanthropist, a former United States Ambassador to Austria, and a director of the Museum of Modern Art. But before all that he was a passionate admirer of German and Austrian art. This collection includes paintings, sculptures, and a wide range of works on paper, as well as dramatic ceiling fixtures, drawing cabinets, flatware, glass, and china, most from German Expressionism or the Bauhaus movement. And the gallery's small size further sets it apart from many of its neighbors; 300 people is a full house.

Lower East Side Tenement Museum

90 Orchard St (at Broome St). Tel. 1-212/431-0233. Tours: Tues-Fri 1-4pm, Sat-Sun 11am-430pm; additional tours Apr-Oct, Thurs at 6 & 7pm; Jun-Aug, Mon 1pm, 2pm, 3pm and 4pm. Call for walking-tour information. Admission $9 adults, $7 students/seniors.

Providing an interesting counterpoint to New York's many mansion-museums, this offbeat winner brings visitors into a typical tenement which was home to 7000 people from 20 nations from 1863 to 1935. It re-creates three cramped apartments belonging to poor immigrants of the early 20th century and interprets the neighborhood's array of immigrant experiences. We're not talking ancient history here: More than a few current local residents who have peeked in recognized their own apartments. Tours depart every 30 minutes and you can combine this museum with a walking tour of the neighborhood, offered on weekends for a small additional charge.

Manhattan's Special-interest Museums

Abigail Adams Smith Museum

421 East 61st St. Tel. 1–212/838-6878. Open Tues-Sun 11am-4pm. Closed Aug. 1795 house-turned-hotel built for daughter of President John Adams illuminates hotel life in the early 19th century.

American Bible Society Gallery

1865 Broadway (at 61st St). Tel. 1–212/408-1200. Open Mon-Wed and Fri 10am-6pm, Thurs 10am-7pm, Sat 10am-5pm. Very good Christian art from the non-Christian world (think samurai Jesus) curated by a top proselytizer.

Museum of Arts and Design

40 West 53rd St. Tel. 1–212/956-3535. Open Tues-Wed and Fri-Sun 10am-6pm, Thurs 10am-8pm. Top work from foremost makers of furniture, glass, textiles, jewelry and more.

American Numismatic Society

Broadway (btw 155th/156th Sts). Tel. 1–212/234-3130. Open Tues-Fri 9am-430pm. 750,000 international coins and medals rivaled only by the largest state collections of Europe.

Americas Society Art Gallery

680 Park Ave (at 68th St). Tel. 1–212/249-8950. Open Tues-Sun noon-6pm. Promoting art and culture of the Western Hemisphere from primitive weavings to abstract avant-garde.

Bard Center for the Decorative Arts

18 West 86th St (btw Central Park West/Columbus Ave). Tel. 1–212/501-3000. Open Tues-Wed and Fri-Sun 11am-5pm, Thurs 11am-8pm.

Two to three annual exhibitions from Roman glass and women designers in the USA, to Indian jewelry, and graphic design in prewar Germany.

Children's Museum of Manhattan

212 West 83rd St (btw Broadway /Amsterdam Ave). Tel. 1–212/721-1234. Open Wed-Sun 10am-5pm.

Five floors of engaging, educational interactive exhibits on the arts, literacy, media, science and the environment.

China Institute Gallery

125 East 65th St (btw Park/Lexington Aves). Tel. 1–212/744-8181. Open Mon, Wed and Fri-Sat 10am-5pm; Tues, Thurs 10am-8pm.

High-quality temporary exhibitions encompassing all areas of Chinese art.

Dahesh Museum of Art

580 Madison Ave. Tel. 1–212/759-0606. Open Tues-Sat 11am-6pm.

The only museum in America dedicated to 19th- and early-20th-century European academic art, which is the continuation of the great Renaissance, Baroque and Rococo traditions. Now in brand new space.

Dia Center for the Arts, 548

West 22nd St (btw Tenth/Eleventh Aves). Tel. 1–212/989-5566. Open Wed-Sun noon-6pm.
Large-scale, long-term exhibitions of contemporary art from brand-name contemporaries.

Dyckman Farmhouse

4881 Broadway (at 204th St). Tel. 1–212/304-9422.
Open Tues-Sun 11am-4pm.
Manhattan's last surviving Dutch-Colonial farmhouse, built circa 1784, decorated with early American furnishings.

El Museo del Barrio

1230 Fifth Ave (btw 104th/105th Sts). Tel. 1–212/831-7272.
Open Wed-Sun 11am-5pm.
Founded by East Harlem's Puerto Rican leaders to preserve and pay tribute to the community's cultural heritage.

Grolier Club

47 East 60th St (btw Park/Madison Aves). Tel. 1–212/838-6690. Open Mon-Sat 10am-5pm.
One of the first organizations in America to treat books and prints as objects worthy of display. There are four exhibitions a year.

Hispanic Society of America

Audubon Terrace (Broadway/ 155th St). Tel. 1–212/926-2234.
Open Tues-Sat 10am-430pm, Sun 1-4pm.
Paintings, decorative arts, archaeology, sculpture and textiles address nearly every aspect of culture in Spain, Portugal, Latin America, and the Philippines.

Isamu Noguchi Garden Museum

32-37 Vernon Blvd., Long Island City. Tel. 718/721-1932.
Open Apr-Oct, Wed-Fri 10am-5pm, Sat-Sun 11am-6pm.
Comprehensive collection of stone, metal, wood and clay artwork by the famous sculptor, in a tranquil setting created by the artist.

Museum for African Art

593 Broadway (btw Houston/ Prince Sts). Tel. 1–212/ 966-1313.
Open Wed-Thurs and Sun 11am-6pm, Fri-Sat 11am-8pm.
Top-notch exhibitions devoted exclusively to historical and contemporary African art.

Museum for African Art

36-10 43rd Ave (at Queens Blvd) Tel 1–718/784-7700. Open Mon & Thurs-Fri 10 am-5pm, Sat-Sun 11am-6pm.
The pre-eminent urban center of folk art scholarship in the nation, with an outstanding permanent collection.

Museum of American Illustration

128 East 63rd St. Tel. 1–212/838-2560. Open Tues 10am-8pm, Wed-Fri 10am-5pm, Sat noon-4pm.
Showcase of 1500 works by such legends as Norman Rockwell, N.C. Wyeth, Rockwell Kent, Bob Peak, Bernie Fuchs, and Brad Holland.

TAXI

115

Museum of Chinese in the Americas
70 Mulberry St, 2nd fl. Tel. 1-212/619-4785. Open Tues-Sun noon-5pm. Chinese-American history through photos, documents, historical displays, and the best collection of opium pipes we've seen.

New York City Fire Museum
278 Spring St (btw Hudson/Varick Sts). Tel. 1-212/691-1303. Open Tues-Sat 10am-5pm, Sun 10am-4pm. Leather buckets, helmets, engines and other artifacts from the late 18th century to the present.

New York Historical Society
2 West 77th St. Tel. 1-212/873-3400. Open Tues-Sun 11am-5pm. Paintings, sculpture, furniture, tools, decorative objects, Tiffany lamps and other home-grown objects from the 1600s to the present day.

Ukrainian Museum
203 Second Ave. Tel. 1-212/228-0110. Open Wed-Sun 1-5pm. Clothing, kilims, ceramics, jewelry, and an outstanding collection of Easter eggs, plus materials documenting Ukrainian immigration in the US.

New York Unearthed
17 State St (near Battery Park). Tel. 1-212/748-8628. Open Wed-Mon 10am-5pm. The South Street Seaport's off-site museum devoted to city archaeology.

New Museum of Contemporary Art
583 Broadway (btw Houston/Prince Sts). Tel. 1-212/219-1222. Open Tues-Wed & Fri-Sun noon-6pm, Thurs noon-8pm. Closed Mon. Dynamic solo exhibitions and landmark group shows that define key moments in the development of contemporary art. A unique and innovative space.

Nicholas Roerich Museum
319 West 107th St. Tel. 1–212/864-7752. Open Tues-Sun 2-5pm.
Major exhibition of paintings by Russian-born artist and cultural philosopher Nicholas Roerich

Yeshiva University Museum
15 West 16th St (btw Fifth/Sixth Aves). Tel. 1–212/294-8330. Open Tues-Thurs 11am-5pm.
Jewish ceremonial objects, art, textiles, rare books, photographs, and ephemera.

#05 Exploring

Digging Deeper

TAXI

119

The Financial District

The Financial District, also known as Lower Manhattan, is the oldest part of the city, as evidenced by the neighborhood's haphazard tangle of streets which hark back to horse-and-carriage days. The settlement of New Amsterdam was founded here by the Dutch West India Company in 1626 mainly for commercial reasons. Almost from the beginning, the little trading post was the marketplace and financial center of the American Colonies, and it hasn't looked back since.

Each morning, bond traders and stockbrokers roll in to this capital of capitalism on suburban trains from all over the Tri-State area. During the day, the district is full of suits with ulcers, battling with tourists for control of the sidewalks. As five o'clock rolls around, the streets become clogged with chauffeur-driven Lincoln Town Cars—coveted industry perks, here to whisk the money men and women back to suburbia. After dark, the Financial District becomes eerily empty and quiet—except for the odd strip club.

When exploring the Financial District, keep an eye out for the free white-and-salmon-colored jitneys run by the Alliance for Downtown New York. The vans loop around Lower Manhattan stopping at major points along the way and can be hailed anywhere along the route.

Several old structures are still hidden amongst the modern

skyscrapers. Chief among these is **Fraunces Tavern**, *54 Pearl St (at Broad; tel. 1-212/425-1778)*, a reconstructed 18th-century publik house imbued with an old Colonial atmosphere. The brick pub was a favorite hangout of George Washington, who bade farewell to his officers in the tavern's Long Room in 1783. Furnished in period style and serving traditional American "fayre," the Tavern is forgettable for lunch, but worth stopping in for a pint and a peak at their small museum cluttered with early Americana. It's open Tues, Wed & Fri 10am-5pm, Thurs 10am-7pm, Sat 11am-5pm. Museum admission $3 adults, $2 students/seniors.

Situated at the southernmost tip of Manhattan, **Battery Park** draws lots of tourists because it's the departure point for ferries to the Statue of Liberty and Ellis Island. It's worth strolling through the green for other reasons as well, not the least of which is to get close to the water and take in some fabulous views. The circular, red sandstone fort in the center of the park is **Castle Clinton**, an 1811 structure that stood just offshore when it was built, but has since been surrounded by acres of landfill. The Castle successively functioned as a theater, immigration center and City Aquarium before being declared a National Monument in the 1940s and made into a small historical museum. Inside, you can see free, continuously running short films on New York's history. This is also where you buy tickets for the ferry to the Statue of Liberty and Ellis Island (*see* Chapter 4/The Top Sights).

The **Staten Island Ferry Terminal**, at the eastern edge of Battery Park is where you board the boats to New York City's other big island. The orange ferries have been making

the 25-minute trip to and from Staten Island since 1905. It's not a comfortable fleet, but it's one of the best sightseeing rides in the city, offering stunning views of New York Harbor, Lower Manhattan, the Statue of Liberty and Ellis Island. Best of all, it's free. Despite what city boosters say, there's not very much particularly worthwhile to do when you reach Staten Island's St. George Terminal, at least in comparison to what's happening back in Manhattan (*see* The Best of Staten Island, below). Think about taking the cruise at sunset or after dark, when you can see Manhattan's office buildings emitting their fluorescent glow.

The Battery Park Esplanade stretches 1.2 miles (1.9 km) along the Hudson River, from Battery Park all the way up to Chambers Street. On warm, sunny days, this is one of the best places to stroll, bike or rollerblade and take in a part of the city that most locals miss. Along the way are several major sculptures by some of the country's foremost artists. Martin Puryear's 73-foot-tall stainless-steel pylon echoes the city's towers, RM Fischer's fanciful stainless steel *Rector Gate* is pure sci-fi, and Ned Smyth's handsome concrete colonnaded court is reminiscent of an ancient temple. The park is part of an enormous commercial and residential complex built entirely on landfill in the 1980s at a cost of $4 billion.

Nearby you'll find the **Museum of Jewish Heritage**, *18 First Place (tel. 1–212/968–1800)*, a dramatic freestanding hexagon housing exhibits related to

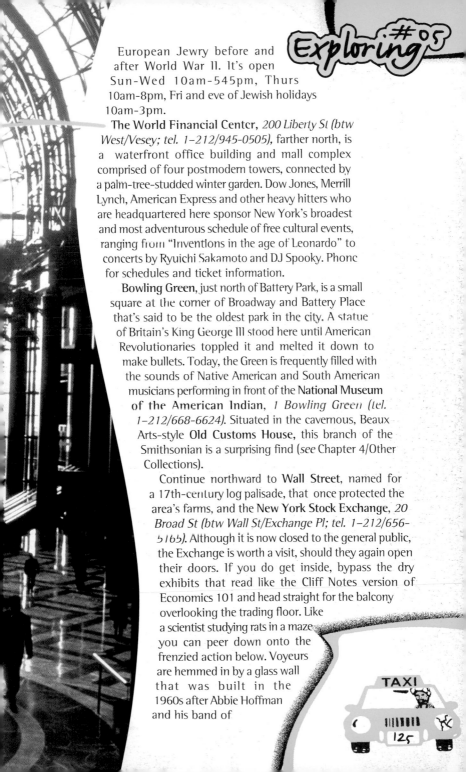

European Jewry before and after World War II. It's open Sun-Wed 10am-545pm, Thurs 10am-8pm, Fri and eve of Jewish holidays 10am-3pm.

The World Financial Center, *200 Liberty St (btw West/Vesey; tel. 1–212/945-0505),* farther north, is a waterfront office building and mall complex comprised of four postmodern towers, connected by a palm-tree-studded winter garden. Dow Jones, Merrill Lynch, American Express and other heavy hitters who are headquartered here sponsor New York's broadest and most adventurous schedule of free cultural events, ranging from "Inventions in the age of Leonardo" to concerts by Ryuichi Sakamoto and DJ Spooky. Phone for schedules and ticket information.

Bowling Green, just north of Battery Park, is a small square at the corner of Broadway and Battery Place that's said to be the oldest park in the city. A statue of Britain's King George III stood here until American Revolutionaries toppled it and melted it down to make bullets. Today, the Green is frequently filled with the sounds of Native American and South American musicians performing in front of the **National Museum of the American Indian,** *1 Bowling Green (tel. 1–212/668-6624).* Situated in the cavernous, Beaux Arts-style **Old Customs House,** this branch of the Smithsonian is a surprising find (*see* Chapter 4/Other Collections).

Continue northward to **Wall Street,** named for a 17th-century log palisade, that once protected the area's farms, and the **New York Stock Exchange,** *20 Broad St (btw Wall St/Exchange Pl; tel. 1–212/656-5165).* Although it is now closed to the general public, the Exchange is worth a visit, should they again open their doors. If you do get inside, bypass the dry exhibits that read like the Cliff Notes version of Economics 101 and head straight for the balcony overlooking the trading floor. Like a scientist studying rats in a maze, you can peer down onto the frenzied action below. Voyeurs are hemmed in by a glass wall that was built in the 1960s after Abbie Hoffman and his band of

TAXI

125

Yippie pranksters dumped bagfuls of dollars onto the traders, causing a near riot.

Federal Hall National Memorial, *26 Wall St (at Nassau; tel. 1-212/825-6888),* a colonnaded building situated almost across the street from the Stock Exchange, marks the site of George Washington's 1789 inauguration and America's first capital. Inside are several historical exhibits, including the Bible on which every American president has placed his right hand and sworn the oath of office. New York's first City Hall was constructed on this site in 1702. Later, when the US Constitution was adopted by the thirteen original states, New York City became the capital of the new nation and City Hall became Federal Hall, the country's administrative headquarters. The departments of State, War and Treasury were all housed here, as was the Supreme Court. Then, in August 1790, the US capital was moved to Philadelphia while the new "Federal City," Washington, DC, was being built on the banks of the Potomac River. The present building was constructed in 1842 as the Customs House of the Port of New York, the busiest port in the nation at that time. It's open Mon-Fri 9am-5pm. Admission is free.

Back on Broadway, at the corner of Wall Street, is **Trinity Church,** *74 Trinity Place (tel. 1-212/602-0800),* the third Episcopal church to stand on land bequeathed to the city by England's King William III. Completed in 1846, the current structure was the tallest building in Manhattan for most of the 19th century. Tombs in the surrounding burial yard date to 1681 and include American founding father Alexander Hamilton amongst other New York notables.

The massive **Equitable Building,** *120 Broadway (btw Pine/Cedar Sts)* is an architectural monstrosity that inspired a 1916 zoning law that requires setbacks and limits building size. It was the largest office building in the city until the completion of the Empire State Building in 1931.

A block north and east sits the **Federal Reserve Bank of New York,** *33 Liberty St (btw William/Nassau; tel. 1-212/720-6130),* another huge, block-like fortress that's said to be the repository of one-third of the world's gold—even more than Fort Knox. You can catch a glimpse of the bullion-filled vaults on a tour of the five heavily guarded underground floors, but you've got to book at least a week in advance.

St. Paul's Chapel, *at the corner of Broadway and Fulton Street,* was George Washington's parish

TAXI

127

church. Consecrated in 1766, this Episcopal God-box still conducts regular services, making it the oldest house of worship in continuous operation in Manhattan. Except for Waterford crystal chandeliers and a few other extravagances, the church has a relatively plain interior that was par for the times. St. Paul's still follows British tradition, offering regular, free noontime classical-music concerts. It's open daily 8am-4pm.

The 60-story **Woolworth Building**, *on Broadway (btw Barclay St/Park Pl),* was completed in 1913 and remained the tallest building in the world for more than a decade. Commissioned by five-and-dime king Frank W. Woolworth, the building is unusual among skyscrapers for having been financed in cash. It's worth stepping into this huge downtown landmark to gape at the cathedral-like lobby, featuring vaulted ceilings encrusted with awesome mosaics.

Across Broadway stands **City Hall**, *Broadway/Murray St (tel. 1-212/788-3000),* a beautiful Federal-style landmark (1803-1812) which houses the offices of "hizzoner," the Mayor. It's open Mon-Fri 9am-430pm. Admission is free. On Broadway at one of the entrances to City Hall Park is a **statue of Nathan Hale** (1893), a Colonial patriot who was executed by the British as a spy. Some observers think that Hale's unbuttoned shirt and rope-bound body smacks of homoeroticism, an amusing commentary given its location beside City Hall.

Don't let the cobblestone streets fool you, because the much-hyped **South Street Seaport** *(btw Pearl, Water, John and Beekman Sts; tel. 1-212/732-7678)* is basically a shopping mall with chain stores and forgettable bars that become after-work singles joints. We like the wooden pier, though, as well as the great views of the Brooklyn Bridge and the collection of life-size sailing and steam ships. It's open Mon-Sat 10am-9pm, Sun 11am-7pm. Some shops are open two hours later in summer and restaurants keep extended hours.

TriBeCa

Encouraged by great restaurants like Nobu, TriBeCa Grill, Montrachet, Chanterelle, and Bouley Bakery; avant performance spaces like The Knitting Factory; and high-profile offices like Miramax Films, TriBeCa has not-so-quietly evolved into one of the city's premier neighborhoods.

When real-estate developers dubbed it the "Triangle below Canal Street" (TriBeCa) in the 1970s, there were fewer than 250 people living in this wasteland, north of the Financial District and south of Greenwich Village. Like SoHo before it, TriBeCa was transformed from scary warehouse district to genteel residential community in the space of a single decade. But unlike SoHo this change didn't happen spontaneously, but was driven by developers determined to make the neighborhood habitable. Lured by the promise of cheap rent, artists and their ilk were the first to take the bait. Galleries and performance spaces opened, along with cafes and small shops catering to the new residents. As infrastructure and services reached critical mass, prices skyrocketed and many of the pioneers were forced to assign their lofts to investment bankers and other rich folk who could afford the enormous rents and monthly maintenance fees.

Once an important transfer point for goods moving through lower Manhattan, TriBeCa is still chock-full of loading docks protruding from beautiful cast-iron buildings, many of which have been renovated as living lofts. Despite its similar history—and shared future—TriBeCa feels very different from SoHo. Sure, upscale restaurants have taken over entire blocks of Franklin and Hudson streets, but for the most part, the stylish shops and eateries are not all lined up in brightly-lit rows as they are in SoHo. More often they are tucked away amongst still-operational commercial spaces. Lots of little streets remain ungentrified, and TriBeCa is still a bit foreboding at night.

TAXI

129

SoHo

The neighborhood South of Houston (SoHo; btw Canal and Lafayette streets and Sixth Ave) is an architectural landmark, foodie paradise, and fashion statement. The fantastic cast-iron buildings that line these streets were converted from factories into living lofts and artists' studios. But that was long ago, before the neighborhood abandoned its boho roots in favor of high-end restaurants and shops. Upwards of two-thousand bucks a month for a small one-bedroom apartment and plenty of pricey shops have twisted this former bohemian stronghold into a bastion of hip urban bourgeoisie. Even the best-known art galleries have fled to Chelsea, though there are still plenty here worth exploring. What remains is one of the world's best places to shop and stroll, a chronically cool neighborhood whose style has come to define an entire genre of fashion designers from Todd Oldham to Miu Miu. Interspersed amongst the boutiques are plenty of Euro-restaurants and happening clubs, as well as the more-than-occasional espresso bar, that now clutter Spring, Mercer, Prince and Lafayette streets.

There are several good museums too. **The New Museum of Contemporary Art**, *583 Broadway (at Houston St; tel. 1–212/219-1222)*, is known for strange, experimental exhibitions by both internationally known (and not) artists. They usually have a great window installation that tips you off to what's happening inside. It's open Tues-Wed and Fri-Sun noon-6pm, Thurs noon-8pm. Closed Mon. Admission $5 adults, $3 students/artists/seniors; free Thurs 6-8pm.

Nearby is **Poet's House**, *72 Spring St. (btw Broadway/Lafayette St; tel. 1–212/431-7920)*, a reading room and resource center with the country's largest collection of poetry. You can leaf through magazines and don Walkman headphones to listen to spoken words from the House's huge collection of tapes. There are lots of live readings here too.

It took but 20 years for SoHo to evolve from a light-manufacturing district to artists' squat to chic, expensive neighborhood. The area was settled surreptitiously in the late sixties and early seventies by creatives who were attracted by low rents and vast spaces with high ceilings, and who were willing to tolerate such squatter hardships as nights and weekends without heat. By 1971 so many of the painters and sculptors were living illegally in their famously spacious lofts that the law finally caught up with the de facto reality: SoHo was a residential district. The neighborhood was officially designated a "mixed use" zone for live/work lofts and an Artist Certification Committee (which still exists to this day, but has no enforcement power) was created to make sure that the area's most desirable spaces went only to working artists. Thus, SoHo became a very privileged place to live. There is still an air of exclusivity in SoHo, perpetuated by bars,

galleries and clubs that are hard to find if you don't already know about their existence. The most happening places are often hidden behind solid steel doors and opaque window treatments, and many are located floors above street level.

Most of SoHo is part of the officially designated Cast-Iron District, an architectural preservation area that protects the unique building style of this formerly industrial neighborhood. The most celebrated structure is the **Haughwout Building**, at the corner of Broadway and Broome Street. Built in 1857 for E.V. Haughwout & Co., a silver and porcelain maker and retailer, it was almost demolished (along with the neighborhood) in the 1960s, but was saved by the Landmarks Preservation Commission, an official body created after the devastating demolition of the grand Pennsylvania Station.

Chinatown

C hinatown is in the midst of radical change. Originally encompassing a few blocks surrounding Mott Street, the neighborhood is bursting at its seams, spilling across its long established borders of Canal, Mulberry, Worth and the Bowery. Over a third of New York's Chinese population of 300,000 lives in or around this district (most of the rest live in Queens). Unlike Little Italy, which seems to have gasped its last breath and is now little more than a strip of touristy restaurants, Chinatown is thriving, growing, and expanding in all directions. At the same time, it's transforming into a kind of Southeast Asiatown, as Vietnamese, Thai, Malay and Cambodian immigrants pour in to toil in the neighborhood's overcrowded sweatshops and hygienically-challenged restaurants.

The first Chinese resident of Manhattan bedded down at 8 Mott Street in 1858. Within 20 years there were more than 2000 Chinese living in the area that would become Chinatown. Since 1883, when the Federal Chinese Exclusion Act was repealed, Chinatown has enjoyed steady, continuous growth. Today it's humming, even by New York standards. Chinatown is a wondrous place; a tangle of narrow streets crammed with exotic-produce markets, street vendors hawking stir-fried noodles, drugstores selling dried seahorses and deer antlers, cheerful pagoda-topped phone booths, and, everywhere you look, an impossible clutter of signs, most of which are in Chinese characters. Restaurants are packed shoulder to shoulder along Chinatown's tiny alleyways (the best are listed in Chapter 8), and Canal Street is awash with vendors hawking knock-off designer watches, sunglasses and handbags, as well as cheap toys and electronics.

There is no better place for an afternoon stroll in New York than Chinatown. While in the neighborhood, visit the **Museum of Chinese in the Americas**, *70 Mulberry St, 2nd fl (tel. 1–212/619-4785)*, then join the locals and burn some incense at the feet of the giant porcelain Buddha at the **Eastern States Buddhist Temple**, *64 Mott St (btw Canal/Bayard Sts). Tel. 1–212/966-6229)*.

Little Italy & Nolita

From 1880 to 1910 the number of Italians in New York rose from about 12,000 to over a half-million. Most settled in the neighborhood between Canal, Houston, Elizabeth and Lafayette streets. But today, little remains of the Little Italy that inspired such tales as *The Godfather*. Few, if any, first-generation Italians call this enclave "home," so the Italian elements feel very contrived (think EPCOT). The only Italian you'll really encounter here is on the signs on the *caffes* and *ristoranti*, the "Kiss Me I'm Italian" T-shirts and, perhaps, the lips of the occasional Italian tourist. A mafioso can't even get gunned down in one of the neighborhood's clam houses anymore.

Still, each autumn, Little Italy puts on its best face, in the form of the **San Gennaro Festival**, an 11-day cacophony of bad music, garish carnival games and delicious sausage-and-pepper sandwiches.

The tomato-rich southern-Italian cuisine that Little Italy is famous for can be quite good here. Also authentico are the restaurant owners, who stand on their Mulberry Street sidewalks pleading with tourists to come in. Check out **Ferrara**, *195 Grand St (tel. 1–212/226-6150)*, America's oldest Italian pastry shop, and **Alleva Dairy**, *188 Grand St (tel. 1–212/226-7990)*, serving great Italian sandwiches with fresh, house-made mozzarella cheese.

But Little Italy is getting squeezed from all sides. Chinatown is encroaching from the south, SoHo is pressing from the west, and a trendy little enclave called NoLIta (North of Little Italy) is expanding on the north. Elizabeth, Mulberry and Mott streets, especially, are blossoming with stylish clothing boutiques and trendy restaurants. It's only a matter of time before Little Italy is a distant memory.

TAXI

135

The Lower East Side

Until recently, the shifting demographics of the Lower East Side reflected the latest waves of immigration to New York. Known for cheap tenement housing, the area between Houston Street, The Bowery and FDR Drive was the first stop in the city for Irish and German immigrants, followed by Eastern European Jews, who dominated the neighborhood from the mid-19th to the mid-20th centuries. In 1920 there were more than 400,000 people living in the Lower East Side, making it one of the most densely populated places in the world. Although the Jews who lived here were poor, their neighborhood was an intellectual hotbed and creative center. Yiddish theater flourished along Second Avenue, where Irving Berlin, the Marx Brothers and George Gershwin performed. Today the Yiddish theaters and most of the kosher food shops are history, but some vestiges of the neighborhood's illustrious Jewish past remain in discount clothing stores on Orchard Street and the random deli (Katz's, *205 East Houston St*), bialy shop (**Kossars Bialystoker**, *367 Grand St*), pickle stand (**Gus'**, *35 Essex St*), matzoh maker (**Streit**, *150 Rivington St*), and knishery (**Yonah Schimmel's**, *137 East Houston St*).

The nearby **Eldridge Street Synagogue**, *12 Eldridge St (btw Canal/Division Sts) (tel. 1-212/219-0888)*, was the first built by Eastern European Jews in America. The synagogue's intricate woodwork, multi-colored stained glass windows and beautiful frescoes contrast dramatically with the low-rent buildings that surround it. The very few members who remain are of the Orthodox congregation K'hal Adath Jeshurun. It's located near the **Lower East Side Tenement Museum** (*see* Chapter 4/Other Collections). The synagogue offers tours Tues and Thurs at 1130am and 230pm, and hourly on Sundays beginning at 11am (last tour 3pm). Admission is $5 adults, $3 students/seniors.

Today the Lower East Side is largely a Puerto Rican stronghold and salsa has replaced klezmer. *Loisaida* (the Spanish pronunciation of "Lower East Side"), as residents refer to it, was decimated by drugs in the 1970s. But it's slowly crawling back to become one of Manhattan's most happening neighborhoods. Black-clad youth, who at one time may have been bound for SoHo or the East Village, are increasingly attracted to this "LoHo" for its (relatively) affordable housing. There has been a very active bar and boutique scene on Ludlow, Orchard, Stanton, and Delancey streets for years now (*see* Chapter 8/Lower East Side Cool). And even good restaurants are moving in. But there's nothing that can even remotely be considered "hip" east of Clinton Street, where things still feel a bit sinister after dark.

Greenwich Village

The neighborhood between Broadway and the Hudson River and 14th and Houston streets is New York's original "Village." Later, the appellation expanded east, creating two distinct and distinctive halves. Both parts are terrific places to explore.

Built in the mid-19th century with beautiful upper-class homes and lots of little churches, shops, theaters, clubs and galleries, the **West Village**, as it is now known, was the first residential district outside of Lower Manhattan to blossom into a pleasant, self-contained community. It's still one of the greatest parts of Manhattan in which to live.

By comparison, the **East Village** east of Broadway—which was formerly known as the upper reaches of the Lower East Side—continues to thrive with lower-income hipsters, unrepentant anarchists and earnest starving-artists living alongside older Ukrainian and Latino immigrants and the more than occasional Wall Streeter who's just here 'cause the rent is right.

The Village, as the entire neighborhood is collectively known, moved from strength to strength as members of the working class settled here at the onset of the Industrial Revolution and the area south of Washington Square Park became a stronghold of Italian immigrants. By most accounts, the neighborhood's legendary gay subculture began to take root about the same time, driven by commerce around the city's west-side docks.

The founding of New York University added to the Village's increasingly liberal atmosphere, which further encouraged all manner of artists, radicals, and bohemians to plant their seeds here.

Writers James Agee and Anais Nin were at the vanguard of Village bohemia. Beat poet Gregory Corso was born in the tenement house at 190 Bleecker Street. And many beatniks who were not

lucky enough to be Villagers by birth later became local residents by choice. Allen Ginsberg and Jack Kerouac came downtown from Columbia University in the 1950s, just about the same time that Norman Mailer and others launched the *Village Voice*. In the 60s hippies ruled these streets, and in the 70s gays launched their own cultural revolution here.

Washington Square Park, at the bottom of Fifth Avenue, is the spiritual and geographical center of the Village; a popular place to hang out for street performers, bongo players, speed-chess players and bogus-weed sellers. The marble **triumphal arch** on the north side of the park, built in 1892, commemorates the centennial of George Washington's inauguration. Most of the Federal-style brownstones surrounding the park are owned by **New York University** (NYU). Founded in 1831, the largest private university in America has colonized the park as part of its unofficial campus.

The twelve-story red stone cube at the southeast corner of Washington Square Park is **Elmer Bobst Library**, *70 Washington Sq. South (tel. 1-212/998-2500)*, NYUs main library. An immensely ugly building, with a forbidding exterior and chilly interior, it's open only to students and staff. You can enter as far as the turnstiles, which will afford you a peak at the enormous interior atrium and patterned marble floor, said to be inspired by a Venetian piazza. **Judson Memorial Church**, *55 Washington Sq. South (tel. 1-212/477-0351)*, on the south side of the park, was designed in 1882 by McKim, Mead and White, one of the city's most celebrated architectural firms. The intricately carved pseudo-Romanesque exterior belies a disarmingly simple interior. The building was renovated with funds provided by King Juan Carlos II of Spain. Further

TAXI

139

west, on a corner of Sixth Avenue, are the **West 4th Street Basketball Courts**, a celebrated urban playground that, in recent times, has been appropriated by corporate sponsors. Unless you've got tons of *chutzpah*, it's unlikely you're going to get a piece of the action at these legendary hoops. Games here are dead serious and professional players can often be spotted mixing it up with the wannabes.

Jefferson Market Library, the neo-Gothic, turreted red-brick building at the corner of Sixth Avenue and 10th Street is a former courthouse said to be inspired by "Mad" King Ludwig's Neuschwanstein castle in Bavaria. The bell in the tower was created to commemorate the victory of Admiral George Dewey in Manila Bay during the Spanish-American War. True to New York form, it's graffitied with the words "To hell with Spain—Remember the Main—1898."

The Village becomes more beautiful the further west you go. Some of the city's most winsome brownstones are located on the leafy streets that angle inward towards the avenues, so that at one point 4th Street crosses 12th Street. Christopher Street, the famous gay thoroughfare, is now only a shadow of it's former self, as the scene long ago moved north to Chelsea.

By contrast, the Village becomes progressively grungier and more colorful the farther east you go from Washington Square Park. It's been that way forever (William S. Burroughs' 1953 classic *Junkie* is set here). The East Village is a great place to roam, exploring cheap restaurants, piss bars and hidden streetwear boutiques. Despite the unfortunate Gap store here and Starbucks there, the neighborhood clings strongly to its "authenticity." And the area's activists remain some of the city's most vociferous, taking on developers and even City Hall at every turn.

Tompkins Square Park *(btw 7th and 10th Sts, and Aves A and B)*, the unofficial epicenter

of the East Village, is a buzz of activity on warm summer weekends, bringing everything from drum circles to chess competitions.

St. Mark's Place, one of the East Village's main drags, has long been the strip where the East Village meets the world. Leon Trotsky once lived in the windowless brick tenement at number 77. These days, the strip is often crowded with suburban kids shopping for street fashions and cheap sunglasses, both of which are always in good supply.

Heading west, St. Mark's Place becomes **Astor Place**, named for 19th-century furrier John Jacob Astor. The giant **Cube sculpture**, at the intersection of Broadway and 8th Street, has become one of the neighborhood's most distinctive landmarks. It's a favorite of skateboarders. Push it, it turns.

Cooper Union College, *Cooper Square (tel. 1–212/353-4000)*, just across the street to the south, is the only private, full-scholarship college in the United States dedicated exclusively to preparing students for the professions of art, architecture and engineering. It was established in the 19th century by industrialist Peter Cooper.

One block away is **Astor Place Hair Stylists**, 2 Astor Place (at Broadway; tel. 1–212/475-9854). This once-traditional barber shop became world-famous in the 70s and 80s for a punk-inspired buzz-cut in which the barbers used electric clippers to "etch" designs into hair: the Yankee's logo, a marijuana leaf, or maybe just a simple off-center part in a closely-cropped head. Try 'em out, it's still their stock in trade.

Turn right up Broadway and walk two blocks to **Grace Church**, *802 Broadway (tel. 1–212/254-2000)*, the cutest Episcopal church in a city full of cute Episcopal churches. It's a Gothic Revival beauty. Farther along, Broadway becomes the city's premiere shopping ground for high-end antiques.

Chelsea

It's an old Manhattan story already: Dilapidated industrial wasteland becomes hip cultural Mecca. As in SoHo and TriBeCa before it, that's exactly what's happened to this former shipping district bounded by Fifth Avenue, the East River, and 14th and 26th Streets. The twist is that the style fiends who've settled into this hot neighborhood here are predominantly gay, thereby relieving the West Village of its position as lone standard-bearer of queer culture in the city. But Chelsea's scene is quite different from its southern neighbor. While the West Village is settled with older gays, who are now quite content to stay at home most nights, Chelsea boys are younger and not as attached to significant others. Eighth Avenue just below 23rd Street is hopping with beautiful muscle men mingling in bars, cafes and gyms.

Dance clubs and stylish restaurants continue to open and prosper in the nearby Meatpacking District, on the border between Chelsea and the West Village, while on the far west side of Chelsea one of the largest sports complexes anywhere occupies the **Chelsea Piers** (*see* Chapter 6/Recreation & Exercise).

Last, and certainly not least, Chelsea has become home to some of the city's best and brightest art galleries, many of which have relocated here from SoHo (*see* Chapter 7/Shopping by Subject).

Gramercy & The Flatiron District

Once home to the Astors and the Roosevelts, the area around Gramercy Park began life in the 1830s as one of New York's most fashionable addresses. Later on, the district attracted many successful writers and intellectuals, leading some to dub it "an American Bloomsbury." Publisher James Harper (of Harper Collins) lived here, as did writers Edith Wharton, Eugene O'Neill and O. Henry. Then the Communist Party moved their headquarters here, followed by Andy Warhol's legendary Factory in the 1960s.

Gramercy Park, at Lexington Avenue and 21st Street, is a private park, open only to neighborhood residents, who are given keys (as are visitors who stay at the Gramercy Park Hotel; *see* Chapter 3/Hotels.

Nearby is the **Theodore Roosevelt Birthplace**, *28 East 20th St (btw Broadway/Park Aves; tel. 1–212/260-1616)*, the reconstructed home of the only president born in New York City. The interior of this beautiful Victorian brownstone was re-created with the help of Roosevelt's sisters and is a great example of how the better half lived in the mid-19th century. It's open Mon-Fri 9am-5pm. Guided tours, which are mandatory, depart on the hour. Admission is $3 adults, free for seniors/children.

The Flatiron District is named for the **Flatiron Building** at Broadway and 23rd Street, the triangular-shaped terra cotta office tower that stands at the district's northernmost prow. At 21 stories, it was the tallest building in the world when it was completed in 1903. Today, the Flatiron District is very much the city's fashion center, home to model agencies, photographers' studios, film labs, and many of the city's hottest restaurants and bars.

TAXI

143

The area between 30th and 59th streets is the city's most densely commercialized. It's also an awesome place to explore. The eastern and western edges of Midtown are largely residential. Inbetween are the theaters of Broadway, the lights of Times Square, several concert halls, the skyscraping headquarters of dozens of Fortune 500 companies, and the majestic architectural cousins: the Chrysler Building, the Empire State and Rockefeller Center.

Fifth Avenue, which cuts through the heart of Midtown, is home to some of the world's finest department stores. It's also the address of **St. Patrick's Cathedral** *(at 50th St),* America's largest Roman Catholic church; **Trump Tower** *(btw 56th/57th Sts),* The Donald's pink-marble and bronze monument to his ego; and the **New York Public Library** *(at 42nd St),* one of the best research libraries in the world. Guarded by *Patience* and *Fortitude,* the famous pair of stone lions, the landmark Beaux-Arts library is also known for excellent book-themed exhibits, which flaunt its extensive holdings.

Bryant Park *(btw 41st and 43rd streets, and Fifth and Sixth avenues),* just behind the library, was the site of the 1853 World's Fair, where Elisha Otis unveiled the elevator and Isaac Singer introduced the sewing machine.

Two blocks east is **Grand Central Terminal** *(Park Avenue and 42nd Street)* a landmark of engineering and Renaissance-style architecture built in 1913. A late-20th-century renovation hosed off 83 years of accumulated grime to reveal one of the city's most impressive pieces of architecture. Check out the constellations of the winter zodiac painted on the vaulted blue ceiling of the station's main concourse. When it was created, many hoped the ceiling would double as an astronomical teaching tool, until it was revealed that the constellations were mistakenly painted backwards, which explains why Pegasus is charging from the west instead of the east.

The Chrysler Building, *405 Lexington Ave (at 42nd St),* on the next block, is a stunning Art Deco gem and the city's first true skyscraper. At 77 stories it was the tallest building in the world when it debuted in 1930. True to its name, the building was constructed as the headquarters of the Chrysler Corporation. Look closely and you can see that it's designed with depictions of racing cars molded into the relief. And the gargoyles which protrude from upper floors are patterned on the 1929 Chrysler cars.

The famous slanted roof of **Citicorp Center,** *601 Lexington Ave (btw 53rd/54th Sts)* is one of the more conspicuous features of Manhattan's skyline. Designed in the 1970s, at the height of the oil crisis, the south-facing slant contains a giant solar panel that was meant to provide most of the building's power. Unfortunately, it never worked.

Nearby, Marilyn Monroe's famous "white dress scene" was filmed over the subway grate in front of the **Loews New York Hotel** on Lexington Avenue and 51st Street.

Central Park

59th to 110th Sts (btw Fifth Ave/Central Park West). Tel. 1-212/794-6564.

It's hard to imagine Manhattan without Central Park. Its spacious greenery is an important counterpoint to the concrete jungle. The huge park ingeniously blends rolling meadows, lakes, woods, formal avenues, and rocky outcroppings, making it a wonderful place to explore. Designed in 1858 by landscape architects Frederick Law Olmsted and Calvert Vaux, the park is New York's pressure valve; the place where urbanites come to run, blade, catch some sun or shade and generally release pent-up city steam.

The best way to get to know the park is on foot. Although most locals consider the park dangerous at night (and some even worry about walking too close to Harlem—ever), there is little to worry about during daylight hours.

The Central Park Visitor Center is located in The Dairy, *(mid-park at 65th St)*, just behind Wollman Rink. Inside is an instructive 12-foot model of the park.

The Wollman Skating Rink *(east side at 63rd St)* is iced in winter and paved for rollers in summer (see Chapter 6/Recreation & Exercise).

Central Park Zoo *(east side at 64th St; tel. 1-212/861-6030)* is divided by climate into three sections: an indoor rain forest, an outdoor temperate zone, and an indoor Arctic area. And there's a giant leafcutter ant farm, of which various chambers are projected on closed-circuit TV.

Sheep Meadow *(west side btw 66th/71st Sts)*, where flocks grazed until 1934, is for sunbathing, picnicking and Frisbee tossing. On warm afternoons, it can attract thousands of people.

The Mall *(east side btw 65th/72nd Sts)* is a formal pedestrian avenue. Most of the statues that line the Promenade—including Ludwig van Beethoven, Thomas Moore, Walter Scott and Robert Burns—commemorate foreigners. They were donated by various groups of prideful hyphenated-Americans.

Bethesda Terrace *(mid-park at 73rd St)* offers an awesomely beautiful vantage over The Lake. It's centerpiece is a giant fountain called Angel of the Waters, which was designed by Emma Stebbins in 1873.

The Balto Statue *(east side at 67th St)*, made famous by a popular animated children's film, is "Dedicated to the indomitable spirit of the sled dogs that relayed antitoxin 600 miles over rough ice, across treacherous waters through Arctic blizzards from Nenana to the relief of stricken Nome in the winter of 1925."

Strawberry Fields *(west side at 72nd St)*, a heart-shaped grove dedicated to John Lennon, is situated adjacent to **The Dakota** *(1 West 72nd Street; at Central Park West)*, the building in which the ex-Beatle lived—and was killed, around 11pm on December 8, 1980.

At **The Lake** *(mid-park btw 72nd/77th Sts)* you can rent a rowboat for a scenic paddle in the shadow of Manhattan's magnificent skyscrapers ($10 per hour; tel. 1–212/517-2233).

The Model Boathouse *(east side at 74th St)* stands at the edge of the small, oval Conservatory Water, where locals come to race radio-controlled sailboats, rentable at $10 per hour. We love this place.

Just north of the Model Boathouse is the **Alice in Wonderland Statue** *(east side at 75th St)*, donated by philanthropist George Delacorte in memory of his first wife, Margarita. An early interactive art piece, it was designed to be played with and crawled upon.

Just across the Conservatory Water from the Model Boathouse is the **Hans Christian Andersen Statue** *(east side at 74th St)*, depicting the children's-story writer with a book in his hands and the Ugly Duckling at his feet.

The **Ramble** *(mid-park btw 74th/78th Sts)*, 37 acres of woodland traversed by numerous winding pathways, is the perfect counterpoint to The Lake. We're told that at night it's a favorite gay-male rendezvous.

Belvedere Castle *(mid-park near 79th St)* is perched on a rocky outcropping above the Great Lawn. Inside you'll find the Henry Luce Nature Observatory displaying local flora and fauna.

The **Great Lawn** *(mid-park btw 80th/85th Sts)* is a giant expanse that's perfect for team sports and sun worshiping.

The **Jacqueline Kennedy Onassis Reservoir** *(mid-park btw 86th/95th Sts)* is encircled by the park's excellent 1.6-mile running track.

Divided into French and English styles, the two-square-block **Conservatory Garden** *(east side near 105th St)* is the finest formal garden in Manhattan. Planted with thousands of flowers, shaded by crabapples, and incorporating two fountains, it's a great place for a romantic stroll.

And just north, at the newly stocked **Harlem Meer** (east side at 108th St), you can actually hook a fish (on a catch-and-release basis). Fishing poles are provided.

Upper West Side

If it weren't for **Lincoln Center**, *64th St and Broadway (btw Columbus/Amsterdam Aves)*, the area west of Central Park would simply be one of the city's richest residential districts. The center of liberal Jewish life in the 1970s, the Upper West Side is changing to accommodate yupscale professionals and young families who appreciate the neighborhood's excellent services and proximity to the park.

The **American Museum of Natural History**, *Central Park West (btw 77th/81st Sts)*, is here (*see* Chapter 4/The Best Museums), and there are some good clothing shops along Columbus Avenue (*see* Chapter 7/Shopping).

At night, Amsterdam Avenue, between 79th and 86th streets sports the neighborhood's best stretch of bars. But even these can be eerily quiet on weekdays.

Third World nannies and ladies who lunch are the stereotypical images of 10021, the city's most prestigious zip code. Madison Avenue shoppers, dripping with Eurogel floss in and out of the world's most expensive designer boutiques while, on Park Avenue, white-gloved doormen hail cabs for their residents. The northern and eastern reaches of the neighborhood are far less exclusive. Second and Third avenues are full of late-model high-rises harboring ambitious executive-assistants, and there are plenty of raucous beer bars for those who can't be bothered to taxi downtown.

The best thing to do here is stroll up **Madison Avenue** (btw 59th and 82nd Sts) and "lick the windows" of Manhattan's finest high-end shops.

Many of the city's best museums—including the Met and the Guggenheim—are located on Fifth Avenue's **Museum Mile** (*see* Chapter 4/ The Best Museums). The neighborhood is also home to **Temple Emanu-El** (*Fifth Ave at 65th St*), the largest synagogue of modern times, built with an interesting early Romanesque/ Byzantine/Near Eastern design.

Other neighborhood sights include the **New York Historical Society,** *2 West 77th St (btw Central Park West/Columbus Ave; tel. 1–212/873-3400),* a research institution that mounts crowd-pleasing exhibitions of Tiffany lamps and Audubon watercolors; the **Mont Vernon Hotel Museum,** *421 East 61st St (btw First/York Aves; tel. 1–212/838-6878),* a small carriage house containing 19th-century period rooms which originally stood on the former estate of the daughter of US President John Adams; and **Gracie Mansion** *(89th St and East End Ave; tel. 1–212/570-4751),* the Mayor's residence in Carl Schurz Park. Tours of the 1779 Federal-style mansion are offered on Wednesdays at 10am, 11am, 1pm and 2pm. Reservations are required and admission is $7 adults; $4 seniors.

TAXI

153

Harlem

Manhattan's largest residential neighborhood, located between the rivers from about 97th to 168th streets, is the spiritual, political and intellectual capital of black America. It's also a community plagued with crime, poverty, drugs and political impotence. Both these aspects attract curious visitors, who come up to see what makes this largely dilapidated corner of the world so famous. Much of the hoopla is historical: Musical greats like Ella Fitzgerald, Dizzy Gillespie, Billie Holliday, Charlie Parker and Tito Puente sung or swung in Harlem.

125th Street, Harlem's main commercial thoroughfare, is home to the **Apollo Theater**, *253 West 125th St (btw Adam Clayton Powell, Jr/Frederick Douglass Blvds; see* Chapter 9/ Major Concert And Theater Venues) and **The Studio Museum in Harlem**, *144 West 125th St (btw Lennox/Seventh Aves; tel. 1–212/864-4500*), which displays art and artifacts of black America and the African Diaspora. Originally created as a studio for working artists, the museum mounts regular exhibitions of traditional and contemporary African, Caribbean, and African-American art. And Harlem residents recently welcomed another business resident to 125th Street, former US President Bill Clinton.

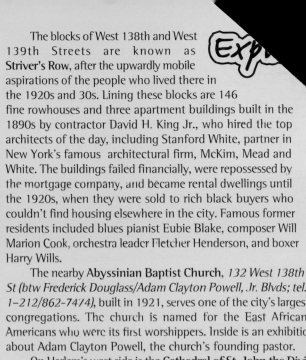

The blocks of West 138th and West 139th Streets are known as **Striver's Row**, after the upwardly mobile aspirations of the people who lived there in the 1920s and 30s. Lining these blocks are 146 fine rowhouses and three apartment buildings built in the 1890s by contractor David H. King Jr., who hired the top architects of the day, including Stanford White, partner in New York's famous architectural firm, McKim, Mead and White. The buildings failed financially, were repossessed by the mortgage company, and became rental dwellings until the 1920s, when they were sold to rich black buyers who couldn't find housing elsewhere in the city. Famous former residents included blues pianist Eubie Blake, composer Will Marion Cook, orchestra leader Fletcher Henderson, and boxer Harry Wills.

The nearby **Abyssinian Baptist Church**, *132 West 138th St (btw Frederick Douglass/Adam Clayton Powell, Jr. Blvds; tel. 1-212/862-7474)*, built in 1921, serves one of the city's largest congregations. The church is named for the East African-Americans who were its first worshippers. Inside is an exhibition about Adam Clayton Powell, the church's founding pastor.

On Harlem's west side is the **Cathedral of St. John the Divine**, *1047 Amsterdam Ave (btw 110th/112th Sts; tel. 1-212/316-7540)*, America's largest Gothic cathedral and the seat of the Bishop of the Episcopal Diocese of New York. Begun in 1892 (and not yet fully completed) the Cathedral is a grand European-style affair, filled with magnificent stained glass and art ranging from Raphael to Keith Haring. It's open daily from 8am-6pm. Admission is free ($1 contribution requested).

The adjacent **Peace Garden** is one of the most whimsical places in the city. The centerpiece is Greg Wyatt's *Peace Fountain*, a strange and wonderful piece designed with a giant crab and jumping giraffes, including one being hugged by Archangel Michael. The small sculptures of animals and other heroes that encircle the larger fountain were created by local schoolchildren, then cast in bronze.

Columbia University, *114th-120th Sts (btw Broadway/Amsterdam Ave; tel. 1-212/854-1754)*, a few blocks away, is not technically in Harlem, but in adjacent Morningside Heights, on the site of the former Bloomingdale Lunatic Asylum—an old (and, some say, not entirely unrelated) Upper West Side institution. In 1938, the physics lab at New York City's only Ivy League school was the site of the world's first artificially induced nuclear chain reaction. Although it was designed by McKim, Mead and White, the campus architecture has been likened to a fortress.

TAXI

155

...ke a guy a lifetime to know Brooklyn t'roo and ...' wrote Thomas Wolfe in the 1930s, "an' even ...1 wouldn't know it all." With more than 2.3 ...esidents, Brooklyn is by far the largest of New York's five boroughs. It's the most diverse too; the world in microcosm, with dozens of distinct cultural communities that dominate particular neighborhoods creating mini nation-states. The area around Atlantic Avenue is inhabited by longtime immigrants from Syria and Lebanon. Brighton Beach, settled with 300,000 Russian speakers from the former Soviet Union, has been dubbed "Little Odessa." Crown Heights, Williamsburg, and Boro Park are home to the largest Jewish populations in America. And Brooklyn's Bedford-Stuyvesant section is home to far more African-Americans than Harlem.

The Gothic towers of the world-famous **Brooklyn Bridge** have welcomed visitors for more than a century (*see* Chapter 4/New York's Greatest Hits). A short walk away, in Brooklyn Heights, you'll find the **Brooklyn Historical Society**, *128 Pierrepont St (at Clinton St; tel. 1–718/224–4111)*, a terra-cotta landmark that's home to *The Honeymooners* television show stage as well as permanent exhibits about Coney Island, the Brooklyn Dodgers baseball team, and the Brooklyn Bridge. It's open Tues-Sat noon-5pm. Subway: 2, 3, 4, 5, A, C, F, M, N, R.

Montague Street, the charming "high street" of the **Brooklyn Heights Historic District,** is filled with restaurants and cafes. The Heights is a 50-block architectural treasure from 19th-century urban America. The **Waterfront Promenade** overlooks the East River and offers superb views of Manhattan.

Set in a 1930s Brooklyn Heights subway station, the **New York Transit Museum**, *130 Livingston St (btw Boerum Pl/Schemerhorn St; tel. 1–718/694-5100)*, features 100 years of transit artifacts and photographs and is home to 18 vintage subway cars. It's open Tues-Fri 10am-4pm, Sat-Sun noon-5pm. Subway: 2, 3, 4, 5, A, C, F, M, N, R.

The **Brooklyn Museum of Art**, *200 Eastern Parkway (at Washington Ave; tel. 1–718/638-5000)*, near the Park Slope section of the borough, is the second largest art museum in New York (after the Met). This Beaux-Arts palace, created by McKim, Mead and White almost

a century ago, features paintings and sculpture from ancient Egypt to contemporary America and includes 28 elaborate period rooms, from a 17th-century Dutch farmhouse to a 1920s Art Deco library. It's open Wed-Fri 10am-5pm, Sat-Sun 11am-6pm. Subway: 2, 3, 4, 5, A, C, F, M, N, R.

Next to the museum is the 526-acre expanse of **Prospect Park**, which includes a zoo, Civil War memorial arch and 1776 Dutch colonial homestead.

There's always something in bloom at the adjacent **Brooklyn Botanic Garden**, *900 Washington Ave (at Eastern Parkway; tel. 1-718/623-7200)*, a 52-acre urban oasis and one of the world's most beautiful and most-visited public gardens. The **Steinhardt Conservatory**, a giant greenhouse containing tropical and desert plants, is a standout, as is the Japanese Garden and the avenue of cherry trees which blossom in brilliant pink each Spring. Subway: 2, 3, D, or Q.

The Coney Island Boardwalk with its world-famous Astroland Amusement Park, Nathan's Famous hotdogs, Disco Skooter, and wide open beach offers another only-in-Brooklyn experience. Stroll the three-mile boardwalk then pop into the **New York Aquarium**, *Surf Ave and West 8th St (tel. 1-718/265-3474)*, which showcases 300 species of marine creatures from around the world. The Sea Cliffs exhibition, a 300-foot-long rocky coastal habitat, is home to walruses, seals, penguins, and sea otters. Subway: D or F to West Eighth Street.

The Concord Baptist Church of Christ, *833 Gardner C. Taylor Boulevard (tel. 1-718/622-1818)*, located off Fulton Street in Bed-Stuy, is the house of worship for the largest African-American congregation in the United States. Nearby restaurants serve soul food, Caribbean specialties, and, increasingly, cuisines harking back to African roots.

The Brooklyn Academy of Music (BAM), *30 Lafayette Ave,* offers a full schedule of adventurous and avant performing arts programs including the annual Next Wave Festival (see Chapter 9/Major Concert And Theater Venues).

Staten Island, A Bucolic Paradise! At least that's what the Convention & Visitors Bureau would like you to believe about the home of Fresh Kills, one of the world's largest garbage dumps. Actually, Staten Island does have expanses of protected wilderness that are so vast it's hard to believe that you're in New York City. Because there was no land link to the island until the Verrazano-Narrows Bridge was built in 1964, the island still feels relatively isolated (and insulated) from the rest of the city. In fact, Staten Island is so different in character from the other boroughs that its residents symbolically elected to secede from the city in 1993.

In 1687 the Duke of York offered the island as a prize in a sailing competition won by the team from Manhattan, which has claimed the island ever since. The best (and most beautiful) way to get there from Manhattan is via the free **Staten Island Ferry**, which departs from Battery Park at the southern tip of Manhattan (subway 1 or 9 to South Ferry).

Before 1898, Staten Island was an independent county called Richmond, after the Duke of Richmond, the illegitimate son of King Charles II. The county seat, Richmondtown, is now the **Historical Richmondtown Restoration**, *441 Clarke Ave (tel. 1–718/351-1611)*, an historic village-turned-museum that's staffed by costumed craftspeople. It's open April-Sept, daily 1-5pm. Take bus S113, S54, or S74 from the ferry landing.

The Garibaldi-Meucci Museum, *420 Tompkins Ave (Rosebank; tel. 1–718/442-1608)*, a National Landmark, is in the former home of the unsung inventor of the telephone. Antonio Meucci received his patent in 1871, five years before Alexander Graham Bell. Even in death Meucci gets second billing at his own museum, to Giuseppe Garibaldi, the famed Italian freedom fighter who was a frequent houseguest before he went back to the Boot to lead his legions to victory and establish the modern Italian state. They are open Tues-Sun 1-5pm Take bus S103 from the ferry landing.

The Conference House, *Hylan Blvd (Tottenville; tel. 1–718/984-6046)*, was the site of an historic meeting in 1776 between British Commander Admiral Lord Richard Howe, his brother General William Howe, and revolutionary leaders Benjamin Franklin, John Adams, and Edward Rutledge. It was the only peace conference held in an attempt to halt the American Revolution. The Billopp House, as it is also known, is now a museum, displaying period furnishings, a 17th-century working kitchen and beautiful rolling lawns. It's open Mar-Dec, Wed-Sun. Take bus S103 from the ferry landing.

The most unusual museum on Staten Island is the **Jacques Marchais Center of Tibetan Art**, *338 Lighthouse Ave (at Richmond Rd; Tel. 1–718/987-3500)*, two Tibetan-style stone buildings containing a large collection of tankhas and religious artifacts. Set in a peaceful garden high on a hillside overlooking New York Bay, the buildings resemble a mountain temple. It is open Wed-Sun 1-5pm. Take bus S113 from the ferry landing.

The Best Of The Bronx

If a tornado whipped through the South Bronx, the joke goes, it would cause millions of dollars in improvement. Home to **Yankee Stadium**, *161st St (tel. 1–718/293-6000)*, "the House that Ruth Built," the southern reaches of the borough remain in burned-out disrepair. But there's also plenty nice in the Bronx, particularly the residential areas in the north. The only New York City borough attached to the United States mainland was named after the Dutch settler Jonas Bronck, who had claimed the region as his farm back in 1636. Today, much of the Bronx is a bedroom community for daily-breaders who commute into Manhattan for work.

The Bronx Zoo, *Bronx River Pkwy-Fordham Rd (tel. 1–718/367-1010)*, America's largest urban zoo, is the most famous tenant in the Bronx. The zoo's Congo Gorilla Forest, a re-creation of an African rainforest, includes shady forests and treetop lookouts for viewing baby lowland gorillas. The Zoo is open daily 10am-430pm. Admission is $8 adults, $5 children 2-12. Subway: 2, 5.

New York Botanical Garden, *200th St and Southern Blvd (Kazimiroff Blvd; tel. 1–718/817-8700)*, is a National Historic Landmark and one of America's foremost public gardens. The glass conservatory features exhibits ranging from desert plant life to rainforest specimens. The garden is best in summer, when the enormous grounds are in full bloom. It's open Tues-Sun and holiday Mon 10am-5pm. Subway: D, 4.

The Edgar Allan Poe Cottage, *East Kingsbridge Rd-Grand Concourse (tel. 1–718/881-8900)*, one of the city's most wistful historic sites, was home to the writer from 1846 to 1849. Many of his famous works, including "Annabel Lee," were written here. Subway: D, 4.

From the perspective of a jaded Manhattanite, Queens has all the disadvantages of being part of New York City (poor schools, potholes, unresponsive government...) without any of the city's cultural benefits. For millions of New Yorkers, however, Queens is home. The borough is a patchwork of dozens of working- and middle-class neighborhoods, the kind in which most New Yorkers live. Downscale places like Woodside, Jackson Heights, Corona, and Flushing are neighborhoods of small wood-frame houses interspersed with 20-plus-story red-brick apartment buildings. Local columnist Jimmy Breslin has quipped that Queens is like "a little bit of Akron picked up and dumped in the middle of New York City." He's only half kidding. The other and, in our minds, more fascinating aspect of Queens is its reputation as an ethnic powerhouse that is home to more than 75 different cultural groups: Astoria has the largest Greek population outside Athens, Jamaica is largely Caribbean, there's a Little India and a Little Colombia in Jackson Heights, and Flushing has developed into one of America's largest Chinatowns.

The borough was named in 1683 after the wife of Charles II of England, Queen Catherine of Braganza. It remained predominantly rural until the beginning of the 19th century, and there are still some huge parks and open spaces left.

Flushing Meadows-Corona Park is most famous for the *Unisphere*, a giant sculpture of Earth from the 1964 World's Fair that has appeared as the backdrop in countless rap videos.

Queens is also the site of **Shea Stadium** (home to baseball's Mets), **Aqueduct** and **Belmont** racetracks, and the **National Tennis Center** (host to the US Open).

The American Museum of the Moving Image, *35th Avenue at 36th St (Astoria)*, one of New York's most popular museums, is also based in Queens, as is the **Isamu Noguchi Garden Museum**, *32-37 Vernon Blvd, in Long Island City (see* Chapter 4/Other Collections). It's hard to believe the beauty and serenity at these gardens, studded with the sculptor's organic-looking statues and fountains, while the warehouse in which Noguchi worked features his brilliant lanterns, stage sets and more.

Organized Tours

Lots of different walking tours are offered every day in Manhattan. The best tours are once-monthly events, or special celebrations of an area or object promoted by a Business Improvement District. Many are free. Look in *The New York Times'* Friday Weekend section, the *Village Voice,* or the *New York Press* for a list of this week's walking tours.

WALKING TOURS =

Big Onion Walking Tours *(tel. 1–212/439–1090)* offers a comprehensive schedule that covers most of Manhattan. Their guides are mostly graduate students in American history from Columbia University. Itineraries run the gamut from the Multi-Ethnic Eating Tour of the Lower East Side to the Gay and Lesbian History Tour.

The Municipal Art Society, *457 Madison Ave (at 51st St; tel. 1–212/935–3960),* runs walking tours which stress excellence in urban design and planning and the preservation of the best of the city's past. Call or stop in to their bookstore for information.

Harlem, Your Way! *(tel. 1–212/690–1687 or 800/382–9363)* is a Harlem-based company that runs popular gospel and jazz tours. They also have neighborhood walking tours that offer an insiders' view of what they call "the black capital of the world."

BOAT TOURS =

Circle Line *(tel. 1–212/563-3200),* the classic New York sightseeing experience, sails all the way around Manhattan island in about three hours. Shorter excursions are also available. The company's eight uncomfortable boats are converted World War II Navy landing vessels. Tours depart Pier 83, at West 42nd Street on the Hudson River, and cost $20 for adults, $10 for children.

NYC Waterway
(tel. 800/533-3779), Circle Line's chief competitor, offers 45-minute tours of New York Harbor departing from South Street Seaport in Lower Manhattan. A longer 90-minute cruise departs from Pier 78, at West 38th Street and 12th Avenue on the Hudson River, and hits Manhattan's highlights.

HELICOPTER TOURS =

Liberty Helicopter Tours *(tel. 1–212/967-6464 or 1-800/542-9933; www.libertyhelicopters.com* buzz around the city and the Statue of Liberty in late-model choppers. Prices start at about $60 per person.

#06 Exercising
Fitness & Sports

ReCreaTioN & eXercisE

Chelsea Piers, on the Hudson River from 17th to 23rd streets (tel. 1–212/336-6000; www.chelseapiers.com), is the best thing to happen to sports in Manhattan. A one-stop sports shop, the complex is a fantastic mini-village that encompasses a golf drivingrange, indoor and outdoor ice rinks, batting cages, swimming pool, the world's longest indoor track, basketball and sand volleyball courts, a huge gym, a swimming pool, and a 10,000-square-foot climbing wall. In addition, there are a couple of restaurants, a mile-long esplanade, and several boating marinas.

Piers 59 through 62 were built at the beginning of the 20th century for the *Lusitania,* the *Ile de France,* and other luxury ocean liners. The *Titanic* was heading here when she sunk in 1912. The piers were abandoned in the 1940s, when newer landings able to accommodate larger ships were built farther uptown. The jetties were transformed into a huge sports complex in 1995. For most critics, the biggest problem with Chelsea Piers is its location on the far west side of Manhattan, a long way from the nearest subway. Fans shrug, however, saying that it's only a $10 cab ride from anywhere.

Bicycling

Manhattan street cycling is not for the timid, but with a helmet and *cojones* you can tangle with the taxis and cover a lot of ground, including zillions of potholes. If a pedal in the park is more your speed, you'll love the miles of relatively flat, winding paths of Central Park. You can rent bikes at **Central Park's Loeb Boathouse** (near East 72nd St; tel. 1–212/517–2233). Three-speed, 10-speed, and tandem bikes start at $10 per hour. They're open daily from 10am to 6pm.

Billiards/Pool

Briefly an upscale fad in the 1980s, pool has thankfully returned to its scummy roots. The best halls are dive-y places with tens of tables, good lighting, and late closing times, if any at all. **Slate Billiards**, 54 West 21st St (btw Fifth/Sixth Aves; tel. 1–212/989-0096) is one of the best in the city.

Bowling

Bowlmor Lanes
110 University Place (btw. 12th/13th Sts). Tel. 1–212/255-8188. www. bowlmor.com. Open Mon & Fri 11am-4am, Tues-Wed 11am-1am, Thurs 11am-2am, Sat 2pm-4am, Sun 2pm-1am.
Packed with college graduates intent on recreational slumming, this 44-laner attracts kitsch-hunting low rollers with disco bowling (Mon 10pm-4am) and other special events. The charge is $6-$7 a game, plus $4 for shoe rentals.

Leisure Time
625 Eighth Ave (at 42nd St). Tel. 1–212/268-6909. Open Mon-Thurs, Sun 10am-11pm, Fri-Sat 10am-2am.
This 30-lane alley and bar in the Port Authority Bus Terminal attracts neighborhood rowdies, suits on their way home from work, and the usual smattering of runaways and chicken-hawkers. Avoid Thursdays; that's league night. Charges are $6 per game and $3.50 for shoe rentals.

Horseback Riding

Claremont Riding Academy, *175 West 89th St (tel. 1–212/724-5101)*, rents horses for riding in Central Park. There are no guides; jockeys must be trained English riders. Horses are available year-round, daily, from 630am until about one hour before dark. They charge $45 per hour.

Climbing

Chelsea Piers (see above) has an amazing 10,000-square-foot climbing wall—one of the largest in the country.

Golf

Although there are no courses in Manhattan, you can practice your swing at Chelsea Pier's tri-level driving range (see above). The hardest-core out-of-town duffers go to the Bronx's Van Cortlandt Golf Course, in Van Cortlandt Park, Park South and Bailey Avenue (tel. 718/543-4595). It's the oldest public course in the US, and looks like it.

Gyms

There is no shortage of health clubs in Manhattan. There will certainly be one (or more) in your neighborhood, and most hotels have special deals with nearby clubs, if they don't have one of their own. When a question to the concierge is answered by a blank stare, go tone those six-pack abs at one of the following high-tech spots, which allow visitors to use the facilities for a day for a price that ranges from $24 to $50:

Downtown: *Crunch Fitness , 623 Broadway (tel. 1–212/420-0507).*
Midtown: *NY Health & Racquet Club, 132 East 45th St (tel. 1–212/986-3100); 20 East 50th St (tel. 1–212/593-1500).*
Upper East Side: *Crunch Fitness, 1109 Second Ave (tel. 1–212/758-3434).*
Upper West Side: *Crunch Fitness, 160 West 83rd St (tel. 1–212/875-1902); Equinox, 344 Amsterdam Ave (tel. 1–212/721-4200).*

In line Skating

Central Park is a paradise for bladers, who skate here daily by the thousands. Distance bladers keep to the road loop, which is closed to cars on weekends. Beginners, acrobats, and figure skaters converge on the bandshell, in the middle of the park at the latitude of 72nd Street. Battery Park City, along the Hudson River in Lower Manhattan is another great place to blade, especially on weekends, when there are fewer cars on the Financial District's streets and you can roll all the way to South Street Seaport.

Each warm Wednesday night starting at 9pm, dozens (and sometimes hundreds) of skaters meet at Union Square Park (14th St, btw Broadway/Park Ave South) for **Night Blade Manhattan,** a group roll through the streets of the city. The **Empire Skate Club** (tel. 212/774-1774) sponsors group skates, speed-skating events, and two-or three-day skating tours. Call for itineraries and start times. In-line skates (as well as conventionals) can be rented at **Blades Board & Skate** locations all over town (*see* Chapter 7/Shopping).

TAXI

169

Jogging

Each morning, Central Park is filled with hoofers charging their way around the Reservoir, a 1.6-mile (2.6 km) gravel path privately paid for by a sporting local resident. Meanwhile, Downtowner suffer around Washington Square Park, along East Park, (which runs from 14th to Grand streets), o the promenade on the West Side from Batter the Chelsea Piers.

Ice Skating

Skyrink at Chelsea Piers. *Tel. 1–212/336-6100.*
Skyrink was cooler when it was located on the 16th floor of a building in Midtown. But, we have to admit the ice is better now that it's part of the Chelsea Piers complex. It's busier too, regularly reserved for hockey leagues and lessons. Monday to Friday from noon to 120pm and on Friday nights (actually Saturday morning) from 1am to 230am and Saturday from midnight to 2am, there's coed hockey, open to anyone with $25, a pair of skates, and full gear, including mask. On Saturday nights from midnight to 2am, Skyrink hosts adult hockey clinics for $20. Reservations are recommended. You have to clear the ice by 4am, when semi-professional figure skaters come in for practice. For more information, call the ice hockey office between 5 and 11pm.

Rockefeller Center Ice Rink
1 Rockefeller Center Plaza (Fifth Ave at 49th St). Tel. 1–212/332-7654.
From October to April you can glide around this rinky-dink rink under the gaze of *Prometheus* and thousands of spectators. It's open daily from 9am-1030pm (until midnight Sat), costs $8.50 adult and $7 children on weekdays, and $11 and $7.50 respectively on weekends. Skates are available for rent (for $6).

Wollman Rink
in Central Park (at 62nd St). Tel. 1–212/439-6900.
A terrific outdoor rink for figure skaters, Wollman is a decent-sized oval, with a dramatic location under the trees and skyscrapers of Central Park South. Rollerskaters and bladers take over from mid-April to mid-September. Admission is $8.50-$11 adults, $4.25-$7 seniors/students; phone for opening hours.

Spectator Sports

So what if both "New York" football teams play in New Jersey, the Dodgers and Giants are long gone, and the Yankees are constantly threatening to leave? Fact is, no city in the world can boast of so many champions in so many sports as New York. We're the best, and we'll kick your ass.

Tickets can be purchased at face value in person or by phone from each team's box office. **TicketMaster** (tel. 1–212/307-7171) sells the same seats with a $3 to $8 service charge. If the game you're looking for is sold out, check with your hotel concierge; it's his/her job to dig something up. Failing that, you can pay a premium (usually 5% on the price) for good seats to almost any event by calling a scalping agency like **Ticket City** (tel. 800/765-3688) or **The Ticket Office** (800/248-9849).

Tickets & Info

New York Giants	1–201/935-8222
New York Knicks	1–212/465-5867
New York Jets	1–516/560-8200
New York Yankees	1–718/293-6000
New York Mets	1–718/507-8499
New York Rangers	1–212/465-6741

Baseball

A large bronze plaque just across the river in Hoboken, New Jersey, asserts that Abner Doubleday invented baseball there in 1845. But, the New York Convention & Visitors Bureau steadfastly claims that the game was first played in New York City's Madison Square Park (where we notice no commemorative plaque exists). Such is the rivalry in sports. In any event, there can be no doubt that the national pastime is New York's game. The first professional leagues started here in the 1870s, and at one time the city had three borough-based teams: the Yankees in the Bronx, the Dodgers in Brooklyn, and the Giants in Manhattan. Today the rivalry is between fans of the Yankees and the Queens-based Mets and each season the city's faithful pray the two teams will slug it out in a Subway Series, as they did in 2000. Tickets cost $10 to $75.

The New York Yankees

Yankee Stadium, Bronx. Tel. 718/293-6000.
From their humble beginnings in 1903 as the New York Highlanders, the Yankees have raked in over 32 American League pennants and twenty-six World Championships, making them the winningest team ever in professional sports. We can think of no truer New York experience than to sit with the diehards in the bleachers and learn the true meaning of a "Bronx cheer." Opened in 1923, the "house that Ruth built" is a classic piece of baseball architecture that still reverberates with the spirits of Yankee's past – Joe DiMaggio, Lou Gehrig, Mickey Mantle, Whitey Ford, Roger Maris and Phil Rizzuto. The Stadium is reached by subway on the 4 or D train to 161st Street.

New York Mets

Shea Stadium, Queens. Tel. 718/507-8499.
They finished dead last in batting, fielding, and pitching in their inaugural season (1962). And except for a couple of extraordinary years since, they haven't exactly been the best team in baseball. But the Mets are likable losers. You gotta love those thunderous jets flying directly over the stadium towards La Guardia Airport, the cool "Home Run Apple" in center field, and their retro "Meet the Mets" theme song. First-base coach Mookie Wilson—who is in the Mets Hall of Fame along with greats like Gil Hodges and Casey Stengel—is always greeted by fans with a heartfelt "Mooooook." And Jerry Seinfeld, the Amazins' most famous fan, can regularly be spotted in a box behind the third-base dugout. If you can't get a good seat, buy the cheapest bleacher ticket, then grease an usher in the boxes. It's done all the time. And think about avoiding the stadium on dangerous Bat Day, when Queens' kids are given half-sized souvenir baseball bats. Take the #7 subway or the Long Island Railroad to Shea.

Football

New York Giants

Giants Stadium, The Meadowlands, East Rutherford, NJ. Tel. 1–201/935-8222.

New York Giants' regular-season games are some of the hardest sports tickets to get. Even in a rebuilding year the "Big Blue Wrecking Crew" brings a fiercely loyal crowd and more than a dash of NFL history into every game they play. That's the result of five National Football League championships and two Super Bowl victories. They made it to Super Bowl XXXV in 2001, but were swatted away by the Baltimore Ravens. Still, the future awaits and the fans are diehards. Buses to the Meadowlands depart from Port Authority Bus Terminal and take about 30 minutes.

New York Jets

Giants Stadium, The Meadowlands, East Rutherford, NJ. Tel. 1–516/560-8200.

Stuyvesant High School Peglegs notwithstanding, there is no professional football played in New York. The Jets have been around since 1960, but it was the "Broadway" Joe Namath era that transformed them into the most beloved footballers in town. Bill Parcells turned the struggling team around and brought it within a game of the Super Bowl in 1998. Early in 2001 he resigned and new coach Herman Edwards rebuilt the team once again. Buses to the Meadowlands depart from Port Authority Bus Terminal and take about 30 minutes.

Ice Hockey

The New York Rangers

Madison Square Garden, 2 Pennsylvania Plaza, Seventh Ave (btw 31st/33rd Sts). Tel. 1–212/307-7171 for tickets or 465-6225 for guest relations.

After a 54-year dry spell, the Rangers finally brought the Stanley Cup to Madison Square Garden in 1994, and have been hot ever since. Fans can be seen lining up at the Garden the night before tickets go on sale, and games are now usually sold out. The institutionalized violence on the ice rarely carries into the stands, but you'd be well advised not to wear an Islanders or Devils cap or to root for your home team if they're not the Rangers. The season runs from October to April.

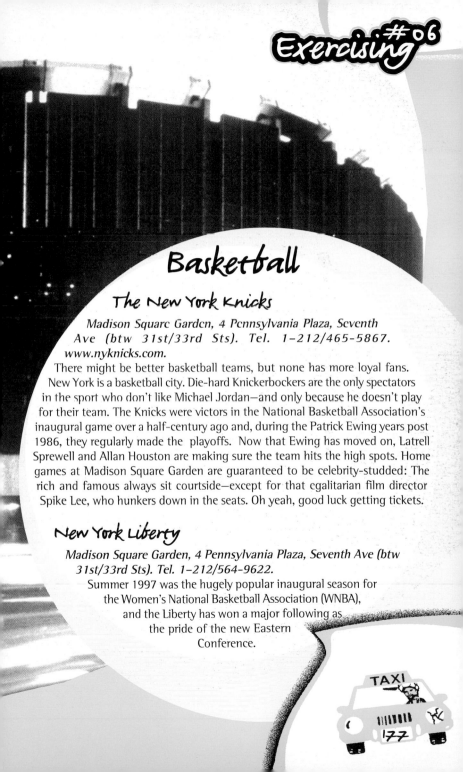

Basketball

The New York Knicks

Madison Square Garden, 4 Pennsylvania Plaza, Seventh Ave (btw 31st/33rd Sts). Tel. 1-212/465-5867. www.nyknicks.com.

There might be better basketball teams, but none has more loyal fans. New York is a basketball city. Die-hard Knickerbockers are the only spectators in the sport who don't like Michael Jordan—and only because he doesn't play for their team. The Knicks were victors in the National Basketball Association's inaugural game over a half-century ago and, during the Patrick Ewing years post 1986, they regularly made the playoffs. Now that Ewing has moved on, Latrell Sprewell and Allan Houston are making sure the team hits the high spots. Home games at Madison Square Garden are guaranteed to be celebrity-studded: The rich and famous always sit courtside—except for that egalitarian film director Spike Lee, who hunkers down in the seats. Oh yeah, good luck getting tickets.

New York Liberty

Madison Square Garden, 4 Pennsylvania Plaza, Seventh Ave (btw 31st/33rd Sts). Tel. 1-212/564-9622.

Summer 1997 was the hugely popular inaugural season for the Women's National Basketball Association (WNBA), and the Liberty has won a major following as the pride of the new Eastern Conference.

TAXI

HorseRacing

Aqueduct

110th St and Rockaway Blvd., Ozone Park, Queens.
Tel. 1-718/641-4700. Admission $2-$4.
Thoroughbred races are held Wednesdays through Sundays from November to May. Take the A subway to the track.

Belmont Park

Hempstead Turnpike and Plainfield Ave., Belmont, Queens.
Tel. 1-718/641-4700. Admission $2-$4.
In addition to hosting the Belmont Stakes, the third leg of the Triple Crown, this park keeps a long summer season from May to October, with races Wednesdays through Sundays. The best way to reach Belmont is via Long Island Railroad's Pony Express from Penn Station.

The Meadowlands

East Rutherford, NJ. Tel. 1-201/935-8500.
Admission $1-$4.
Open all year, the Meadowlands features trotters from January through August and thoroughbreds from September through December. Races are held Tuesdays through Saturdays. To reach the track, take the bus from Port Authority Bus Terminal.

Soccer

MetroStars

Giants Stadium, The Meadowlands, East Rutherford, NJ. Tel. 1-201/935-3900.
It took all of four minutes for New York's fledgling professional soccer team to become local heroes. In May 1996, trailing badly in the second half of their fourth game, the MetroStars stormed from behind, scored three goals in four minutes, then won the game in a shoot-out. The team is led by head coach Octavio Zambrano, the winningest coach in the league. The soccer season runs from April through October.

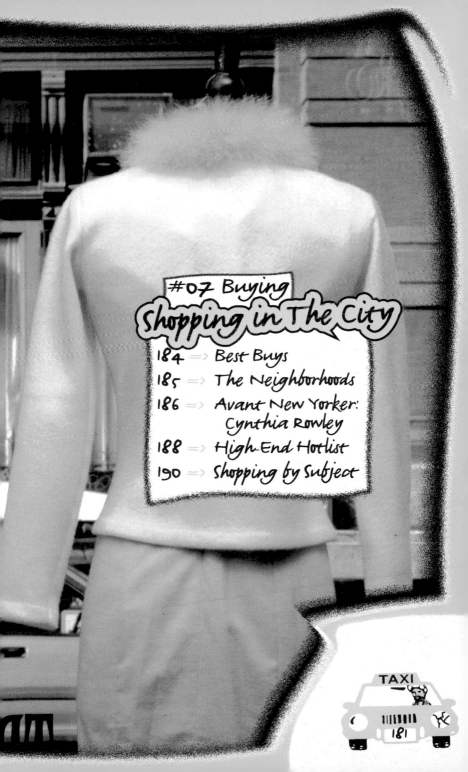

#07 Buying

shopping in The City

TAXI

181

Along with Paris, and perhaps Hong Kong, New York City is one of the shopping capitals of the universe. Despite stock-market swings, conspicuous consumerism and binge shopping remain strong. And, for better or worse, globalization has made it possible to find almost anything you want in New York, often at lower prices than in London, San Francisco, or Paris.

As every dedicated clothes-hound knows, shopping isn't just about saving money. It's a holistic, sensual experience that one just can't put a price on—especially if you're using someone else's credit card. New York City remains the world capital for clothing. And for the sheer pleasure of urban hunting-and-gathering, this city remains one of the best on the planet. With few exceptions, New York has resisted the global trend toward urban "mallification," allowing shoppers to floss in and out of boutiques all day while strolling around some of the city's most exciting streets.

TAXI

Opening Hours

Shops are generally open Monday through Saturday from about 930 or 10am to 7 or 9pm, and Sunday until 6pm. Many stores, especially department stores, keep longer hours on Thursdays.

The Best Buys

Comedian Jack Benny once quipped that the trouble with New York is that "it's so convenient to everything I can't afford." But the truth is you can get practically anything in New York for less money than you'd pay anywhere else. To Europeans, this city often looks like one giant red-tag sale.

Orchard Street (btw Houston/Canal Sts), on the Lower East Side, is where bargains were invented. There you'll find high-end designer fashions as well as basic family apparel at about 25% off the retail price. The street is jam-packed with shoppers on Sundays, and only about half the stores are open on Saturdays (many observe the Jewish Sabbath), so it's best to go mid-week to avoid the crowds (see Discount Shopping, below).

Knock-Offs

There's nothing in America quite like **Canal Street**. Walk its length through Chinatown (btw Broadway/Bowery) and you'll find lots of fake designer accessories at dirt-cheap prices. This is the place to hunt for Rolex, Cartier, Tag Heuer, and other "high-end" watches for about $20. Name-brand bags like Gucci, Hermès, Chanel, and Louis Vuitton are readily available, as are sunglasses with names like Cartier, Ralph Lauren, and others. You're expected to bargain here: Offer half-price.

The Neighborhoods

Madison Avenue from the high 50s to the low 80s is New York's most legendary shopping strip, packed shoulder to shoulder with the biggest names in fashion (see High-End Hotlist, below). On this rarefied avenue of international couture, platinum-card customers dress up to shop, and are required to ring door-bells to enter practically every store. The Upper East Side is also home to the city's best thrift shops.

Many of Madison Avenue's newest arrivals relocated from **Fifth Avenue**, a former high-end stomping ground that transformed itself into a proletariat shopping center. We are happy to report that, with the closing of the Coca-Cola Store and the Warner Bros. Shop, the lowbrow chain trend is now in retreat. Fifth Avenue is in the process of reinventing itself once again with luxury shops that are worthy of the street's stalwart department stores like Saks, Lord and Taylor, Bergdorf Goodman, and Henri Bendel.

The **Upper West Side**, particularly along Columbus Avenue in the 70s, is full of mid-priced fashion shops like Betsey Johnson and Kenneth Cole, aimed squarely at people from Generation Jones.

Meanwhile, **SoHo** has developed into earth's swankiest mall, home to a slew of expensive, stylish boutiques that appeal to the moneyed hipsters of the world. The art-gallery edge has moved elsewhere—primarily to Chelsea—but SoHo remains the best place to shop for avant fashions from "downtown" designers like Todd Oldham and Miu-Miu.

Among newer shopping neighborhoods, **NoLIta** (North of Little Italy) and the **Lower East Side** are currently the hottest, blending funkiness and sophistication with prices that even downtowners can almost afford. These are the places to look for small boutiques by local designers like Kelly Christy, Cynthia Rowley, and Tracy Feith.

Greenwich Village remains the top destination for urban streetwear, especially on Broadway (btw 8th/Houston Sts) and along 8th Street (btw Sixth Ave/Broadway). Serious tightwads should check out the streets of the East Village between Second Avenue and Avenue A, which are honeycombed with lots of little vintage shops. And stylish men should head to Christopher Street, deep in the West Village, where stores cater to guys with fashion sense.

TAXI

185

Avant-New Yorker: Cynthia Rowley

Although she was born in Illinois, Cynthia Rowley has made her mark in New York, where she is known for her wit, originality, and sophisticated collections that run the gamut from inexpensive little T-shirts and fun prints to imported leathers and cashmeres. A media darling, Cynthia has been a guest on The David Letterman show and many other shows, and even once designed a cover for the late *George* magazine. Recipient of the Council of Fashion Designers of America's New Fashion Talent award, Rowley is known in the industry as the "Queen of Theme" for creative introductions of new collections— like the time she simulcast her fashion show on the Times Square Jumbotron. With almost 30 Cynthia Rowley stores around the world, this designer's star is shooting.

*Avant*Guide_* Is there a New York style?

*Cynthia Rowley_* People look a little bit edgier here. New York style is very practical for our urban environment. It's cosmopolitan and chic—sort of "fast fashion." And the cliché is true: People wear a lot of black here. Black is not only sleek, it's very practical in New York, as are accessories like messenger bags. The clothes fit the lifestyle. New Yorkers walk a lot and take subways. Unlike other parts of the country, where people teeter on high heels, New Yorkers wear shoes you can walk in and dress for their unique environment. I would also say that what most people think of as "American style" is really "New York style." It's clean, modern sportswear that's both practical and casual.

A*G_ What's the future of New York fashion?

C.R_ I think that things will get earthier. Life in this city isn't going to get any easier and fashions will always be practical. But New Yorkers are also strongly influenced by other cultures. In the ▮▮▮▮▮'ll often see established urban designs mixed with ironic influences like bowling tops or Hawaiian surfer shirts.

A*G_ Describe your perfect day in New York.

C.R_ Well, even just going to work I have a pretty perfect day, but I suppose I'd get up and have breakfast at Kitchenette (73 West Broadway; tel. 1–212/267–0740), which is in my neighborhood [TriBeCa]. Then I would take a long walk, checking out the stores in NoLIta and SoHo. I'd stop into the Cynthia Rowley store and say "hi" to everybody, walk all the way up to the Sixth Avenue Flea Market (only for some inspiration, because I have too much junk already), then go to the Museum of Modern Art or the Whitney or the galleries in Chelsea. In the evening, I'd go to Pó (31 Cornelia St; tel. 1–212/645–2189) for dinner, then home to watch a movie on my new outdoor movie screen! It's actually the neighboring building's big, ugly addition that we now project movies onto. On day two, I'd take the Circle Line around Manhattan. I know it's kitschy, but I love it!

High-End Hotlist

agnès b
*1063 Madison Ave
(btw 80th/81st Sts)
Tel. 1–212/570-9333*

Armani A/X
*568 Broadway (at Prince St)
Tel. 1–212/431-6000*

Betsey Johnson
*251 East 60th St (btw Second/
Third Aves). Tel. 1–212/319-7699*

Bottega Veneta
*635 Madison Ave (at 59th St)
Tel. 1–212/371-5511*

Burberry's
*9 East 57th St (btw Fifth/
Madison Aves). Tel. 1–212/371-5010*

Calvin Klein
*654 Madison Ave (at 60th St)
Tel. 1–212/292-9000*

Celine
*667 Madison Ave (at 61st St)
Tel. 1–212/486-9700*

Chanel
*15 East 57th St (btw Fifth/Madison
Aves). Tel. 1–212/931-2950*

Christian Dior
*21 East 57th St (at Fifth Ave)
Tel. 1–212/931-2950*

DKNY
*655 Madison Ave (at 60th St)
Tel. 1–212/223-3569*

Dolce & Gabbana
*825 Madison Ave
(btw 68th/69th Sts)
Tel. 1–212/249-4100*

Emanuel Ungaro
*792 Madison Ave
(at 67th St)
Tel. 1–212/249-4090*

Emilio Pucci
*24 East 64th St (btw Fifth/
Madison Aves). Tel. 1–212/752-4777*

Emporio Armani
*601 Madison Ave (btw 57th/
58th Sts). Tel. 1–212/317-0800*

Ermenegildo Zegna
*743 Fifth Ave (btw 57th/
58th Sts). Tel. 1–212/421-4488*

Escada
*717 Fifth Ave (at 56st St)
Tel. 1–212/755-2201*

Etro
*720 Madison Ave (btw 63rd/
64th Sts). Tel. 1–212/317-9096*

Fendi
*720 Fifth Ave (at 56th St)
Tel. 1–212/767-0100*

Gianfranco Ferre
*845 Madison Ave (at 70th St)
Tel. 1–212/717-5430*

Gianni Versace
*647 Fifth Ave (btw 51st/
52nd Sts). Tel. 1–212/317-0224*

Giorgio Armani
*760 Madison Ave (at 65th St)
Tel. 1–212/988-9191*

Givenchy
*710 Madison Ave (at 63rd St)
Tel. 1–212/772-1040*

Gucci
*685 Fifth Ave (at 54th St)
Tel. 1–212/826-2600*

Hermès
*691 Madison Ave (at 62nd St)
Tel. 1–212/751-3181*

Issey Miyake
992 Madison Ave (at 77th St)
Tel. 1-212/439-7822

Jaeger
818 Madison Ave
(btw 68th/69th Sts)
Tel. 1-212/794-0780

Kenzo
80 Wooster St (at Spring St)
Tel. 1-212/966-4142

Krizia
769 Madison Ave (at 66th St)
Tel. 1-212/879-1211

La Perla
777 Madison Ave
(btw 66th/67th Sts)
Tel. 1-212/570-0050

Laura Ashley
398 Columbus Ave (at 79th St)
Tel. 1-212/496-5110

Laura Biagiotti
4 West 57th St (btw Fifth/
Sixth Aves). Tel. 1-212/399-2533

Les Copains
801 Madison Ave (btw 57th/
58th Sts). Tel. 1-212/327-3014

Liz Claiborne
650 Fifth Ave (at 51st St)
Tel. 1-212/956-6505

Louis Feraud
703 Fifth Ave (btw 53rd/
54th Sts). Tel. 1-212/758-8822

Louis Vuitton
49 East 57th St (btw Park/
Madison Aves). Tel. 1-212/371-6111

Max Mara
813 Madison Ave (btw 68th/
69th Sts). Tel. 1-212/879-6100

Missoni
1009 Madison Ave (at 78th St)
Tel. 1-212/517-9339.

Moschino
803 Madison Ave (btw 67th/68th Sts)
Tel. 1-212/639-9600

Prada
841 Madison Ave (at 70th St)
Tel. 1-212/327-4200

Ralph Lauren/Polo
867 Madison Ave (at 72nd St)
Tel. 1-212/606-2100

Romeo Gigli
21 East 69th St (btw Madison/
Park Aves). Tel. 1-212/744-9121

Salvatore Ferragamo (women)
661 Fifth Ave (btw 52nd/
53rd Sts). Tel. 1-212/759-3822

Shanghai Tang
714 Madison Ave (btw 53rd/54th Sts)
Tel. 1-212/888-0111

Tiffany & Co.
727 Fifth Ave (at 57th St)
Tel. 1-212/755-8000

Valentino
747 Madison Ave (at 65th St)
Tel. 1-212/772-6969

Yves Saint Laurent
855 Madison Ave (at 71st St)
Tel. 1-212/988-3821

#07 Buying

Shopping By Subject

Antiques

The **Sixth Avenue Flea Market**, in parking lots on Sixth Avenue between 24th and 26th streets (tel. 1–212/243-5343), is the best and biggest flea market in Manhattan. The antiques part, closer to 26th Street, features furniture, collectibles, vintage clothing, and plenty of miscellaneous junk. It's open during good weather year-round, Saturday and Sunday from 9am to 5pm, though most vendors arrive unofficially as early as 7am. Admission is $1.

An identical parking lot, directly south, is open only on Sundays and sells kitchenware, furniture, glasses, personal artifacts, pottery, glassware, jewelry, and art. Admission is free.

A **smaller lot on 25th Street**, east of Sixth Avenue, has fewer vendors and a somewhat smaller crowd, but the offerings can be just as glorious. They have furniture, clothing, accessories, and more.

The Showplace, 40 West 25th St (tel. 1–212/633-6010), is like an indoor extension of the outdoor market, with a small cafe downstairs. It's open Saturday and Sunday only from 830am to 530pm.

The Garage, 112 West 25th St (btw Sixth/Seventh Aves; tel. 1–212/647-0707) is just that: a two-story parking garage, which transforms on weekends into yet another bustling antiques venue. It's open Saturday and Sunday from 8am to 5pm.

The Metropolitan Art & Antiques Pavilion, 110 West 19th St (tel. 1–212/463-0200), offers weekend "theme" shows which range from antiquarian books to vintage fashions.

The SoHo Antiques Fair, at Broadway and Grand Sts (tel. 1–212/682-2000) is a good general market for antiques and collectibles and a lively addition to the downtown weekend scene. It's open Saturday and Sunday from 9am to 5pm.

Uptown you'll find the **Manhattan Arts & Antiques Center**, 1050 Second Ave (at 56th St; tel. 1–212/355-4400), a serious (and we mean seriously expensive) 100-dealer venue with ultra-fine European, American, and Oriental antiques. It's open Monday to Saturday from 1030am to 6pm, Sunday noon to 6pm.

alleries

Most New York galleries specialize in 20th-century art. The city is, after all, one of the world's primary centers for contemporary art.

There are three major areas in Manhattan in which galleries cluster:

Chelsea has relatively recently become the hottest gallery area and many of the biggest names in SoHo have moved here into the massive warehouses that line the streets between 20th and 26th west of Ninth Avenue. Long home to taxi brokers, AOL-Time Warner cable trucks, and whore-hunting curb crawlers, these blustery stretches in the low 20s have been speedily gentrified into one of Manhattan's coolest neighborhoods.

SoHo and **TriBeCa** (around West Broadway) are still on the gallery-goers list, but they're not nearly as hot as they used to be.

The galleries in **Midtown** (on 57th Street, east of Fifth Avenue) are mostly upscale, Old World art houses dealing in Old Masters and paintings and sculpture by well-known European artists.

Art Now Gallery Guide, a free monthly listing exhibits at scores of New York galleries, is available at many of the spaces listed below. *Time Out New York* and *New York* magazines also have excellent listings on what's on this week.

Most galleries are closed Sundays, and all keep shorter hours (or are closed entirely) in summer. If you are planning a crawl and have your heart set on a particular place, it's a good idea to telephone ahead to avoid disappointment.

303 Gallery
525 West 22nd St (btw Tenth/Eleventh Aves). Tel. 1–212/255-1121. Open Tues-Sat 10am-6pm.

Although small on space, 303 is a giant when it comes to avant artists specializing in multimedia works. In one installation Biennialist Rikrit Tiravanija filled the gallery's storage rooms and offices with kettles of soup, and moved all the stuff that's usually in the back rooms into the exhibition space.

Andrea Rosen
525 West 24th St (btw Tenth/Eleventh Aves). Tel. 1–212/627-6000. Open Tues-Sat 10am-6pm.

Rejuvenated after moving from SoHo to Chelsea, Andrea Rosen can always be counted on for exhibitions that are interesting and daring. One artist in her stable, John Coplans, is working on a lifelong project photo-documenting the aging process of his own body.

Art in General
79 Walker St (btw Broadway/Lafayette St). Tel. 1–212/219-0473. Open Tues-Sat noon-6pm. Closed July/Aug.

One of the best galleries in which to see art stars of the future, Art in General has long been associated with cutting-edge creatives from around the world. Group exhibitions are frequently organized by guest curators.

Artists Space
38 Greene St (btw Grand/Broome Sts), 3rd Fl. Tel. 1–212/226-3970. Open Tues-Sat noon-6pm. Closed Aug.

A great place to see up-and-comers on the SoHo scene, Artists Space's group shows give unknown artists their first shot at the limelight. Performance artist Laurie Anderson shows here too.

Barbara Gladstone
515 West 24th St (btw Tenth/Eleventh Aves). Tel. 1–212/206-9300. Open Tues-Sat 10am-6pm.

There's always something exciting going on at Gladstone, the dealer of the moment and groomer of some of earth's best and brightest talents. The emphasis is currently on high tech.

Bonakdar Gallery

521 West 21st St (btw Tenth/Eleventh Aves). Tel. 1–212/414-4144. Open Tues-Sat 10am-6pm.

Yet another SoHo transplant to Chelsea, Bonakdar occupies a huge space, which can accommodate dinosaur-sized works by conceptual and other artists. British prankster Damien Hirst has been shown here.

David Zwirner

525 West 19th St (at Eleventh Ave). Tel. 1–212/966-9074. Open Tues-Sat 10am-6pm.

This gallery highlights cutting-edge artists known for excellent technique and painstaking attention to detail. Paintings are the gallery's mainstay, though recent exhibits have included Raymond Pettibon's cartoonish drawings, and a group show of conceptual photography from the 60s and 70s.

Deitch Projects

76 Grand St (btw Wooster/Greene Sts). Tel. 1–212/343-7300. Open Tues-Sat noon-6pm.

Terrific, large-scale contemporary art explodes behind a deceptively small door. Expect to find provocative objects and installations that don't hang on walls. One infamous example included a performance artist who barked at visitors from inside a doghouse. And Theresita Fernandez transformed the gallery into a cavernous and dry light-blue swimming pool. Yoko Ono shows here.

Dia Center for the Arts

548 West 22nd St (btw Tenth/Eleventh Aves). Tel. 1–212/989-5566. Open Wed-Sun noon-6pm. Closed July/Aug. Admission $6.

This large, four-story Euro gallery is almost single handedly responsible for the art scene in Chelsea. Opened in 1987, Dia is a four-story warehouse of conceptualism and minimalism accommodating large works and installations. Their Printed Matter Bookstore is the country's most important distributor of artist-made books.

Exit Art
475 Tenth Ave (at 36th St), 2nd fl. Tel. 1–212/966-7745. Open Mon-Sat noon-8pm, Sun noon-6pm.

One of the biggest spaces in SoHo, Exit Art is a very cool upstairs loft specializing in the unusual and provocative. One theatrical installation by 15 artists called "Let the Artists Live" created little home/studios where the artists lived for over a month.

Feature Inc.
76 Greene St (btw Broome/Spring Sts). Tel. 1–212/941-7077. Open Tues-Sat 11am-6pm. Closed July/Aug.

Feature Inc. is known for staunch individualism and eclectic taste that runs the gamut from abstract sculpture and contemporary paintings to Indian Tantra paintings and 80s punk photography. One of their main artists, Tom Friedman, creates abstract sculpture from things like pencils, toothpicks, and ABC (already been chewed) bubble gum.

Jack Tilton
49 Greene St (btw Grand/Broome Sts). Tel. 1–212/941-1775. Open Tues-Sat 10am-6pm.

Tilton's über-unconventionalists are very à la mode, and most seem to hail from Europe and Asia. You can often see something wild and extravagant here like Nicole Eisenman's large-scale installations, created out of cartoonish drawings.

Mary Boone
754 Fifth Ave (btw 57th/58th Sts), 4th fl. Tel. 1–212/752-2929. Open Tues-Sat 10am-6pm.

1980s art-world darling Mary Boone moved uptown and became a honey of the Establishment with a stable that includes Julian Schnabel, David Salle, and Jean Michel Basquiat. There are lots of newcomers too.

Matthew Marks
522 West 22nd St (btw Tenth/Eleventh Aves). Tel. 1–212/243-1650.
523 West 24th St (btw Tenth/Eleventh Aves). Tel. 1–212/243-0200.
Both spaces open Tues-Sat 10am-530pm.

A giant among giants, Marks has two airy Chelsea spaces, each of which cater to the city's current crop of A-listers, including Ellsworth Kelly, Nan Goldin, Brice Marden, and Richard Serra.

Metro Pictures
519 West 24th St (btw Tenth/Eleventh Aves). Tel. 1-212/206-7100. Open Tues-Sat 10am-6pm.
This wonderful triplex space usually has three separate exhibitions happening simultaneously. Some of America's biggest names show here (Mike Kelley, Robert Longo, and Cindy Sherman), along with lesser-knowns like Gary Simmons, who found fame for his statues of Ku Klux Klansmen as little lawn jockeys.

Paula Cooper
534 West 21st St (btw Tenth/Eleventh Aves). Tel. 1-212/255-1105. Open Tues-Sat 10am-5pm, Fri 10am-noon.
Paula Cooper, who opened SoHo's first commercial gallery, is now in a dramatic Chelsea space that's so white-hot it's worth visiting no matter what's hanging. It's a massive room capable of displaying the large-scale photographs of Andres Serrano and huge multimedia installations by Robert Gober and Robert Wilson.

PostMasters
459 West 19th St (btw Ninth/Tenth Aves). Tel. 1-212/727-3323. Open Tues-Sat 11am-6pm.
One of Chelsea's newest arrivals, this top experimental space is good at keeping its fingers on the pulse of the next century. Digital and multimedia art is a specialty.

P.P.O.W.
555 West 25th St (at Eleventh Ave), 3rd fl. Tel. 1-212/647-1044. Open Tues-Sat 11am-6pm.
Penny Pilkington and Wendy Olsoff curate top shows in their two-room gallery. The emphasis is on female artists, and even non-buyers are allowed to relax on the couch in the "killing room."

Buying

Auctions:

Me and My Gavel
by Nicholas D. Lowry

Since the center of the world's art market shifted from London to New York during the 1980s, New Yorkers don't have to limo far to bid on world-class art and collectibles.

At almost all auction houses, goods are exhibited for preview during the week leading up to the sale. Previews are announced in the *Weekend* section of Friday's *New York Times*, admission is free, and the public is welcome to attend.

Catalogues, which are printed for every auction, are excellent exhibit guides. In addition to telling you what you're looking at, each item carries a price estimate; like Jeff Koons' life-size porcelain sculpture of Michael Jackson with a monkey which sold for $5.32 million—higher than its catalogued estimate.

There are only two household names in auctions, **Christie's**, *20 Rockefeller Plaza (49th St, btw Fifth/Sixth Aves; tel. 1–212/636-2000)*, and **Sotheby's**, *1334 York Ave (btw 71st/72nd Sts; tel. 1–212/606-7000)*, both of which are headquartered in the Big Apple. Fueled by giddy Wall-Streeters and dot-commers, these two monoliths poured millions of dollars into their extraordinary showrooms just before the end of the Clinton administration. The result is two impressive (and impressively snooty) showplaces in which all the booty is stocked, displayed, and sold. Auctions here deserve their reputations as pretentious, stuffy affairs. During high-profile events and major sales, like the annual modern-art auctions, velvet ropes and burly bouncers separate the Great Unwashed from well-healed bidders like a rabbi separates milk from meat. And the heaviest hitters are safeguarded from generic rich people in fully-catered "sky boxes" above the general crowd. To get in you've got to order tickets in advance; they're free, but required for admission.

New York is also home to several auction houses where pomp plays second fiddle to the actual material being sold. **Swann Galleries**, *104 East 25th St (btw Park/Lexington Aves; tel. 1–212/254-4710)* is a family-run boutique auction house that specializes in things on paper: books, maps, photographs, posters, autographs, etchings, engravings, lithographs, and the like. They have an auction almost every week of the year, which means that there's always something interesting on display.

Tepper Galleries, *110 East 25th St (btw Park/Lexington Aves; tel. 1–212/677-5300)*, located in the same building as Swann, is an estate clearer, selling everything from chandeliers and silverware to paintings and furniture. They have an auction every other Saturday from 10am to 8pm, each of which contains roughly 1200 lots. Their "catalogues" are simply photocopied sheets and if the atmosphere was any less casual it would be a rodeo.

William Doyle Gallery, *175 East 87th St (tel. 1–212/427-2730)*, on the Upper East Side, is also a generalist auction house dealing in estate properties, but it's a classier operation that gets hold of better estates.

Kiehl's

109 Third Ave (btw 13th/14th Sts).
Tel. 1–212/677-3171 or 1–800/543-4572.
Open Mon-Wed and Fri 10am-630pm, Thurs
10am-730pm, Sat 10am-6pm.

Long before the Body Shop and other purveyors of "green" cosmetics, there was Kiehl's, founded in the East Village in 1851 as a homeopathic pharmacy. Taken over by a former apprentice, a Russian Jewish émigré who studied pharmacology at Columbia University, Kiehl's gradually grew into a natural-cosmetics store, selling herbal-based moisturizers, shampoos, eye creams, masques, facial cleansers, talcs, lipsticks, and toners—all of which are packaged in trademark no-frills containers and sold at Lancôme prices. The pharmacy also purveys all kinds of tinctures and homeopathic remedies. It's great fun to browse this quirky shop where free samples are generously thrust upon customers, who are encouraged to try before they buy.

Sephora

Rockefeller Center, 636 5th Ave (at 50th St).
Tel. 1–212/245-1633. Open Mon-Sat 10am-8pm, Sun
11am-7pm.

The New York flagship of this fast-growing beauty supermarket is an awesome trove of thousands of products from almost 500 different labels. All the major fragrances, cosmetics, and skin-care products are here, along with a helpful staff and terrific in-store soundtrack.

    Branches: Sephora Soho, 555 Broadway. Tel. 1–212/625-1309. Open Mon-Wed & Sat 10am-8pm, Thurs-Fri 10am-9pm, Sun noon-7pm; **Sephora Flatiron**, 119 Fifth Ave. Tel. 1–212/674-3570. Open Mon-Sat 10am-8pm, Sun noon-7pm; **Sephora Times Square**, 1500 Broadway. Tel. 1–212/944-6789. Open Mon-Tues 10am-10pm, Wed-Sun 10am-midnight. **Sephora 34th Street**, 130 West 34th St. Tel. 1–212/629-9135. Open Mon-Sat 9am-830pm, Sun 11am-7pm.

Books

Barnes & Noble

Union Square North (at 17th St). Tel. 1-212/253-0810. Open daily 10am-10pm.

Manhattan, the birthplace of Barnes & Noble, contains several well-stocked superstores. The Union Square shop, in a beautiful four-story 1881 building, is a particularly wonderful place to browse. In addition to books, you'll find music, software, a newsstand, cafe, and lots of comfortable chairs for lounging.

Branches: **105 Fifth Ave** (at 18th St). Tel. 1-212/807-0099. Open Mon-Fri 930am-745pm, Sat 930am-615pm, Sun 11am-545pm; **675 Sixth Ave** (at 21st St). Tel. 1-212/727-1227. Open Mon-Sat 9am-11pm, Sun 10am-10pm; **4 Astor Place** (btw Broadway/Lafayette St). Tel. 1-212/420-1322. Open Mon-Sat 10am-11pm, Sun 10am-10pm; **1280 Lexington Ave** (at 86th St). Tel. 1-212/423-9900. Open Mon-Sat 9am-11pm, Sun 10am-9pm; **600 Fifth Ave** (at 48th St). Tel. 1-212/765-0590. Open Mon-Fri 830am-9pm, Sat 10am-8pm, Sun 10am-7pm; **1972 Broadway** (at 66th St). Tel. 1-212/595-6859. Open daily 9am-midnight; **2289 Broadway** (at 82nd St). Tel. 1-212/362-8835. Open Sun-Thurs 9am-11pm, Fri-Sat 9am-midnight.

Books of Wonder

16 West 18th St (btw Fifth/Sixth Aves). Tel. 1-212/989-3270. Open Mon-Sat 10am-7pm, Sun noon-6pm.

BoW is the best children's bookstore in the city, bar none. This is the place to go for interactive learning books, terrific picture books, and other materials for toddlers and young adults. Check out the Thursday-night speaker series.

Gotham Book Mart

41 West 47th St (btw Fifth/Sixth Aves). Tel. 1-212/719-4448. Open Mon-Fri 930am-630pm, Sat 930-6pm.

This store is a literary landmark, established in 1925 by the legendary Frances Steloff, friend to James Joyce, Tennessee Williams, DH Lawrence, Henry Miller, and many other literary lions, who often stopped into this wonderfully cluttered and bookish store. Their portraits and letters can be found tucked away on any available wall space. Today it still offers a huge selection of new and used books and it still employs knowledgeable book lovers. Organization is not great and the atmosphere is stuffy to the point of being claustrophobic. But great philosophy, poetry, and fiction sections give credence to the sign outside, which reads "Wise Men Fish Here."

Oscar Wilde Memorial Bookstore

15 Christopher St (btw Sixth/Seventh Aves). Tel. 1-212/255-8097. Open Mon-Fri 11am-8pm, Sun noon-7pm

This neighborhood landmark is one of the best gay bookshops in America. Novels and nonfiction titles are augmented with videos, T-shirts, key chains, and other crap.

Rizzoli

31 West 57th St (btw
Fifth/Sixth Aves). Tel.
1-212/759-2424. Open
Mon-Sat 10am-730pm,
Sun 11am7pm.

Easily among the most
beautiful bookshops in
the city, Rizzoli is
known for large-format
art books and high-end
titles of all kinds. The
store's interiors could
be the subject of
a coffee-table book of
its own.

St. Mark's Comics

11 St. Mark's Pl (btw
Second/Third Aves).
Tel. 1-212/598-9439.
Open Mon 11am-
11am, Tues-Sat
10am-1am, Sun
11am-11pm.

New York City's leading
comic-book store has
a huge selection of
everything from
Superman to erotic
manga. And the pierced
and peroxided staff looks
scarier than many
superheroes' nefarious
enemies.

Strand Bookstore

828 Broadway (at 12th St).
Tel. 1-212/473-1452. Open
Mon-Sat 930am-1030pm, Sun
11am-1030pm.

The Strand is one of the largest
second-hand bookshops anywhere,
claiming to have eight miles of
books on display. The best deals
here are the review copies of recently
published books, which sell for 50%
off. They're displayed on tables
upfront and on racks downstairs.
Although it seems rather
overwhelming, the store's stock is
organized by subject. Strand also
operates a rare-book department,
which is accessed via another
entrance on Broadway.

Branch: 95 Fulton St (btw
William/Gold Sts). Tel. 1-212/732-
6070. Open Mon-Fri 930am-9pm,
Sat-Sun 11am-8pm.

TAXI

Argosy Books

116 East 59th St (btw Park/Lexington Aves). Tel. 1-212/753-4455. Open Mon-Fri 10am-6pm, Sat 10am-5pm.

One of the few remaining outlets in the city for out-of-print and rare books, Argosy has six cluttered stories filled with centuries-old volumes and first editions. When we were looking for a copy of *Peter Pan*, all they could come up with was a first edition signed by the author, for about $500. There is also an extensive print department known for antique maps.

TAXI
203

Clothing-Basics

Anthropologie
375 West Broadway (btw Spring /Broome Sts). Tel. 1–212/343-7070. Open Mon-Sat 11am-8pm, Sun 11am-6pm.

The same folks who gave us Urban Outfitters (see below) offer high-quality basics for post-Xers. Sturdy fabrics, muted colors, and simple styles are made for matching.

Branch: 85 Fifth Ave (at 16th St).

APC
131 Mercer St (btw Prince/Spring Sts). Tel. 1–212/966-9685. Open Mon-Sat 11am-7pm, Sun noon-6pm.

Parisian basics for men and women include top-quality cotton T-shirts, great turtleneck sweaters, black leather jackets, and oiled motorcycle jeans in a variety of colors. The initials stand for Atelier Production and Creation. You get the idea.

Club Monaco
160 Fifth Ave (at 21st St). Tel. 1–212/352-0936. Open Mon-Fri 10am-8pm, Sat 10-7, Sun noon-6pm.

Great black-and-white clothes that look like Prada for a fraction of the price. Club Monaco was the vanguard of quality knock-off design stores (like Zara) that can be found all over the city.

Jeffrey
449 West 14th St (btw Ninth/Tenth Aves). Tel. 1–212/206-1272. Open Mon-Wed and Fri 10am-8pm, Thurs 10am-9pm, Sat 10am-7pm, Sun 1230-6pm.

It's worth the hike to former Barneys shoe buyer Jeffrey Kalinsky's emporium way west on 14th Street. For obvious reasons his s... department... fetishist's dre... Christian Lo... beauties by F... & Gabbana. A... there are plenty of power outfits from Gucci, Prada, Jil Sander, et al to wear with them. The merchandise shows well against the concrete walls. Prices, of course, are sky high.

Original Levi's Store
750 Lexington Ave (at 59th St). Tel. 1–212/826-5957. Open Mon-Sat 10am-8pm, Sun noon-6pm.

The city's largest selection of Levi's jeans and other paraphernalia sprawls across this huge Lexington Avenue shop. All colors and styles are stacked to the rafters, and the staff will custom fit your purchases.

Urban Outfitters
374 Sixth Ave (at Waverly Pl). Tel. 1–212/677-9350. Open Mon-Sat 10am-10pm, Sun noon-9pm.

Clothier to college types across America, Urban Outfitters is known for inexpensive, trend-setting basic wear at fair prices. They've also got funky candles, funny books, and a huge variety of playful gift items.

Clothing Clubwear

Hotel Venus

382 West Broadway (btw Spring/Broome Sts). Tel. 1–212/966-4066. Open daily noon–8pm.

This Patricia Field's shop is club-kid central, filled with glamourpuss-sleazy garments for clubbing, vamping, and vogueing. Untraditional materials run the gamut from plastic and fur to Spandex and feathers, and most of the women's clothes are available in men's sizes. A salon in back specializes in weaves and dyes. Lots of outrageous make-up and wigs are guaranteed to turn heads when parading into clubs like Studio Filthy Whore.

Intermix

210 Columbus Ave (btw 69th/70th Sts). Tel. 1-212/769-9116. Open Mon-Sat 10am–7pm Sun noon–6pm.

"Sex and the City" style designer clothing fills the racks of this trendy shop, popular with media types and models who eat nothing. Look for tops, dresses, jeans, shoes and lots of accessories by designers like Marc Jacobs, Jimmy Choo, Diane von Furstenberg, and Tocca, as well as plenty of names you've never heard of.

TAXI

207

Clothing – Designer Boutiques

SoHo still has plenty of big-name boutiques, but if you want cutting-edge design and outrageous fun then cruise the storefronts along Mott, Elizabeth, Ludlow, and Orchard Streets. This is where you'll discover the "new" designers in spades. Check out Zao, for example, at 175 Orchard Street. It's the wave of the future—shopping as entertainment that's meant to keep you offline.

agnès b
103 Greene St (btw Prince/Spring Sts). Tel. 1-212/925-4649. Open daily 11am-7pm.
New York's schmashion mavens have embraced this epitome of basic Parisian style as their own. The classic styling and sturdy construction is designed to last a lifetime.
   Branches: 13 East 16th St (at Fifth Ave). Tel. 1-212/741-2585. Open daily 11am-7pm; **1063 Madison Ave** (btw 80th/81st Sts). Tel. 1-212/570-9333. Open daily 11am-7pm, Sun noon-6pm.

Anna Sui

113 Greene St (btw Spring/ Prince Sts). Tel. 1-212/941-8406. Open Mon-Sat 1130am-7pm, Sun noon-6pm.

Anna Sui has the uncanny ability to simultaneously appeal to both LA and NYC with collections that are a little bit high fashion and a little bit rock 'n' roll. Think sequined skirts, leather pants, and other flashy female fashions. We like the pink-and-black shop too.

Bebe

1044 Madison Ave (btw 79th/ 80th Sts). Tel. 1-212/ 517-2323. Open Mon-Fri 10am-8pm, Sat 10am-7pm, Sun 11am-6pm.

Up-to-the-moment derivatives mean moderately priced knockoffs of the top designer styles. Look for well-tailored dresses, suits, tops, and other feminine wearables that will get you past the velvet ropes.

Betsey Johnson

138 Wooster St (btw Prince/Houston Sts). Tel. 1-212/ 995-5048. Open Mon-Sat 11am-7pm, Sun noon-7pm.

In addition to Johnson's trademark skintight flesh-wrappers, you'll find plenty of feminine urban trashwear made with leather, lace, and fishnet. Check out her line of peek-a-boo lingerie.

Branches: 248 Columbus Ave (at 72nd St). Tel. 1-212/362-3364. Open Mon-Sat 11am-7pm, Sun noon-7pm; 251 East 60th St (btw Second/Third Aves). Tel. 1-212/319-7699. Open Mon-Sat 11am-7pm, Sun noon-7pm.

Calvin Klein

654 Madison Ave (at 60th St). Tel. 1-212/292-9000. Open Mon-Sat 10am-6pm (Thurs until 8pm), Sun noon-6pm.

The only real way to enter this attitude-laden megastore is with a manner that's so disarmingly casual it throws the black-clad model-slash-salespeople off-guard. Clothes are now sold alongside Calvin's chic-simple furnishings and housewares.

TAXI

209

Chanel

15 East 57th St (btw Fifth/Madison Aves). Tel. 1–212/355-5050. Open Mon-Fri 10am-630pm (Thurs until 7pm), Sat 10am-6pm, Sun 11am-5pm.

A uniformed doorman greets highbrow shoppers as they enter this chi-chi shop of clothing, accessories, shoes, and scents.

Comme des Garćons

520 West 22nd St. (btw Tenth/Eleventh Aves). Tel. 1–212/604-9200. Tues-Sat 11am-7pm, Sun-Mon noon-6pm.

Comme des Garćons is so funky that their bridge line looks like other designers' haute couture. The complicated designs are positively wild in contrast to the shop's spare, concrete cube interior.

Cynthia Rowley

112 Wooster St (btw Spring/Prince Sts). Tel. 1–212/334-1144. Open Mon-Wed 11am-7pm, Thurs-Fri 11am-8pm, Sat 11-7pm, Sun noon-6pm.

Both sophisticated and sensible, Rowley's patterns are ceaselessly creative and the fabrics are always comfortable. Sexy dresses are often embroidered or beaded, and wonderful, whimsical accessories include purses, lipstick bags, totes, and shoes. We love this shop.

TAXI
211

DKNY

*655 Madison Ave (at 60th St).
Tel. 1–212/223-3569. Open
Mon-Sat 10am-7pm (Thurs
until 9pm), Sun noon-6pm.*
Believe it or not, there was no
DKNY shop in NYC until late
1998; the designer was sold
exclusively by department stores
and other retailers. This beautiful
Madison Avenue space rights
that wrong, offering the
complete line of Donna Karan
goods.

Dolce & Gabanna

*434 West Broadway (btw
Spring/ Prince Sts). Tel.
1–212/ 965-8000. Open
Mon-Sat 11am-7pm, Sun
noon-6pm.*

Domenico Dolce and Stefano
Gabbana stay at fashion's peak
with clubby creations that seem
to have found their way onto the
back of every film and music
star. The shops themselves are
bastions of waifdom and are
definitely worth perusing.
 Branch: 825 Madison Ave (btw
68th/69th Sts). Tel. 1–212/249-
4100. Open Mon-Sat 10am-
7pm.

Emporio Armani

*110 Fifth Ave (at 16th St).
Tel. 1–212/727-3240. Open
Mon-Sat 11am-8pm, Sat
11am-6pm, Sun noon-5pm.*
 Armani's Fifth Avenue
 shop, located in a classic

Stanford White building, features
less-pricey lines that include those
trademark crisp suits.
 Branch: 601 Madison Ave (btw
57th/58th Sts). Tel. 1–212/317-
0800. Open Mon-Fri 10am-8pm,
Sat 11-7, Sun noon-6pm.

Fendi

*720 Fifth Ave (at 56th St).
Tel. 1–212/767-0100. Open
Mon-Sat 10am-6pm (until
7pm Thurs), Sun noon-5pm.*
The entire product line—
handbags, shoes, and
accessories—of the famous
Italian luxury-goods company
is under one roof at this
flagship American store.

Givenchy Boutique

*710 Madison Ave (at 63rd
St). Tel. 1–212/688-4338.
Open Mon-Wed and Fri-Sat
10am- 6pm, Thurs 10am-
7pm, Sun noon-6pm.*
Ready to wear, accessories and
fragrances at this snazzy space
on East 63rd means lots of
colorful outfits, fun Pumpkin
bags with drawstring closures,
and trademark fragrances Ysatis,
Amarige, Organza, and more.

Helmut Lang

*80 Greene St (btw Spring/
Broome Sts). Tel. 1–212/925-
7214. Open Mon-Sat 11am-
7pm, Sun noon-6pm.*
Spare surroundings and minimalist
clothes are the hallmarks of this
top-of-the-line Austrian clothier.
A fashion designer's designer, Lang
presents his entire collection here,
along with the occasional sale rack.

Kelly Christy
235 Elizabeth St (btw Houston/Prince Sts).
Tel. 1-212/965-0686. Open Tues-Sat noon-
7pm; Sun noon-6pm.
Kelly Christy is the city's hippest hat maker,
using innovative fabrics and styles for designs
that are hand-fitted to your head. Toppers
start at about $200.

Label
265 Lafayette St (btw Prince/Spring Sts).
Tel. 1-212/966-7736. Open daily noon-
7pm.
Unique streetwear for feminine skaterats
doesn't get more fashionable than the
offerings at this cool and slender SoHo
shop. Sexy separates and dresses are
emblazoned with pop-culture silk screens
and other urban motifs. And the clothes
are priced to move.

Marc Jacobs
163 Mercer St (btw Houston/Prince
Sts). Tel. 1-212/343-1490. Open Mon-
Sat 11am-7pm, Sun noon-6pm.
Despite (or maybe because of) outrageous
prices, Jacobs' perfect designs are some of
the city's most coveted. Clean and simple
is the order of the day, with plain striped
tees, luxurious cashmere tanks, and the
like.

Miu Miu
100 Prince St (btw Mercer/Greene Sts).
Tel. 1-212/334-5156. Open Mon-Sat
11am-7pm. Sun noon-6pm.
Prada's second wave is a bridge-line
that's just a bit funkier and a wee
bit less expensive than its parent.

TAXI

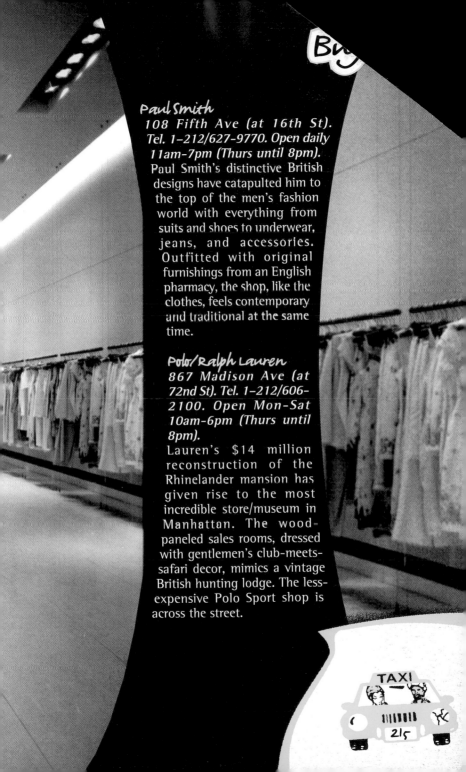

Paul Smith

*108 Fifth Ave (at 16th St).
Tel. 1–212/627-9770. Open daily
11am-7pm (Thurs until 8pm).*
Paul Smith's distinctive British
designs have catapulted him to
the top of the men's fashion
world with everything from
suits and shoes to underwear,
jeans, and accessories.
Outfitted with original
furnishings from an English
pharmacy, the shop, like the
clothes, feels contemporary
and traditional at the same
time.

Polo/Ralph Lauren

*867 Madison Ave (at
72nd St). Tel. 1–212/606-
2100. Open Mon-Sat
10am-6pm (Thurs until
8pm).*
Lauren's $14 million
reconstruction of the
Rhinelander mansion has
given rise to the most
incredible store/museum in
Manhattan. The wood-
paneled sales rooms, dressed
with gentlemen's club-meets-
safari decor, mimics a vintage
British hunting lodge. The less-
expensive Polo Sport shop is
across the street.

TAXI

215

if designer shopping and bargain hunting is one of your main reasons for visiting New York, get your hands on a copy of *S&B Report*! Available at larger newsstands in the city (*see* Magazines, below), the booklet details the city's current bargains and showroom sample sales. Serious shoppers in search of low prices on high-style should also turn to the "Sales and Bargains" column in *New York* magazine and the "Shoptalk" page in *Time Out New York*.

At the turn of the century, the Lower East Side was the city's wholesale-clothing district. On Sundays wholesalers opened their doors to the public and consumers were able to buy from them directly. Stores in this neighborhood still have a wholesale flavor to them, with outdoor clothing racks, hodge-podge window displays, and prices that are far lower than they are uptown. Orchard, Delancey, Grand, and Essex streets are the boundaries of the Lower East Side Shopping District, six square blocks famous for discounted apparel, leather goods, fabrics, and linens. The area has some 300 businesses selling Escada, Ungaro, Valentino, Guess, Liz Claiborne, Kenar, and other designer labels. Harris Levy, on Grand Street, is a linen store that has been in the same family for four generations. Fine & Klein, on Orchard Street, is an old-time landmark for handbags and leather goods. Hosiery and lingerie at no-frills prices can be found at Louis Chock on Orchard Street. This store has been around since the corset was cutting-edge. Be aware that most shops here are closed Friday afternoons and Saturdays to observe the Jewish Sabbath, and Sundays are still zoos.

Pick up a copy of the free *Lower East Side Shopping Guide* at the **Lower East Side Information Center**, *261 Broome Street (btw Orchard/Allen Sts; tel. 1–212/226-9010 or 1–866/224-0206).* It's open Sunday to Friday, 10am to 5pm.

Century 21

*22 Cortlandt St (btw Broadway/Church St). Tel. 1-[...]
9092. Open Mon–Wed 745am–8pm, Thurs 745am[...]
Fri 745am–8pm, Sat 10am–8pm, Sun 11am–7pm.*

A fashion zoo if ever there was one, Century 21 is famous with
bargain hounds for last season's designer collections at massively
reduced rates. Intrepid shoppers elbow their way through
unorganized racks and bins of Romeo Gigli, Helmut Lang, D&G,
Jil Sander, and others, priced 50% and more off original retail.
Even New York Yankees caps are discounted here (to $5.97).
Located across the street from the World Trade Center site,
Century 21 attracts everyone from diplomats and slumming royals
to international visitors and Wall Street secretaries on their lunch
hours. Dressing rooms are scarce (and nonexistent for men). The
trick here is to arrive without a jacket or any other bulky clothing
so you can try things on over what you are wearing.

Filene's Basement

*620 Sixth Ave (btw 18th/19th Sts). Tel. 1–212/620–3100.
Open Mon–Sat 10am–9pm, Sun 11am–7pm.*

Unsold stock and irregular merchandise with designer labels find
final resting places in one of this Boston-based chain's shops.
It's great for basics—T-shirts, socks, pantyhose, and umbrellas
can be found for up to a third off regular retail.

Branch: 222 Broadway (btw 79th/80th Sts). Tel. 1–212/873-
8000. Open Mon–Sat 10am–9pm, Sun 11am–6pm.

Loehmann's

*101 Seventh Ave (at 16th St). Tel. 1–212/352–0856. Open
Mon–Sat 9am–9pm, Sun 11am–7pm.*

Immortalized by Erma Bombeck's book *All I Know About
Animal Behavior I Learned in Loehmann's Dressing Room,* this
frenzied, five-story off-price Mecca sells designer fashions at
30% to 65% off traditional retail. Frieda Mueller
Loehmann started selling women's skirts and
blouses at a discount out of her Brooklyn home
in 1920. This Chelsea shop is the flagship of
what is now a 75-store chain.

Thrift Shops

There is some seriously good thrifting in New York. Housing Works, a nonprofit supporting people living with AIDS, has three stores around town and always seems to have the best furniture, clothes, and collectibles. Other top thrift stores are clustered on the Upper East Side, where the rich and famous donate their unwanted tuxedos and taffetas.

Council Thrift Shop, 246 East 84th St (btw Second/Third Aves). Tel. 1–212/439-8373. Open Mon-Wed and Fri-Sat 11am-6pm, Thurs 11am-8pm, Sun noon-430pm.

Good Old Lower East Side Thrift Shop, 17 Avenue B (at 2nd St). Tel. 1–212/358-1041. Open Mon-Thurs 10am-6pm, Fri-Sat 11am-8pm.

Housing Works Thrift Shop, 143 West 17th St (btw Sixth/Seventh Aves). Tel. 1–212/366-0820. Open Mon-Sat 10am-6pm, Sun noon-4pm.

Housing Works Thrift Shop, 202 East 77th St (btw Second/Third Ave). Tel. 1–212/772-8461. Open Mon-Fri 10am-7pm, Sat 10am-6pm, Sun 1-5pm.

Housing Works Thrift Shop, 306 Columbus Ave (btw 74th/75th St). Tel. 1–212/579-7566. Open Mon-Fri 11am-7pm, Sat 10am-6pm, Sun 1-5pm.

Memorial Sloan-Kettering Thrift Shop, 1440 Third Ave (btw 81st and 82nd Sts). Tel. 1–212/535-1250. Open Mon-Fri 10am-515pm, Sat 11am-445pm.

Spence-Chapin Thrift Shop, 1473 Third Ave (btw 83rd and 84th Sts). Tel. 1–212/737-8448. Open Mon-Fri 10am-7pm, Sat 9am-5pm, Sun noon-5pm.

Clothing – Vintage

Alice Underground

481 Broadway (btw Grand/Broome Sts). Tel. 1–212/431-9067. Open daily 11am-730pm.

One of Manhattan's largest vintage shops is also one of the best. Top-quality basics are always on the racks, along with plenty of unusual finds.

Rue St. Denis

174 Ave B (at 11th St). Tel. 1–212/260-3388. Open daily noon-730pm.

Excellent-condition vintage can outfit any aspiring hipster from top to toe. Nothing here is cheap, but it's all far less than buying it new—if you could even find this stuff anymore.

Screaming Mimi's

382 Lafayette St (btw Great Jones/4th Sts). Tel. 1–212/677-6464. Open Mon-Sat noon-8pm, Sun 1-7pm.

Vintage so classic and in such good condition, you'll swear it's new. But, they don't make those funky sequined dresses anymore, do they? Good selection of vintage shoes too.

There may be no better street in the world for shoes than the block of West 8th Street, between Fifth and Sixth avenues. More than a dozen shoe shops stock well-made knockoffs of all the latest styles, most at decent prices. You might also check out the following:

Shoofly

465 Amsterdam Ave (at 86th St). Tel. 1-212/580-4390. Open Mon-Sat 11am-7pm Sun noon-6pm.

When you need to shoe your kid in top urban style, Shoofly gets stepping with hip rain boots, classic Mary Janes, and designer sneakers—almost 100 brands in all. Prices can be steep, but what do you expect for European Pepinos and offerings from the likes of Moschino and Dolce & Gabbana? Other accessories too, including mittens, colorful booty socks, gloves and hats, all within reach of the tiniest hands.

John Fluevog

250 Mulberry St (at Prince St). Tel. 1-212/431-4484. Open Mon-Sat 11am-7pm, Sun noon-6pm.

Very cool shoes for the urban jungle. Funky men's and women's styles for club-and streetwear. There always seem to be a lot of Japanese tourists here, so it must be stylish.

Kenneth Cole

353 Columbus Ave (btw 76th/77th Sts). Tel. 1-212/873-2061. Open Mon-Fri 10am-8pm, Sat-Sun 11am-7pm.

Great styling and a chic aesthetic keep Kenneth Cole at the head of foot fashions for both men and women. Most designs are created in-house. Unfortunately, the staff isn't particularly helpful, but it's hard to have it all.

Otto Tootsi Plohound

137 Fifth Avenue (btw 20th/21st Sts). Tel. 1-212/460-8650. Open Mon-Fri 1130am-730pm, Sat 11am-8pm, Sun noon-7pm.

You know this place... great shoes and very cool styles, most from France and England. Prices are high and the staff is unhelpful, but fashion slaves have no choice but to come here.

Branch: 413 West Broadway (btw Prince/Spring Sts). Tel. 1-212-925-8931.

Department Stores

The behemoths Macy's and Bloomingdale's have been mid-range New York institutions for over a century. Saks Fifth Avenue, Bergdorf Goodman, and Henri Bendel duke it out on the higher end of the market, while Lord & Taylor caters to the lower end of the spectrum. Something is almost always on sale at every department store. Major sales are held around holidays, especially after Christmas.

Barneys
660 Madison Ave (btw 60th/61st Sts). Tel. 1-212/826-8900. Open Mon-Fri 10am-8pm, Sat 10am-7pm, Sun 11am-6pm.

Once the best-known downtown shop for men's clothes, Barneys moved uptown—both figuratively and literally—stocked top-quality brands for both sexes, and maintains the best selection of cutting-edge designers. Look for good prices on casual wear on the top floor. PS: They have the best Christmas windows in the city.

Bergdorf Goodman
754 Fifth Ave (btw 57th/58th Sts). Tel. 1-212/753-7300. Open Mon-Sat 10am-7pm (Thurs until 8pm), Sun noon-6pm.

Bergdorf's is beautiful, like walking into a lively museum. People dress up to shop here, and the selling floors are laid out like a collection of boutiques. Although the store is a favorite with old folks with older money, Bergdorf has worked hard in recent years to attract younger shoppers. Their men's store is located across the street.

Saks Fifth Avenue
611 Fifth Ave (btw 49th/50th Sts). Tel. 1-212/753-4000. Open Mon-Fri 10am-7pm (Thurs until 8pm), Sat 10am-630pm, Sun noon-6pm.

Saks is a great store. They have terrific selections of women's designer wear and excellent, if conservative, Men's Store offerings. The window displays are legendary, and prices are not too far out of this world.

Bloomingdale's

Lexington Ave (at 59th St). Tel. 1–212/705-2000. Open Mon-Fri 10am–830pm, Sat 10am-7pm, Sun 11am-7pm.

Open since 1879, Bloomingdale's is one of the most venerable names in Manhattan. Although it's always a madhouse on the ground floor (and it's almost impossible to walk through the huge cosmetics department without getting spritzed), the upper decks (except for the shoe departments) are more sedate and staffed with responsive help. The store's turn-of-the-century Victorian/Art Deco building itself has become an icon, now miniaturized in the form of teapots, candy tins, and handpainted Limoges boxes. Throughout the city one can regularly spot shoppers clutching Bloomie's trademark Medium Brown Bags. Others can't figure out what all the excitement is about: Andy Warhol once said, "Death is like going to Bloomingdale's. It's nothing."

Henri Bendel

714 Fifth Ave (at 56th St). Tel. 1–212/ 247-1100. Open Mon-Sat 10am-7pm.

The epitome of elegance, Henri Bendel's beautiful townhouse oozes with sophistication. The 1920s-Paris-meets-the-new-millennium atmosphere is created with rich woods, magnificent Lalique windows, and fabulous oval staircases in lieu of escalators. They stock pretty much the same stuff as Saks and Bergdorf's—at competitive prices—but somehow everything looks a little bit better here.

Lord & Taylor

424 Fifth Ave (btw 38th/39th Sts). Tel. 1–212/391-3344. Open Mon-Tues 10am-7pm, Wed-Fri 10am-830pm, Sat 10am-7pm, Sun 11am-7pm.

Open since 1826, L&T's 10 floors display the fashions of many American designers. The store is known for great women's collections and some of the best windows in town. The men's sections are relatively thin, and the decor is not particularly special.

Macy's

Herald Square (at 34th St/Broadway). Tel. 1–212/695-4400. Open Mon-Sat 10am-830pm, Sun 11am-7pm.

Occupying an entire city block, Macy's boasts of being the "world's largest department store," a claim also made by Harrods in London. Ten mammoth selling floors of fashion and home furnishings fill this retail elephant with perpetual shopping traffic jams. The Cellar, a basement food and housewares department, remains one of the store's highlights. Macy's seems to be a bit less expensive than rival department stores, but a salesperson can be as absent as a cop when you need one. In November, the store sponsors the tremendous Thanksgiving Day Parade, and each April they hold their legendary Flower Show, which turns the entire store into a giant, aromatic bouquet.

Manhattan Mall

Sixth Ave at 33rd St. Tel. 1-212/465-0500.
Open Mon-Sat 10am-8pm, Sun 11am-6pm.
Anchored by lowbrow stores, the first mall in Manhattan is a thoroughly horrible place filled with boring suburban shops that appeal to God knows whom. Leave this nine-level, neon-ringed non-event for the mallrats, Ricki Lake girls, and other teen-angst rebels.

South Street Seaport

Pier 17 (East River at Fulton St). Tel. 1-212/732-7678.
Open Mon-Sat 10am-9pm, Sun 11am-8pm. Open two hours later in summer; restaurants keep extended hours.
Hard as we may try, it's just impossible for us to recommend even the nicest of malls in a city so overflowing with dynamic shopping neighborhoods. In addition to a slew of suburban-style chain stores, this 12-block cobblestoned riverside development contains a few historic ships, a seafaring museum, some forgettable restaurants, and daily "entertainment."

Trump Tower

725 Fifth Ave (btw 56th/57th Sts). Tel. 1-212/832-2000. Open daily 10am-10pm (stores close earlier).
The Donald's pink-marble and bronze monument to his ego is filled with flamboyant high-end shops befitting Lifestyles of the Rich and Tasteless. Perpetually filled with Euros, it's worth stopping in if only to see what all the fuss is about.

World Financial Center

Battery Park City, 200 Liberty St (btw West/Vesey Sts).
Tel. 1-212/945-0505. Most shops open Mon-Fri 10am-7pm,
Sat 11am-5pm, Sun noon-5pm.
A huge waterfront office and shopping complex, WFC consists of four postmodern towers connected by a large palm-treed winter garden. The Center is home to Dow Jones, Merrill Lynch, American Express, and other major Financial District players. There are about 40 upscale shops and restaurants here, most of which are geared towards bankers and traders. Lots of excellent, free cultural events and happenings are scheduled here too.

An American Craftsman

790 Seventh Ave (at 52nd St). Tel. 1-212/399-2555. Open Sun-Thurs 10am-10pm, Fri-Sat 1030am-11pm.

This one-of-a-kind shop offers the individual creations of more than 900 American craft artists. Wood, jewelry, pottery, textile, and other media are represented. Check out the Rothbard puzzle boxes.

Evolution

120 Spring St (btw Greene/Mercer Sts). Tel. 1-212/343-1114. Open daily 11am-7pm.

The wonders of nature, all beautifully displayed, include fossilized trilobites, exotic seashells, mounted butterflies, amber beetles, various horns and feathers, and an infamous collection of human skulls and skeletons.

FAO Schwarz

767 Fifth Ave (at 58th St). Tel. 1-212/644-9400. Open Mon-Wed 10am-6pm, Thurs-Sat 10am-7pm, Sun 11am-6pm.

This play palace is so awesome that most kids believe it when their parents tell them they're actually in a toy museum. Three floors full of frivolity include house-sized stuffed animals, mini-Porsche automobiles that actually work, a wall of M&M chocolate candies sorted by color, and all manner of toys and games.

Star Magic

745 Broadway (at 8th St). Tel. 1-212/228-7770. Open Mon-Sat 10am-10pm, Sun 11am-9pm.

Great for gizmophiles, Star Magic is a wacky shop dealing in all kinds of lowbrow celestial kitsch. Where else can you find freeze-dried Space Strawberries, sun-activated holographic spinners, and glow-in-the-dark galaxies you can affix to your ceiling?

Tannen's Magic Shop

24 West 25th St (btw Broadway/Sixth Ave). Tel. 1-212/929-4500. Open Mon-Fri 10am-530pm, Sat 10am-4pm.

One of the largest and most respected magic shops in the world, Tannen's sells everything from thumb tips and reels to levitation devices, plus plenty of unique items created for exclusive sale in this store. Get a copy of their catalogue.

#07 Buying

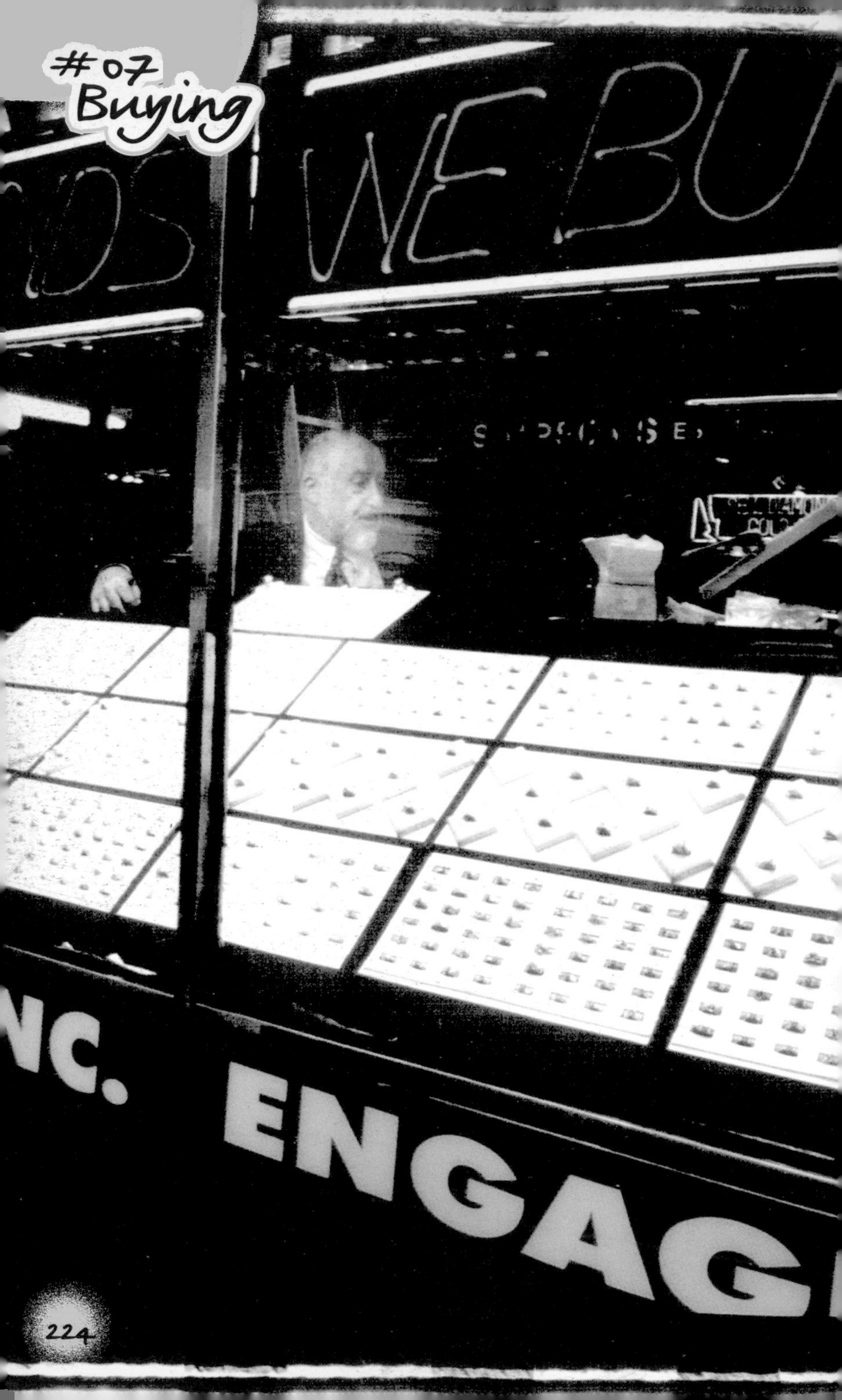

When it comes to diamonds, New York is a woman's best friend. The 47th Street Diamond District (between Fifth and Sixth Aves) includes more than 2600 independent businesses on a single block. Diamonds are cut, set and sold on the street's "exchanges," basically little shopping malls comprised of clusters of booths. Forty-seventh Street makes for incredible browsing. When it comes to buying, however, beware! It's a good idea to know something about stones (or bring someone who does) and ask to see the Gemological Institute of America's report, which should be available for any rock you wish to buy. Most shops close for Sabbath, from Friday afternoon through Sunday morning.

You might also check out the internationally known prestige jewelers on Fifth Avenue, including **H. Stern**, *645 Fifth Ave (at 51st St; tel. 1–212/688-0300)*, **Maurice Badler**, *578 Fifth Ave (btw 45th/46th Sts; tel. 1–212/575-9632)* and **Wempe**, *700 Fifth Ave (at 55th St; tel. 212 397-9000)*.

#07 Buying

Music

Breakbeat Science
181 Orchard St (at Houston St). Tel. 1-212/995-2592. Open Sun-Wed 1-8pm, Thurs-Sat 1-9pm.

All jungle all the time, Breakbeat Science is the vinyl-only headquarters for an unmatched selection of drum 'n' bass. Obscure albums and pre-releases are their specialty.

Disc-O-Rama Clearance Store
146 West 4th St (btw Sixth Ave/MacDougal St). Tel. 1-212/ 477-9410. Open daily 10am-930pm, Sat 10am-1030pm, Sun 11am-730pm.

You wouldn't know it from the outside, but this excellent shop carries a huge selection of the best-priced CDs in the city. They've got everything, and few titles ever top $12.

Fat Beats
406 Sixth Ave (btw 8th/9th Sts). Tel. 1-212/673-3883. Open Mon-Thurs noon-9pm, Fri-Sat noon-10pm, Sun noon-8pm. Closed last Sun of each month.

Hip-hop here is so phat it's obese. There's also an excellent selection of reggae, acid jazz, and trip-hop. Look in the "used" bins for good prices on hard-to-find classics.

Satellite
259 Bowery (btw East Houston/Prince Sts). Tel. 1-212/ 995 1744. Open Mon-Sat 1-9pm, Sun 2-8pm.

A one-stop shop for house, techno, jungle, trip-hop, and other club styles, this DJ-run shop doubles as a clearing-house for info on upcoming parties.

Tower Records
692 Broadway (at 4th St). Tel. 1-212/505-1500. Open daily 9am-midnight.

The best of the chain stores stocks plenty of indie stuff along with major labels. It's a huge space, with a separate shop for classical, plus a store next door where overstocked items are priced under a buck.

Virgin Megastore
1540 Broadway (btw 45th/46th Sts). Tel. 1-212/ 921-1020. Open Sun-Thurs 9am-1am, Fri-Sat 9am-2am.

You could easily spend hours combing through CDs, books, videos, and CD-ROMs in this expansive tri-level complex in the heart of Times Square. There are lots of listening booths to hear new music, but beware the greasy headphones.

Branch: 52 East 14th St (Union Square). Tel. 1-212/598-4666.

4 8th Street between Sixth and Seventh avenues is electric-guitar heaven. It's also one of the best places in the nation for keyboards, drums, woodwinds, and other instruments. The two biggest names here are **Manny's**, *156 West 48th St (tel. 1-212/819-0576)* and **Sam Ash**, *160 West 48th St (tel. 1-212/719-2299)*. Between them, these mega-shops carry everything for the musician from guitar picks to MIDI systems. Their selection of acoustic instruments is unparalleled, and their DJ tables, lighting packages, and software selections aren't too shabby either. Manny's is open daily; Sam Ash closes on Sunday.

Paper Goods

Kate's Paperie

561 Broadway (btw Prince/Spring Sts). Tel. 1-212/941-9816. Open Mon-Sat 10am-7pm, Sun 11am-7pm.

The most celebrated stationery store in the city stocks everything from hand-made papyrus art paper to silly printed toilet wipe. Look for beautiful rice papers, seductively bound journals, and even kites and hatboxes.

Branches: 8 West 13th St (tw Fifth/Sixth Aves; tel.: 1-212/633-0570); 1282 Third Ave (btw 73rd/74th Sts; tel.: 1-212/396-3670)

Magazines

Universal News

676 Lexington Ave (at 56th St). Tel. 1-212/750-1855. Open daily 7am-midnight. 977 Eighth Ave (btw 57th/58th Sts). Tel. 1-212/459-0932. Open daily 6am-midnight.

These amazing magazine malls stock over 7000 international and domestic newspaper and magazine titles, conveniently arranged by subject.

TAXI

Sex/Lingerie

Brasmyth
905 Madison Ave (btw 72nd/73rd Sts). Tel. 1-212/772-9400. Open Mon-Sat 10am-7pm.
Everything you've ever wanted to know about bras (and panties) can be found in this Upper East Side shop stocking literally hundreds of brands from around the world. One lucky on-site tailor customizes shoppers' selections for a perfect fit.

Pink Pussycat Boutique
167 West 4th St (btw Sixth/Seventh Aves). Tel. 1-212/243-0077. Open Sun-Thurs noon-midnight, Fri-Sat noon-330am.
The famous Pink Pussycat is well stocked with sexual aids, toys, lubricants, condoms, and trashy lingerie made of latex and leather. Ask to see The Mule.

TAXI

229

Sports

Blades Board & Skate

659 Broadway (btw Bleecker/Third Sts). Tel. 1–212/477-7350. Open daily 10am-8pm.

Boarders and in-liners get their wheels at these well-stocked shops. They've also got snowboards and clothing that are way too cool for skool.

Branches: 120 West 72nd St (btw Amsterdam/West End Aves). Tel. 1–212/787-3911. Open Mon-Sat 10am-8pm, Sun 11am-6pm; **160 East 86th St** (btw Lexington/Third Aves). Tel. 1–212/996-1644. Open Mon-Sat 11am-8pm, Sun 11am-6pm; **Chelsea Piers, 30th St** (btw Sixth/Seventh Aves). Tel. 1–212/336-6199. Open Mon-Sat 10am-8pm, Sun 11am-7pm.

Paragon Sporting Goods

867 Broadway (at 18th St). Tel. 1–212/255-8036. Open Mon-Sat 10am-8pm, Sun 11-630pm.

From baseball to yoga, Paragon carries clothing and equipment for almost every activity imaginable. They've got a great selection of expensive, name-brand gear from Patagonia, The North Face, and Sierra Designs. In short, it's the best sporting-goods shop in the city.

Richard Metz Golf

12 East 46th (btw Madison/Fifth Aves). Tel. 1–212/759-6940. Open Mon-Fri 930-6pm Sat 10am-6pm, Sun 11am-5pm.

Golf equipment is usually much cheaper in the US than elsewhere in the world. This off-course pro shop has a huge selection of clubs, discounted approximately 20%.

Toga Bike Shop

110 West End Ave (at 64th St). Tel. 1–212/799-9625. Open daily 11am-7pm.

Toga sells Cannondale, Specialized, and Litespeed bikes for 40% to 75% less than European retail. And they'll box them for checking onto the plane.

Village Chess Shop

230 Thompson St (btw 3rd/Bleecker Sts). Tel. 1–212/475-9580. Open daily noon-midnight.

Knights, bishops, pawns, and eggheads come together in this cramped Village landmark. They sell boards, mats, clocks, and accessories, and a partner seems to always be on hand for quality in-shop play.

B & H Photo

420 Ninth Ave. (btw. 33rd/34th). Tel. 1–212/444-5000. Open Mon-Thurs 9am-7pm, Fri 9am-1pm, Sun 10am-5pm. Closed Sat.

This is where the city's professional photographers come to purchase their equipment. It is a vast store which sells almost every brand of digital and 35mm camera, plus a full range of video and other filmmaking equipment, from lighting to color processors. This is the place to buy film in bulk at very low prices.

J & R Music & Computer World

15-23 Park Row. Tel. 1–212/732-8600. Open Mon-Sat 9am-730pm, Sun 1030am-630pm.

Occupying several adjacent buildings, this store makes a great one-stop shopping destination for cameras, computers, sound systems, appliances, and recordings. Prices are excellent and the sales help knowledgeable. It's located one block south of City Hall.

Willoughby's Camera

136 West 32nd St (btw Sixth/Seventh Aves). Tel. 1–212/564-1600. Open Mon-Thurs 830am-7pm, Fri 830am-4pm, Sun 10am-7pm. Closed Sat.

Willoughby's has a huge stock of photo equipment, at good to excellent prices. They also sell video cameras and computers.

Video

Evergreen Video

37 Carmine St (btw Bleecker/Bedford Sts). Tel. 1–212/691-7362. Open Mon-Thurs 10am-10pm, Fri 10am-11pm, Sat noon-11pm, Sun noon-10pm.

In addition to stocking hard-to-find and out-of-print titles, Evergreen boasts one of the best selections of independent and foreign films. They sell DVD and laser discs too.

Kim's Video

6 St. Mark's Pl (btw Second/Third Aves). Tel. 1–212/505-0311. Open daily 10am-midnight.

Known for cult and classic films, Kim's is the best-stocked video shop in the city, with thousands of offbeat titles.

Tower Video

1961 Broadway (at 66th St). Tel. 1–212/496-2500. Open daily 9am-midnight.

With a video selection to rival their audio offerings, Tower stocks a fine range of blockbusters, foreign-language, and alternative titles.

Branch: 383 Lafayette St (at 4th St). Tel. 1–212/505-1166. Open daily 9am-midnight.

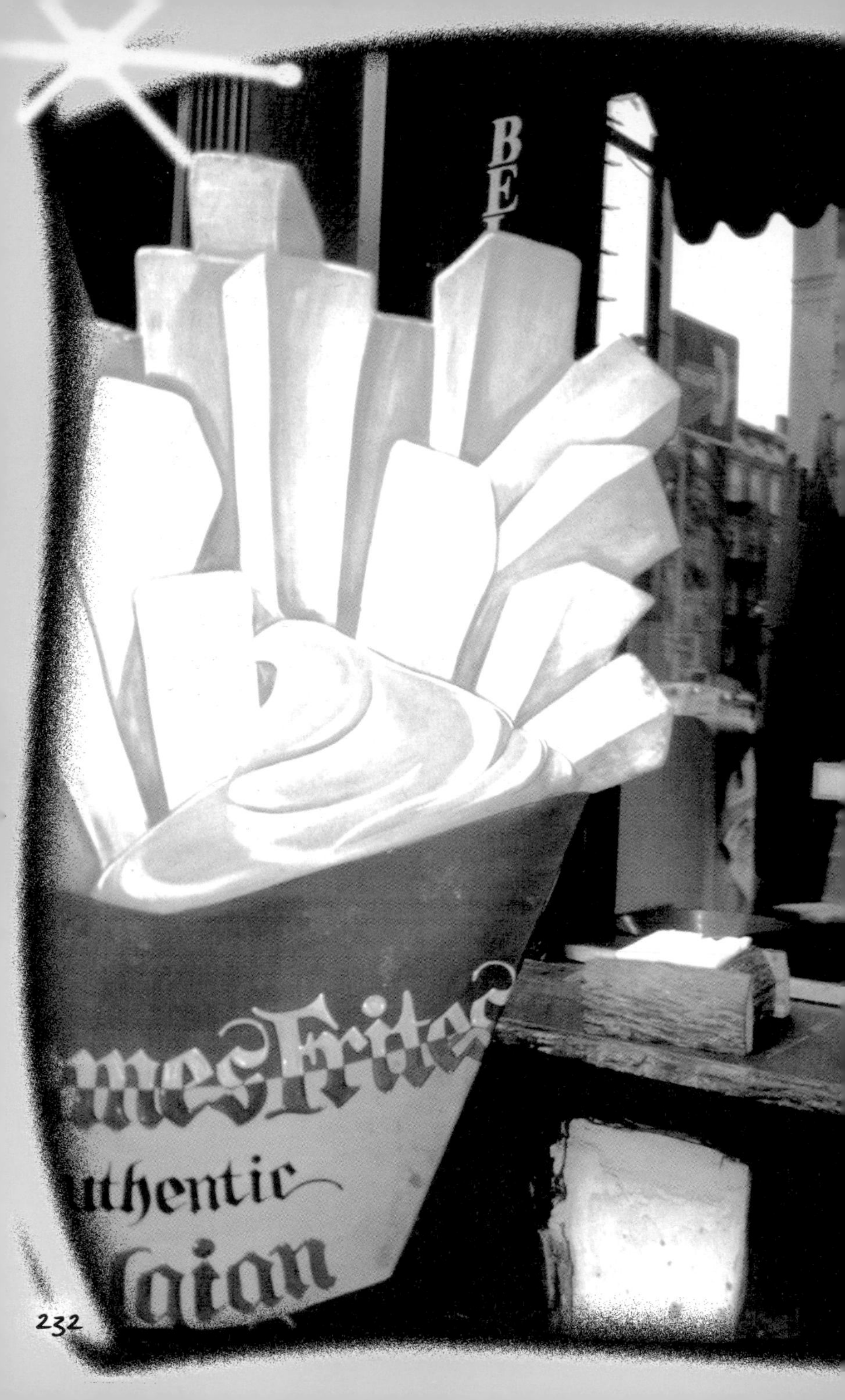
mesFrite
uthentic

#08 Eating
The Restaurant Scene

TAXI

It's not news that great cuisine from practically every corner of the globe can be tasted in New York. More startling is the fact that only relatively recently have New Yorkers come to fully embrace "fusion" cuisine and those multicultural combinations that have long ruled the kitchens of California.

The Pacific Rim, in particular, has taken New York by tsunami. Many, if not most, of the city's top chefs—including Jean-Georges Vongerichten (Jean-Georges, JoJo, Vong, The Mercer Kitchen) and Nobu Matsuhisa (Nobu) are enthusiastically scrambling East and West. Top-rated Gramercy Tavern is known for excellent sea urchin fondue, and even that bastion of the establishment, The Four Seasons, serves macadamia-encrusted tuna in miso-soy sauce. "Wraps," those gourmet-burrito descendants of specialty pizzas, are so ubiquitous you can find them on menus both down and haute. And, when they want to attract the up-and-in, new-fashioned restaurateurs know they better stock some kind of dim-sum-style appetizer and offer entrees that are ginger glazed or shiitake-mushroomed.

A kind of post-ironic retroism is the second characteristic of contemporary New York dining. Rich foods, strong drinks, designer ties, and sexy dresses are in. Complex entrees—richly flavored with time-consuming stock reductions—are remarkably common, though they routinely top $30 and more. Wine lists are also improving all over town. The sommelier at Lespinasse has doubled the cellar, *grands crus* Burgundies have been added to the trove at Montrachet, and Jean-Georges has a list strong enough to match its inventive cuisine. Unfortunately, finding a bottle under $20 is impossible, even in the roughest restaurants. Martinis, cosmopolitans, and increasingly nuevo-Latino concoctions are the aperitifs of choice, and stinky cigars are still ridiculously popular meal-enders.

It's now safe to say that some of the best dining in the world is in New York, the result of a confluence of "hyperlatives": America's best chefs, finest ingredients, and prettiest people converge nightly in Manhattan's top restaurants.

The Reservations Game

As surely as death and taxes, there's always a restaurant of the moment; one in which every night is like a movie premiere, filled with film stars, models, musicians, the media clite, athletes, restaurateurs, "garmentos," and generic rich people. Within the first two weeks of opening, everyone will trample through, before quickly heading off to the Next New Thing. If you want to be there too, it's time to use some muscle, work the phones, and call in favors. When white-hot slows to simmering, street-wise mortals can get reservations about a week in advance. Unless you have connections, or don't mind being seated at 6 or 11pm, we advise you to reserve a table as far in advance as possible. (The country code for the USA is 1; the city code for Manhattan is 212. From Great Britain dial 00-1-212 plus the local number.)

Smoking

Smoking is illegal in most restaurants, but nicotine-addicts are still allowed to get their fix at the bar, as long as dining tables are at least six feet away. Some places have carved out separate dining rooms for tobacco-users, so puff-buffs should inquire about smoking policy when making reservations.

Tipping

Listenup, Europeans! American servers expect a minimum 15% of the total bill. In New York City it's easy to calculate the expected tip—just double the sales tax (8.25%) that's tacked on to the bottom of every check.

Coveted Tables: Avant-Guide to Getting One

For a Tough Reservation:

Restaurant: Good afternoon, Haute Restaurant, may I help you?

Avant✴Guide: Hello, who am I speaking to?

Restaurant: (caught slightly off-guard) This is Joanne.

Avant✴Guide: (with feigned recognition) Oh, hi Joanne! This is (your name). I need a table for four tonight at nine o'clock, can you do it? Say yes.

Restaurant: (laughs) Well, we're booked solid, Ms. (your name), but I'll see what I can do. Can you hold on a moment?

Avant✴Guide: Thank you very much, it's really important.
(Short pause.)

Restaurant: Ms. (your name), we can fit you in at 8:30, is that OK?

For a Really Tough Reservation:

Restaurant: Good afternoon, Haute Restaurant, may I help you?

Avant✴Guide: Hello, who am I speaking to?

Restaurant: (caught slightly off-guard) This is Joanne.

Avant✴Guide: (with feigned recognition) Oh, hi Joanne! This is Randy Thomas at CKA Talent. I'm calling for my client (your name). She needs a table for four tonight at nine o'clock, can you do it? Say yes. (Continue with above script.)

Specialties of the House

Hot dogs, pizza, and bagels, the three foods that are most often associated with the Big Apple, are all "street" eats that are often consumed while walking—a distinctly New York habit.

The NYC Convention & Visitors Bureau claims that the hot dog was invented by Nathan Handwerker for Nathan's Famous in 1900. Today those unpretentious little "pimp steaks" are sold on street carts throughout the city. It usually costs a buck, and is served in a steamed bun topped with any combination of mustard, ketchup, relish, and sauerkraut.

Pizza by the slice, another New York institution, is by far the city's most popular meal. Quality varies from outstanding to offensive, but it's always cheap and filling. Finding a great slice is not as easy as it used to be. Most of New York's pizza places are no longer Italian-owned, and many pies are now made with canned sauce and fake cheese.

Bagels have sunk in quality over the last decade as well. Steaming is the culprit, a cooking process that's cheaper than boiling, with inferior results. Most of the bagels you now see are plump, fluffy rolls that have little resemblance to the dense breads of the real McCoy. Nouveau flavors like jalapeño-cheddar only add insult to injury. Three of Manhattan's best bagelries are Columbia Hot Bagels (2836 Broadway at 110th St), Tal Bagels (979 First Ave at 53rd St), and H&H Bagels (2239 Broadway at 80th St).

Cheaper Eats

There's no question that the city's best bargains are ethnic eats; nowhere in the world is it more appropriate to "think globally and eat locally," to paraphrase a popular bumper sticker. Many of New York's best "melting pot" restaurants are listed below.

You should also know that most of the city's restaurants offer lunch menus that are 25% to 50% cheaper than the dinner prices quoted below. In addition, most top restaurants offer special set-price early-dinner menus. These are usually three-course affairs, involving an appetizer, entree, and dessert for $20-$40 per person. That's a real bargain, but you've got to eat early, as the restaurant expects you to vacate your table by 8pm or before.

Kibbles & Bits

✴ Lunch is usually 25-50% cheaper than dinner. During the summer look for the promotional $20 prix-fixe luncheon at many top restaurants.

✴ Although we may say some nasty things in the reviews below, we enthusiastically recommend all the restaurants we list.

✴ You can drink the water.

Our reviewers have no relationship to any establishment in this guide. All visits are anonymous, and expenses are paid by Avant-Guide.

Where To Dine When Dining Alone

Of course you can eat solo in any restaurant: A good book or *PAPER* magazine can be far better companions than some human beings we've shared tables with. When dining alone, we shy away from quiet places with stuffy service in favor of lively surroundings and bar chairs. Here's where to go when you're on your only.

TAXI

237

Restaurants by Area, Price & Cuisine

The cost ($) reflects the average cost of a dinner with tip.

$ = Under $15
$$ = $16-$25
$$$ = $25-$30
$$$$ = $30-$49
$$$$$ = Over $50

CHELSEA

261: El Cid = = = = = = Spanish	$$
280: Empire Diner = = American	$$
254: Red Cat = = Mediterranean	$$

CHINATOWN

274: Big Wong = = = = Chinese	$
259: Canton = = = = Chinese	$$
274: Golden Unicorn = Chinese	$
276: Goody's = = = = Chinese	$$
264: Joe's Shanghai = = Chinese	$$

FINANCIAL DISTRICT

| 277: Menchanko-ti= = Japanese | $$ |

FLATIRON/GRAMERCY

243: Chicama = = New Peruvian	$$$
245: Gramercy Tavern = = = = Continental/American = =	$$$
280: L'Express = = = = = French	$$
245: Mesa Grill = = = = = = = Southwestern USA = = = =	$$$
248: Patria = = = = New Latino	$$$
249: Tabla = = = = New Indian	$$$
272: Taj = = = = New Indian	$$$
249: Union Pacific French-Asian	$$$$$

GREENWICH VILLAGE

256: Angelica Kitchen Healthist	$$
256: Bar Pitti = = = = = Italian	$$
257: Blue Hill = = = = American	$$$
257: Blue Ribbon Bakery American	$$$
253: BondSt = Japanese-Latino	$$$
250: Chez Es'Saada North African	$$$
260: Chow Bar = = = Chinese-Latino	$$$

CHELSEA (right column)

273: Corner Bistro = = American	$
244: Gotham Bar & Grill = = New Mediterranean = = =	$$$$
276: Gray's Papaya = Hot dogs	$
274: Haveli = = = = = = Indian	$$
263: I Coppi = = = = = Italian	$$$
263: Il Mulino = = = = = Italian	$$$
253: Indochine = = Pacific Rim	$$
264: Iso= = = = = = = Japanese	$$$
265: John's Pizzeria = = = Pizza	$
265: Komodo = = Asian-Latino	$$
266: Little Basil = = = = = Thai	$$
267: Lupa = = = = = = Italian	$$
267: Mexicana Mama's Mexican	$$
268: Mi Cocina= = = = Mexican	$$
269: Pearl Oyster Bar = = = = American Seafood = = = =	$$
269: Pink Teacup = = Barbeque	$$
277: Pommes Frites = Belgian Fries	$
271: Second Avenue Deli Jewish	$$
262: The Grange Hall American	$$
272: Time Cafe = = = American	$$
267: Snackbar= = = = American	$$

HARLEM

| 271: Sylvia's = = = = = = = Soul | $$ |

LOWER EAST SIDE

253: 71 Clinton Fresh Food = = New American= = = = = =	$$$
276: Katz's Deli = = = = Jewish	$$
271: Sammy's Roumanian Jewish	$$$

MEAT PACKING DISTRICT

| 280: Florent = = = = = = French | $$ |
| 251: Pastis = = = = = = French | $$ |

MIDTOWN EAST

250: Asia de Cuba Asian-Latino $$$

273: Cosí Sandwich Bar = Sandwiches $

261: Dawat = = = = = = Indian $$

244: Felidia = = = = = = Italian $$$

240: Le Cirque 2000 = = = = =
     New American= = = = = $$$$

277: Menchanko-ti= = Japanese $$

269: Rosa Mexicano = Mexican $$$

240: The Four Seasons American $$$$

268: The Oyster Bar = = = = =
     American Seafood = = = = $$$

MIDTOWN WEST

242: 21 Club = = = =American $$$$

259: Carmine's = = = = Italian $$$

259: Carnegie Deli = = = Jewish $$

273: Cosí Sandwich Bar=Sandwiches $

265: John's Pizzeria = = = Pizza $

265: Kang Suh = = = = Korean $$

277: Menchanko-ti= = Japanese $$

270: Ruby Foo's = Asian-Latino $$

272: Virgil's Real Barbecue= =
     Barbeque = = = = = = = = $$

270: Zenith = Asian Vegetarian $$

NOLITA

260:Crudo= = = = = = = = = Fish $$

261: Ghenet = = = = Ethiopian $$$

266: MeKongVietnamese-American $$

268: Nyonya = = = = Malaysian $$

276: Pho Bang = = Vietnamese $

254: Rialto = = = New-American $$

277: Rice = = = = = Pan-Asian $$

266: WD-50 = = New-American $$$$

TRIBECA

247: Nobu = = Japanese-Latino $$$$

254: Odeon = French-American $$$

270: Salaam Bombay = = Indian $$$

SOHO

256: Aquagrill American Seafood $$$

252: Balthazar= = = = = French $$$

279: Blue Ribbon = = American $$$

279: Cafe Noir = = = = =
     = = = = French-Moroccan $$

263: Honmura An = = Japanese $$$

264: Jean Claude = = = French $$

266: Lucky Strike= = = = = = =
     American-Continental = = $$

281: Palačinka = East European $

269: Pão = = = = = Portuguese $$

UPPER EAST SIDE

242: Aureole = = New American $$$$

243: Daniel = = = = = French $$$$

265: John's Pizzeria = = = Pizza $

241: Park View at the Boathouse
     New American= = = = = = $$$

282: Payard Patisserie & Bistro=
     French = = = = = = = = = $$$

281: Sarabeth's = = = American $$

UPPER WEST SIDE

281: Barney Greengrass= Jewish $$

278: Big Nick's = = = = = Greek $

273: Gabriela's = = = = Mexican $$

262: Gennaro = = = = Italian $$

276: Gray's Papaya = Hot dogs $

247: Jean-Georges = = = = = =
     New International = = = = $$$$

265: John's Pizzeria = = = Pizza $

270: Ruby Foo's = Asian-Latino $$

281: Sarabeth's = = = American $$

241: Tavern on the Green = = =
     New American= = = = = = $$$

BROOKLYN

248: Peter Luger = Steak = = =
     $$$

TAXI

239

The Four Seasons

99 East 52nd St (btw Park/Lexington Aves). Tel. 1–212/754-9494. Reservations vital. Lunch Mon-Fri noon-2pm; dinner Mon-Fri 5-930pm, Sat 5-11pm. Main courses $28-$55. AE, MC, V.

Manhattan's only landmarked restaurant is a modernist architectural gem and has been a New York phenomenon since 1959. There are two dining rooms, each with its own unique flavor. The rosewood-wrapped Grill Room is king of lunch. It's a grand, important space with leather banquettes and comfortable bar stools that have been warmed by the world's most powerful asses, titans of industry and moguls of entertainment who come here daily to jaw over lobster chowder and tuna burgers. Come nightfall, diners stroll past an enormous Picasso tapestry into the Pool Room, a breathtaking marble-clad temple with tall ceilings, perfect lighting, and a large, gurgling centerpiece pool. At once spacious and intimate, it's one of the most romantic rooms in the city.

Over the years, almost everyone has eaten here, from presidents and kings to rock and film stars. Of course, there have been plenty of mortals too. Dinners here are lengthy, orchestrated affairs often accompanied by several bottles of wine. Food is old-skool American with a modernist twist. True to the restaurant's name the menu changes seasonally, though one item that never disappears is roast duck. Carved tableside, this signature dish is moist and meaty inside, but has a magnificent skin that crackles like a potato chip. It's one of the best things we've ever put in our mouths. Not everything that comes from the kitchen is so memorable, but desserts are great and the chocolate soufflé is tops.

The Four Seasons regularly wins polls for best service. Tirelessly accommodating, the servers can recite every menu item and preparation right down to the last sprig of parsley. The wine list is one of New York's best and, although most bottles are pricey, there are several good ones available for under $35.

Le Cirque 2000

In the New York Palace Hotel, 455 Madison Ave (btw 50th/51st Sts). Tel. 1–212/303-7788. Reservations vital. Lunch Mon-Sat 1145am-245pm; dinner Mon-Sat 545-11pm, Sun 530-1030pm. Main courses $27-$40. AE, MC. V.

When Sirio Maccioni, the irrepressible proprietor of Le Cirque 2000, moved his show to the historical Villard Houses, he was trailed not only by the stars and socialites who have been with him for 25-plus years, but by an entirely new flock of high-flying diners, who swoop in nightly to see what all the fuss is about.

Much ink has been spilled about the Buckingham Palace-meets-Jetsons décor, a lavish three-ring circus that encompasses two dining rooms and a bar. Over-designed to the point of garishness, the decoration includes gilded ceilings, neon-ringed torcheres, jewel-hued carpets, and pre-Raphaelite murals. The single-armed purple throne-like chairs, which are festooned with clown buttons, had their seatbacks lowered following complaints that they obstructed sight lines. That's a good thing, considering that there's such great people watching, especially on weekends.

It's Sirio's and his sons' circus, but the

chefs are their major acts. In the 80s Daniel Boulud and Sottha Khunn created such signature dishes as scallop black-tie and paupiette of sea bass with potato and truffles. Today, Pierre Schaedelin, a protégé of Alain Ducasse, commands the kitchen, turning out dishes that are light on seasoning and sauces but densely flavored and show stopping on the plate. Winners include veal chop sautéed au jus with wild mushrooms, lobster anything, and a consommé with foie-gras ravioli that's so fragrant it threatens to levitate from the table. It's hard to select a dessert from the list of chocolate or fruit delights. Detractors say service lags unless you're a friend of Sirio's or sipping very expensive wine from the huge list that includes several bottles over $6000.

Park View at the Boathouse

in Central Park, at East 72nd St/Central Park Dr (entrance at East 72nd St/Fifth Ave). Tel. 212/517-2233. Reservations recommended. Lunch Mon-Fri 11am-330pm, Sat-Sun 11am-4pm; dinner Fri-Sat 530-830pm. Main courses $24-$32. AE, MC, V.

One of New York's best locations has a great restaurant to match. The Boathouse is a small, wood-framed building on the shore of The Lake in the middle of Central Park. The view from the outdoor dining deck is unparalleled, and lunchtime tables get mighty scarce when the weather turns nice. Chef Alan Ashkinaze cooks delicious and creative contemporary-American dishes. Favorite starters include a rich chestnut soup flavored with smoked duck and chives. The hearty Boathouse short ribs, a traditional favorite, are braised in cabernet for maximum tenderness. But we love the fish dishes: seared striped bass enhanced by sherry-vinegar sauce and caramelized fennel, or Arctic char with a preserved lemon and parsley jus served with artichokes and wild mushrooms. On Friday and Saturday after 7pm, a free mini-bus shuttles diners to the restaurant from the park entrance at Fifth Avenue and 72nd Street.

Tavern on the Green

Central Park West (at 67th St). Tel. 1-212/873-3200. Reservations recommended. Lunch Mon-Fri noon-330pm; dinner Sun-Thurs 530-1045pm, Fri-Sat 5-1130pm; brunch Sat-Sun 10am-3pm. Main courses $26-$44. AF, MC, V.

As wonderful and magical as it is kitschy and tourist-mobbed, Tavern on the Green is probably the most famous restaurant in New York. The enchanting Central Park locale is the primary draw: Summer dining on a patio illuminated by twinkling lights wrapped around trees is hard to beat. Winter meals in the cluttered, flower-filled, lodge-like interior has its own special charm: Eating in the abundantly chandeliered Crystal Room is an event. Tavern on the Green is legendary in hospitality-industry circles as the nation's highest-grossing restaurant, serving a half-million people a year. Despite crowds, both service and food are quite good, at times even excellent.

The New American menu creates old favorites with avant ingredients. Specialties include crab cakes with fresh lump crabmeat and seasonal condiments like orange-mango beurre blanc. The chicken pot pie is as meaty and flavorful as we've ever had. During warmer

months, you can try what *New York* magazine called the "city's best barbecue," grilled outdoors from mid-April through mid-October, then dance to a DJ under the trees from 9pm.

Aureole

34 East 61st St (btw Madison/Park Aves). Tel. 1-212/319-1660. Reservations vital. Lunch Mon-Fri noon-230pm; dinner Mon-Fri 530-11pm, Sat 5-11pm. AE, MC, V.

Little has changed here in the cool decade or so since chef/owner Charlie Palmer opened Aureole in an elegant Upper East Side townhouse. One doesn't mess with success. The dining room is still plushly fabulous, the wait staff still snobbish and efficient, and the New American cuisine still fresh and inventive. Aureole is consistently ranked one of the top restaurants in the city. Its upscale, flower-packed dining room attracts suits at lunch and celebrators at dinner.

Chef Palmer is known for complex concoctions and architectonic presentations. Indeed, Aureole serves some of the tallest food in town. Signature dishes include the perfectly roasted caramelized Clark Farm chicken with chanterelles and herbs accompanied by gnocchi and red Swiss chard. Another hallmark dish is butter-braised lobster over lobster cannelloni with celery-root mousseline and wilted baby spinach. The truffle oyster pan roast is but one of a long list of winning appetizers. And desserts are three-dimensional affairs that should not be missed. Aureole offers a value-packed four-course fixed-price lunch, which on warm days, is best enjoyed in the restaurant's intimate courtyard garden.

"21" Club

21 West 52nd St (btw Fifth/Sixth Aves). Tel. 1-212/582-7200. Reservations recommended. Lunch daily noon-2pm; dinner daily 530-10pm. Main Courses $39-$42. AE, MC, V.

Except, perhaps, for the Yankees, a more venerable New York institution we can not imagine. Catering to the comfort-addicted since the days of Humphrey Bogart and F. Scott Fitzgerald, "21" has functioned as the unofficial commissary for society lunchers and business tycoons for well over half a century. The historic townhouse, which is fronted by dozens of lantern-boy lawn jockeys and filled with a whimsical assortment of toy planes, trains, and automobiles, remains essentially the same as it ever was. But the wonderful career wait staff, powerful cocktails, and updated American menu are now pulling in a younger crowd. Each diner is enthusiastically greeted by a bevy of welcomers, then guided to the historic bar, a former speakeasy with oak-paneled walls and red-and-white-checked cloth-draped tables. The atmosphere is both upscale and casual, and feels very much like an old country house.

Uniformly excellent dishes are equally divided amongst old and new classics. The former celebrates an age when blissfully unaware diners guiltlessly indulged on fist-sized medallions of beef flambéed with cognac and Dijon, and includes aged sirloin, meaty English game pot pie, and the most expensive hamburger in New York ($27). Newer, lighter meals include crisp, baked black sea bass with truffled potatoes and champagne sauce; pan seared halibut with curried lentils, balsamic vinegar and fresh mint; and a rich grilled swordfish in a spicy paprika sauce. The renowned wine cellar is extraordinarily huge, remarkably expensive, and markedly strong in Burgundies and Bordeaux.

Chicama

In ABC Carpet and Home, 35 East 18th St (btw Fifth/Madison Aves). Tel. 1–212/505-2233. Lunch daily noon-3pm; dinner Mon-Thurs 6pm-midnight, Fri-Sat 530pm-1am, Sun 530-10pm. Ceviche bar open daily from noon-closing. Main courses $18-$39. AE, MC, V.

Douglas Rodriguez, the current king of Nuevo Latino cuisine, was named one of the best chefs in New York by the James Beard Foundation. A transplant from Miami, Chef Rodriguez's Latin party rocks this high-volume rustic restaurant with the city's first ceviche bar and a eucalyptus wood-burning rotisserie. The space is as colorful as the food is spiced. Peruvian rugs drape from ceiling beams, santos enliven the walls, and a large cluster of hand-blown glass lanterns illuminates the bar, where mojitos are the drink of choice. Named for Peru's major fishing port, Chicama specializes in seafood piled high at the ceviche bar, which is open throughout the day. There are about 10 different varieties to choose from, including Ecuadorian (with shrimp, roasted tomatoes, and chilies) and Thai (with squid, tuna, lemongrass, ginger, lime leaves, and basil). Other signature dishes include oysters Rodriguez, a mouthwatering explosion of sweet plantain, bacon, and saltwater. Dinner should end with a plate of churros accompanied with chocolate and sweet-milk dipping sauces.

Daniel

60 East 65th St (at Park Ave) Tel. 1–212/288-0033 or 288-0499. Reservations vital. Dinner Mon-Sat 530-10pm. Prix-fixe dinner $85-$160. AE, MC, V.

One of the very best restaurants in New York, with prices to prove it, Daniel is a culinary icon, known for extraordinary cuisine. After directing the kitchen at Le Cirque throughout the 1980s, Lyon-born Daniel Boulud opened his own eponymous restaurant, which became an instant institution. His specialty is classic French seasonal cuisine, updated with inventive sauces and surprising flavor combinations—re-inventions, whose roots are still recognizable. Here, the foie-gras terrine—a dish that has made its way onto the menu at practically every expense-account restaurant in town—is paired with caramelized apples and fig-and-plum chutney flavored with port. It's a memorable appetizer that has become something of a signature dish here. Other excellent starters from Daniel's seasonal menus include intensely-flavored curried cream of cauliflower and apple soup, and rich bluefin tuna tartar with Sevruga caviar, wasabi, cucumber, and watermelon radish in a delicate lemon coulis. Entrees run the gamut from inspired fish dishes like roasted halibut with porcini, salsify, and country bacon to intensely spiced rib-eye steaks in mustard beef jus. The final component of a decadent eight-course tasting menu is a seven-part dessert that concludes with

a basket of warm madeleine cookies, a plate of homemade chocolates, and a multi-tiered tray of mixed petits fours. The French-heavy wine cellar stocks more than 600 selections, with the best on the budget end around $50 (some even as low as $30). With great food and sublime service, the biggest gripe about Daniel used to be the drab dining room, but that is ancient history in the new Renaissance-inspired digs at Park Avenue and 65th Street. Jackets are required (and ties are requested!).

Felidia

243 East 58th St (btw Second/Third Aves). Tel. 1-212/758-1479. Reservations recommended. Lunch Mon-Fri noon-245pm; dinner Mon-Thurs 5-11pm, Fri-Sat 5-1130pm. Main courses $25-$34. Prix-fixe lunch $30. AE, MC, V.

Owner Lidia Bastianich is New York's answer to New Orleans' Emeril Lagasse. She co-owns four other restaurants here and elsewhere, appears regularly on the Food Channel in *Lidia's Italian Table*, sells her own brand of Italian sauces, and even designs tours to Italy. Her terracotta-and-brick Manhattan launching pad opened in 1981 and has secured a reputation for many as the premier Italian restaurant in the city. Certainly, the dishes deliver a hefty punch of flavor thanks to the quality of the ingredients and the traditional Italian preparations, which are designed to intensify natural flavors, not mask them. You've never really tasted a tomato until you savor a bowl of Felidia's deceptively simple tomato soup. Although the kitchen originally focused on cuisine from Istria, the menu has expanded to encompass food from throughout Italy. The exciting six-course regional tasting menus are well worth the money. Practically every dish is a winner—fresh handmade pastas (ravioli stuffed with braised artichokes with black truffle sauce), pan roasted fishes like the salmon served over braised leeks and potatoes with a mustard chive sauce, or braised meats. And the enormous, 600-strong wine list reads like an encyclopedia of Italian wines.

Gotham Bar & Grill

12 East 12th St (btw Fifth Ave/University Pl). Tel. 1-212/620-4020. Reservations recommended. Lunch Mon-Fri noon-215pm; dinner Mon-Thurs 530-10pm, Fri-Sat 530-11pm, Sun 530-945pm. Main courses $28-$38. AE, MC, V.

Many of NYCs finest chefs have earned their toques under the tutelage of Alfred Portale, whose ingenious freestyle California-Mediterranean mélange has been delighting connoisseurs for almost two decades. Gotham's whimsical architectonic presentations never fail to provoke. Piled high on the plate like culinary skyscrapers, the restaurant's plates are epitomes of "fooditecture." Rack of lamb is Portale's signature dish, but it could just as well be halibut with braised escarole, roasted garlic, cranberry beans in a champagne vinaigrette, or the almost impossibly rich Chinese spiced duck breast accompanied by seared foie-gras, roasted peaches, baby bok choy, and snow-pea pods. There is always a vegetarian special on offer, though it may not be listed on the menu. The bottom line is that food here is always exciting, right to the last forkful of Valrhona chocolate tartlet. The older, suburban crowd is less thrilling and the cavernous and clamorous postmodern dining room feels a bit dated. Service is tops and the wines are well chosen. Note too that Gotham is known for a particularly generous fixed-price lunch.

Gramercy Tavern

42 East 20th St (btw Broadway/Park Ave).
Tel. 1-212/477-0777. Reservations recommended. Lunch Mon-Fri noon-2pm; dinner Sun-Thurs 530-10pm, Fri-Sat 530-11pm. Main courses $25-$34. Prix-fixe from $70. AE, MC, V.

Danny Meyer's second venture after his extraordinarily successful Union Square Cafe is more fun and less conservative than its older sibling, but the cuisine still ranks up there. Chef Tom Colicchio's Continental/American kitchen is equally comfortable dishing out foiegras with sour cherries, spiced loin of lamb, or ragout of sea urchin and crab, all of which is accompanied by a serious selection of beers and wines by the glass. And there's always a special menu for vegetarians. Let the *New York*-magazine-reading trend-followers have the high-priced dining rooms with their antiques, tapestries, and fixed-price menus. We prefer to eat in the boisterous Tavern Room, a casual and rustic ante-chamber where the menu is both less finicky and less expensive and the trendiest-looking diners are likely to be members of the media elite. Don't skip desserts—they are another reason this restaurant scores.

Mesa Grill

102 Fifth Ave (btw 15th/16th Sts). Tel. 1-212/807-7400. Reservations recommended. Lunch Mon-Fri noon-230pm, Sat-Sun 1130am-3pm; dinner daily 530-1030pm. Main courses $18-$29. AE, MC, V.

Other restaurants may come and go, but Bobby Flay's Mesa Grill continues to deliver the subtle, spicy, and sweet flavors of the Southwest. We love the palate-piquing combinations, like the spice-rubbed pork tenderloin with bourbon ancho-chile sauce and blue-corn crusted red snapper with buttermilk chipotle sauce and roasted red pepper relish. For starters, let the barbecue duck and habanero chile sauce explode from the corn pancake. Flay continues to come up with winning, inventive dishes that burn into the memory like the 16-spice chicken in caramelized mango garlic sauce served with a plantain tamale. Weekend brunches offer similarly spicy specialties (tequila-smoked salmon quesadilla, and chicken and sweet potato hash served with a green chile hollandaise). In addition to a great selection of predominantly American wines, the bar boasts top-shelf tequilas and an extensive list of margaritas. The quietest seats in the house are up on the balcony of this soaring Flatiron District space decked out in southwestern colors, ranging from clay reds to avocado greens. We prefer to be in the middle of the rodeo, on banquettes decorated with cowboys on bucking broncos.

Jean-Georges

In the Trump International Hotel Tower, 1 Central Park West (btw 60th/61st Sts). Tel. 1–212/299-3900. Reservations recommended. Lunch Mon-Fri noon-230pm, dinner Mon-Sat 530-11pm. Main courses $28-$38. Prix-fixes: lunch $35-$45; dinner $85-115. AE, MC, V.

Jean-Georges Vongerichten is one of the century's great masters of contemporary cooking. His combinations are so extravagantly inventive they're almost mystifying. Witness, for example, seared sea scallops in a sweetish raisin-caper emulsion served with grilled, caramelized cauliflower. These are unlikely but wonderful combinations of ingredients that few would every think of mixing. Garlic soup contains frog's legs and is flavored with thyme. A rich lobster tartine is accented with pumpkin seeds and pea shoots. The loin of venison is flavored with juniper and candied orange seasoning, and turbot is sauced with Château Chalon, a relatively obscure white wine from France's Arbois region. A master of herbs, Jean-Georges seasons many dishes with extracts and essences foraged from local fields and farms. And frequent tableside preparations bring culinary theater to the eyes as well as the palate. There's a reasonably priced 300-plus-strong wine list in which you can get away with a bottle for about $35.

As you might imagine, scoring one of only 64 seats in this stylishly streamlined restaurant is no easy feat. Servers in black Nehru jackets scamper between well-spaced tables in a chic-simple setting designed with muted colors and soaring floor-to-ceiling windows overlooking Central Park. There are about 30 more chairs in the adjacent Nougatine, a (nominally) more casual space with a sparkling exhibition kitchen and active bar that attracts a younger crowd. In summer, tables spill out into Mistral, the front terrace overlooking busy Columbus Circle.

Nobu

105 Hudson St (btw Franklin/N. Moore Sts). Tel. 1–212/219-0500. Reservations recommended. Lunch Mon-Fri 1145am-2pm; dinner daily 545-10pm. Main courses $30-$33. AE, MC, V.

Chef Nobu Matsuhisa, a Japanese-Peruvian Los Angeleno, is perfectly pedigreed to introduce a new kind of fusion artistry to New York. The stunningly delicious results are perfect yin-yang combinations like raw yellowtail with jalapeño peppers, barely cooked sashimi drizzled with garlic-and-ginger-flavored olive oil, and monkfish-liver paté with soy dressing and a gleaming dollop of caviar. Squid pasta—delicate segments of squid and asparagus glazed with butter and garlic sauce—is an extraordinary taste treat you won't soon forget. And you can do no wrong ordering the multi-course Ōmakase menu (from $40 at lunch; from $60 at dinner). The self-consciously stylish dining room is at once stunning and stereotyped. The wall of black pebbles, stenciled beech-wood floor, and dramatically lit centerpiece sushi bar is

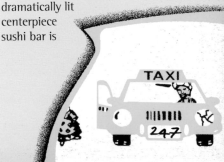

TAXI

247

the look that Hollywood types have come to expect. And, judging by how many A-list personalities grace this space, the design is spot-on. Regulars begin with shots of Masu Sake, served tequila-style in small cedar cups with salted rims. Desserts here, like green tea crème caramel, are actually good—a rarity at sushi houses. The main complaint about Nobu is the difficulty of getting a table (assuming you can even get through on the phone). Make reservations as far in advance as possible, come for lunch, or arrive alone with your eye on a single seat at the sushi bar. The other option is to go to Next Door Nobu, which operates on a first come, first-served basis.

Patria

250 Park Avenue South (at 20th St). Tel. 1-212/777-6211. Reservations recommended. Lunch Mon-Fri noon-230pm; dinner Mon-Thurs 6-11pm, Fri-Sat 530pm-midnight, Sun 530-1030pm. Main courses $23-$36 AE, MC, V.
One of Nueva York's leading Nuevo Latino restaurants, Patria wows its patrons with a winning trio of great looks, samba rhythms, and terrific flavors. To start, simply drink down the tangy Yucatan shrimp ceviche, which arrives in a sizable martini glass; a super seductive combination of orange, lime, achiote, jalapeños, and tomato. Entrees, which are stylishly presented, include incredibly moist suckling pig cooked in red-bean broth. And the sauce that's paired with the short ribs of veal is deliciously spiked with horseradish. The dining room is a dramatic, high-volume space that, paired with an excellent staff, makes for a festive evening. It helps the party too that their extensive wine list includes plenty of reasonably priced bottles from Argentina, Chile, and other southerly vineyards. The least noisy tables are on the ground floor below the bar.

Peter Luger Steakhouse

178 Broadway (btw Bedford/Briggs Sts), Brooklyn. Tel. 1-718/387-7400. Reservations recommended. Kitchen open Mon-Thurs 1145am-945pm, Fri-Sat 1145am-1045pm. Main courses $20-$31. No cards.
One of the oldest and greatest steakhouses in America, Peter Luger sets the standard by which all other steaks must be judged. Choices are kept to a minimum. Aged porterhouse—a fancy word for a thick T-bone—is the only cut they serve. There are no menus. It's just steak for however many people are sitting at the table. A few other items are available (lamb chops, fresh fish), but why? Steaks arrive perfectly charred on the outside and deliciously tender within. How do they do it? Dry-aged beef is blasted under molten-hot broilers that seal in the flavor. Ample portions are then served communally, on a giant platter with a pond of juice. Spoon on some of Luger's sweet, horseradish-laced sauce and you have a steak that's worthy of one's last meal. Forget the dreary starters, limit side dishes to potatoes and creamed spinach, and resign yourself to a wine list that is unremarkable, at best. Prices are high, Williamsburg (Brooklyn) is a schlep, credit cards are not accepted, and the service is insultingly horrible—even nasty. It's proof that we will put up with a lot for the Holy Grail of a luscious steak.

Tabla

11 Madison Ave (at 25th St). Tel. 1–212/889-0667.
Reservations recommended. Lunch Mon-Fri noon-230pm; dinner
daily 530-1030pm. Main courses $18-$25. Prix-fixe $65, $75,
and $90. AE, MC, V.

Calling it "New Indian" doesn't do justice to this exquisite two-story restaurant/bar where the décor and the flavors are exotic indeed. A grand staircase leads to the main dining room overlooking Madison Square Park. It's extraordinarily comfortable. Tables are large and generously spaced, and surrounded by suitably rich coral and jade decor. Chef Floyd Cardoz hails from Bombay, but he brings the flavors of South India to his tables—tamarind, kokum, clove, cinnamon, and black pepper. Forget any samosa you've ever tasted when you order the duck samosa sparked by wonderful pumpkin-and-orange chutney and almonds. Sometimes the menu wanders away from India, as in such appetizers as venison carpaccio with chanterelles, which is presented on

Union Pacific

111 East 22nd St (btw Park Ave South/Lexington Ave).
Tel. 1–212/995-8500. Lunch Tues-Fri noon-145pm; dinner
Mon-Thurs 530-10pm, Fri-Sat 515-1030pm. Main Courses
$22-$32. Prix-fixe from $70. AE, MC, V.

This dining room is serenity itself, incorporating numerous Zen-like Pacific elements, from falling water to a bucolic bridge which leads into the dining room. Chef/owner Rocco DiSpirito turns out creative French-Asian cuisine, trip-hopping his way with deep flavors and contrasting textures. Foiegras with garlands of green papaya spiked with a tamarind sauce is a good example of his talent, as is the wonderful tuna tartare accompanied by wasabi and crunchy Asian pears. Fish is a highlight here, sometimes sauced with golden raisins and tart anchovy vinaigrette. There's a superb selection of cheeses and magnificent desserts like white chocolate risotto and mango-and-papaya carpaccio with pineapple sherbet.

a bed of chestnut-studded frisee. And you've probably never had a curry as alluring as the taro-crusted wild striped bass with sides of baby bok choy and wild mushrooms. And vegetarians will appreciate the that there's a separate, though pricey, meatless menu. Service is attentive but unobtrusive, a trademark of all of owner Danny Meyer's operations. Wines are good too, with a emphasis on the rieslings and gewurztraminers that can stand up to spices. We particularly enjoy eating at the Bread Bar on the first floor, where a limited a la carte menu (and slightly lower prices) attracts a younger, more boisterous crowd.

TAXI

249

Asia de Cuba

In Morgans Hotel, 237 Madison Ave (btw 37th/38th Sts). Tel. 1-212/726-7755. Reservations vital. Lunch Mon-Fri noon-330pm; Dinner Sun-Wed 530-1130pm, Thurs-Sat 530pm-1am. Main courses $25-$30. AE, MC, V.

Good food and a great celebratory atmosphere make Asia de Cuba one of our favorite NYC dining experiences. This is a destination restaurant, designed for revelry. The focal point of the ground-level dining room is a long, 34-seat communal alabaster table that rarely fails to develop into a happy party of like-minded strangers. The fête is encouraged by the city's most extensive rum bar, stocked with quality sugar distillates that can be sipped neat or mixed into any number of garish umbrella drinks. The restaurant's Asian/Latino fusion cuisine is as fun and delicious as the atmosphere. Witness dishes like tuna tartare picadillo style served on wonton crisps, coriander-crusted flat iron steak, and Hunan whole crispy fish stuffed with crab escabeche. High prices and a super-stylish white-on-white decor limits the crowd to wealthy, black-clad suits and creatives and their gorgeous partners. Outlying four-seaters and the balcony bar are more egalitarian.

Chez Es'Saada

42 East 1st St (btw First/Second Aves). Tel. 1-212/777-5617. Reservations recommended. Kitchen open Mon-Thurs 6pm-midnight, Fri-Sat 6pm-1am. Main courses $22-$28. AE, MC, V.

One of those raging few fashion-crowd restaurants in which the gorgeous staff consistently outshines the beautiful patrons, Chez Es'Saada is nothing if not sexy. Slip through an unmarked door into the restaurant's ground-floor bar, a neo-North African space fitted with a half-dozen mosaic-covered tables. A rose-petal-strewn staircase leads to vaulted basement dining lounges where exotic cocktails are strong and food is superb. Chez Es'Saada dishes out urban-rustic French-Moroccan cuisine, the closest thing there is in New York to nouveau-Tangieri cooking. To accomplish this, the kitchen whips really good ingredients into traditional dishes. Chicken bisteeya (phyllo-wrapped pie) and grilled lamb with couscous are the best of the small list of specialties. As the night heats up, a DJ launches groovy world-beats and the Chez becomes one of the hippest lounges around. We like it.

Pastis

9 Ninth Ave (at Little 12th St). Tel. 1–212/929-4844. Reservations not accepted. Breakfast daily 9am-noon; lunch Mon-Fri noon-5pm, dinner daily 6pm-midnight; late supper Sun-Thurs midnight-2am, Fri-Sat midnight-3am. Main courses $9-$18. AE, MC, V.

The fact that Brian McNally started his career in the theater is apparent in all of his restaurants. Above everything, each has an off-Broadway appeal that takes a slice of life from another city and installs it into mainstream New York life. Although the restaurant's mirrors, marble-topped credenzas, zinc bar, signs, and other accouterments may have come from Pennsylvania or some other state, they look like they're straight out of old Les Halles. Rather then feeling like a fish out of water in the raw and gloomy Meatpacking District, upscale Pastis is beginning to define this trend-leaning neighborhood. Despite McNally's supposed intention to make this place a neighborhood spot for working folk, celebrities arrive by the limo-load and the restaurant is buzzing. Culinarily, it's classic blue-collar bistro—onion soup with a thick crust of cheese, croque monsieur served on a wooden board, skate with capers in black butter, roast leg of lamb with flageolets, and steak frites served with béarnaise. And house wines are served by the carafe, accompanied by sturdy tumblers. Show up at off-hours or expect to wait.

Balthazar

80 Spring St (btw Broadway/Lafayette St). Tel. 1–212/965-1414. Reservations vital. Breakfast daily 730-1045am; lunch Mon-Fri noon-230pm; dinner Mon-Sat 545-1145pm, Sun 530-1045pm; brunch Sat-Sun 1130am-330pm. Main courses $19-$25. AE, MC, V.

Once the most happening place in town, Balthazar has settled in to the top 10. That's a good thing, because the more this place cools down, the better it gets, just like Keith McNally's earlier hits, Lucky Strike and Pravda. A brilliantly faux brasserie, Balthazar is Paris par excellence. Golden light bounces off huge ormolu mirrors illuminating red leather banquettes, distressed tile flooring, and handsome, white-aproned waiters. Airy and energetic, the dining room feels much older than it is. And nobody minds having to wait at the three-deep bar. Ultimately, good food is what keeps them coming back for more, and Balthazar delivers with flavorful and creative renditions of brasserie classics. Some dishes are less successful than others, but most are winners, including the house's specialty shellfish platter, a decadent two-tier plateau des fruits de mer brimming with oysters, clams, sweet jumbo shrimp, scallop ceviche, sea snails, and more (about $60 for two). Other excellent entrees include sautéed skate with capers, steak au poivre, and roasted, bacon-wrapped monkfish. And while most appetizers are forgettable, the warm goat cheese and caramelized onion remains one of the tastiest treats in recent memory. You could easily forego a starter and fill up on the delicious round bread that's baked in the adjoining Balthazar Bakery. Desserts are tops, and while the all-French wine list offers no bargains, several drinkable whites are priced under $30.

Indochine

430 Lafayette St (btw Astor Pl/4th St). Tel. 1–212/505-5111. Reservations recommended. Kitchen open Mon–Thurs 530pm–midnight, Fri–Sat 530pm–1230am, Sun 530–1130pm. Main courses $14–$21. AE, MC, V.

Indochine practically invented the hip New York French/Colonial dining scene and it sometimes seems that everything tastes like Indochine these days. A hotspot of the 80s known for saté and celebs, Indochine has taken on all comers and remains as hot as a chili-oil stir fry. The restaurant's black-clad, table-hopping loyals are obviously partial to clubby booths, beautiful servers, and massive floral arrangements. Models are still ordering nothing but can be seen everywhere. And over a decade later the delicate Franco-Vietnamese food still feels inventive, if not exotic. There is an interesting variety of crunchy handrolls, paired with piquant dipping sauces (mango-tamarind et al), plus tangy Asian salads and small dishes. Filet of sole is steamed in a banana leaf and bathed in coconut milk flavored with lime leaves, and sweet-and-sour soup is loaded with shrimp, pineapple, tamarind, and tomatoes. It's all good. Wines are not too dear, and interesting beers are also available.

71 Clinton Fresh Food

71 Clinton St (btw Rivington/Stanton Sts). Tel. 1–212/614 6960. Reservations vital. Kitchen open Mon–Thurs 6–10pm, Fri–Sat 6–1130pm. Main courses $19–$25. AE, MC, V.

Chef Wylie Dufresne, a protégé of Jean-Georges, had both the courage and the foresight to open this small Loisada storefront restaurant in what was, until recently, a foodie wasteland. Success is his reward as securing a table in this trendy, 30-seater is not an easy feat. The menu is seasonal. Winter, for example brings beer-braised short ribs, hanger steaks with garlic-mustard spaetzle, and juicy veal chops that are paired with a chutney-like dressing. The wine list is short, but several good ones are available by the glass. None of the tables are particularly good ones in this cramped and noisy dining room, but nobody seems to care—the food is good, the vibe is groovy.

BondSt

6 Bond St (btw Broadway/Lafayette St). Tel. 1–212/777-2500. Reservations recommended. Kitchen open Mon–Sat 6pm–midnight, Sun 6–11pm. Main courses $18–$26. AE, MC, V.

A recent venture by the Midas-touched Indochine, Republic, and Bar d'O people, BondSt is a chic, tri-level space that, for hipsters, has become some of the most coveted real estate in the city. Here beautiful people serve THE beautiful people. Built with sleek unadorned woods and low-tech tables, the twin dining rooms and slate sushi bar are simple almost to the point of being rustic. It's a fun space that's great for groups. The food too is conspicuously minimalist neo-Japanese, created by ex-Nobu chefs. In addition to sushi and sashimi in all its incarnations you might find grilled ribeye steak with a rich tamarind red wine sauce and pan-roasted cod with Peruvian potato, baby beets, and sundried tomato in a coolly luscious lemongrass-cucumber broth. Traditional tatami rooms are available upstairs, while the cellar contains the lounge, where sakétinis are the drink of choice.

TAXI

253

Red Cat

227 Tenth Ave (btw 23rd/24th Sts). Tel. 1-212/242-1122. Dinner Mon-Thurs 530-1130pm, Fri-Sat 530pm-midnight, Sun 5-10pm. Main courses $14-$22. AE, MC, V.

This Chelsea hotspot gets going early in the evening with a boisterous artsy-boho-club crowd, most of whom work in the neighborhood. Diners are attracted by the reasonably priced but bold-flavored Mediterranean-American cuisine, the warm welcome, the stylish, narrow crimson room lit by oversize Moroccan lanterns, and the lack of any bogus attitude. Many regulars begin with a warm salad of grilled endive with blue cheese which bursts with caramelized balsamic flavor. Steamed and roasted Manila clams flavored with red pepper, smoked ham, and sherry is another winning starter. Mains run the gamut from sliced baby lamb with grilled red onions and sour cherries to mustard-crusted trout and pan crisped skate wing. And definitely order a side of parmesan fries doused with mustard aioli. If you're alone, this is a great place to dine at the bar.

Rialto

265 Elizabeth St (btw Houston/Prince Sts). Tel. 1-212/334-7900. Reservations recommended. Lunch daily 11am-430pm; dinner daily 530pm-1230am. Main courses $9-$22. AE, MC, V.

At first glance, Rialto is a New York neo-bistro of the most common sort: a casual setting with lots of little tea candles, mirrors angled off the wall, and decent bistro fare. But this breezy spot has struck a chord with younger trendies who have made it one of the busiest restaurants in NoLIta. In warm weather, the charming urban garden is the place to be. And the New American menu is just avant enough to make it interesting. Standout starters include rich and creamy potato-garlic soup and fabulous grilled wild-mushroom sausage. Portobello napoleon with polenta cake, roasted peppers, yellow squash, zucchini, and spinach is a delicious signature entree. Juicy turkey burgers and hamburgers can always be found on the menu and are consistently excellent.

Odeon

145 West Broadway (btw Thomas/Duane Sts). Tel. 1-212/233-0507. Kitchen open Mon-Fri noon-2am, Sat 11am-3am, Sun 1130am-2am. Main courses $15-$29. AE, MC, V.

Famous since Warhol's day, Odeon was the first hip New York bistro. Immortalized in Jay McInerney's novel *Bright Lights, Big City*, this downtown hangout is almost single-handedly responsible for making TriBeCa a neighborhood. Today it's a downtown fixture known to everyone from local families to top celebs who come here for swanky steak frites and monster martinis. Success persists because Odeon refuses to rest on its laurels. The tried-and-true brasserie menu features perfect steak au poivre, a wonderful seared-tuna sandwich enriched with arugula and wasabi mayonnaise, fine country salads, and big juicy burgers. Not incidentally, there's a great bar, which still sees plenty of star power. People-watching improves by the hour, culminating with a late-night party of club kids and fashionistas. The gregarious staff works hard to maintain the quality and consistency that has made this place an institution.

Angelica Kitchen

300 East 12th St (btw First/Second Aves). Tel. 1–212/228-2909. Reservations accepted only for six or more. Kitchen open daily 1130am-730pm. Main courses $9-$12. No cards.

Animal-liberationists and their friends swear by this bustling East Village macro-vegetarian temple to meatlessness. It's tough to produce good-tasting macrobiotic cuisine, but Angelica Kitchen succeeds. It goes beyond the bland bowls of steaming brown rice, beans, tofu, and seaweed to include sugar- and dairy-free world-beat creations with Asian and South American influences. Everyone loves the soba noodles and the sea vegetables, and regulars swear by the three-bean chili made with lentils and kidney and pinto beans. Creative soups and sandwiches are also served, plus a short list of inventive and tasty desserts. The atmosphere is ascetic, portions are generous, and the price is right.

Aquagrill

210 Spring St (at Sixth Ave). Tel. 1–212/274-0505. Reservations recommended. Lunch Tues-Fri noon-3pm; dinner Tues-Sat 6-1045pm, Sun 6-1030pm; brunch Sat-Sun noon-345pm. Main courses $20-$26. AE, MC, V.

Aquagrill is all about the sea and being seen. A great SoHo location and an amazingly extensive oyster bar (24 varieties at last count) play to all manner of downtown fish-lovers and shellfish-ionados. Good chefs and top ingredients converge daily in Aquagrill's hard-working kitchen where a fresh ocean catch like halibut, cod, monkfish, and tuna is brought in each morning and handled with utmost care. Winning starters include warm octopus salad and seared tuna carpaccio. Move on to the bouillabaisse filled with snapper, shrimp, mussels, clams, scallops, and lobster in a garlic saffron tomato broth, or the grilled falafel-crusted salmon in a lemon coriander vinaigrette. Of course, you can also choose your *poisson* and have it cooked to your specifications: roasted, poached, or grilled. Side dishes are as good as the main courses, and we usually order several. Try the soft-truffle polenta, yellow Finnish potato hash, and sautéed spinach. Good lighting, comfortable seating and fair prices help make Aquagrill a king of all things fishy. It's especially great in summer, when tables spill onto a sidewalk terrace.

Bar Pitti

268 Sixth Ave (btw Bleecker/Houston Sts). Tel. 1–212/982-3300. Reservations accepted only for three or more. Kitchen open daily noon-midnight. Main courses $14-$20. No cards.

The dining room's tiled floor and wood tables are attractive enough, but Bar Pitti is unbeatable in summer, when the restaurant's glass facade opens and the tables that take over the sidewalk fill with actors, artists, and fashion folk. There are few better places in the city to watch the world waddle by. In every other respect this is just an unpretentious Tuscan trattoria, serving decent meals at reasonable prices. Regulars ignore the menu and wait for one of the kind, harried waiters to prop a blackboard on a spare chair and tick off the day's specials. Pasta is the restaurant's finest course. Portions are small, as they are meant as *primi piatti*, but flavor is as large as it gets. The kitchen's trademark dish, spaghetti with clam sauce, regularly finds its way onto the specials board. And a wonderful pasta marinara proves that, in the right hands, even simple meals can become high cuisine. Meat courses run the gamut from beef and chicken to veal and pork. Whatever you choose, side it with sautéed spinach, some of the very best in town.

Blue Ribbon Bakery

33 Downing St (at Bedford St). Tel. 1-212/337-0404. Reservations accepted only for five or more. Kitchen open Tues-Sun noon-2am. Main courses $10-29. AE, MC, V.

Don't be fooled by the simple Village-y atmosphere of this small spot. Local neighborhood people line up to get in to the unadorned dining room. It's owned by the same folks who conceived Blue Ribbon and Blue Ribbon Sushi, and they have lent their imaginations to the menu, which offers an array of small plates, sandwiches made with great house made breads, and an eclectic assortment of mains. There's a touch of New Orleans in several of the last, like the intense grilled catfish with chorizo, bacon, collard greens, sweet potatoes, and corn tartar, or the New Orleans-style barbecue shrimp. You could almost have a different small plate every night of the year and still not have exhausted the menu— Serrano ham, leek vinaigrette, and marinated salmon, for example. The chocolate chip bread pudding may cost more than you bargained for, but it's worth it. Cheese lovers will also relish the ten-odd choices on hand. There's an extensive wine list to accompany everything.

Blue Hill

75 Washington Pl (btw MacDougal St/Sixth Ave). Tel. 1-212/539-1776. Reservations recommended. Kitchen open daily 6-11pm. Main courses $18-$26. MC, V.

There is something very alluring about this small subterranean dining room. It's sleek and minimal, wrapped in ocher-neutral colors. The gorgeous floral arrangements and the candlelit ambience add to the romance. There is nothing gimmicky about this place. It's named after a farm in Massachusetts and the cuisine is strictly seasonal, using local ingredients only when they are available—corn shoots in June, rhubarb in spring, and so on. Consequently it's a very focused menu (five appetizers and seven mains). Among the appetizers there might be Cape Cod scallops perked up with a warm beet salad, cranberry juice, and horseradish, or luscious braised endive, port wine, and raspberry vinegar. The poached duck might arrive on a pool of spinach and roasted yellow beets, or on a puree of winter squash and Swiss chard leaves and stems. Salsify, pearl onions, and carrots *en cocotte* set off the rack and loin of lamb. Warm chocolate bread pudding sided with vanilla ice cream and chocolate sorbet closes everything perfectly. Blue Hill is a great restaurant.

ICATESS

STAURAN

854

Carnegie Deli

854 Seventh Ave (btw 55th/56th Sts). Tel. 1-212/757-2245. Reservations not accepted. Kitchen open daily 630am-4am. Main courses $7-$17. No cards.

This legendary Yiddish cafeteria is known to its fans for skyscraper sandwiches, which are so staggeringly huge that diners have to practically unhinge their jaws to eat them. Pastrami and corned beef are the specialties of this house - on rye of course, with plenty of mustard. Other Jewish traditionals here are good, but not great. The best of the lot are chicken soup with baseball-sized matzo balls, cheese blintzes, potato pancakes, and what is perhaps the best, most creamy cheesecake in the entire world. One slice is so big that if you eat the whole thing alone you might suffer from a "food-over," which is like a hangover, but worse. The Carnegie's authentic New York, no-frills atmosphere is one of its quirky attractions. But, unlike the old days, when surly service was an integral part of this deli's *gestalt*, today's wait staff is inauthentically attentive. The clientele has changed too, as tourists are in the majority at the height of lunch and dinner. Arrive late to avoid the crowds—the kitchen is open until 4am.

Canton

45 Division St (btw Bow[...] Sts). Tel. 1-2[...] open Wed-Thu[...] noon-10pm. C[...] courses $14-$1[...]

Good food served in excruciatingly plain surroundings sums up the majority of the restaurants in Chinatown. While you will probably find an acceptable meal at almost any chopstick house you stumble into, Canton has been a reliable choice for decades, consistently wowing diners with fair prices, extraordinarily friendly service, and some of the best Cantonese fare in NYC. Once you are seated in the spare, blue-clothed dining room, the hostess will walk you through a menu of South China hits that sound familiar but taste far better than the glutinous rice toppers dished out by most other places. Although we've never had a bad meal here, standouts include plump butterfly shrimp, pungent ginger chicken, and whole sea bass with Chinese vegetables.

Carmine's

200 West 44th St (btw Broadway/Eighth Ave). Tel. 1-212/221-3800. Kitchen open Sun-Mon 1130am-11pm, Tues-Sat 1130am-midnight. Main courses $17-$29. AE, MC, V.

A parody of southern-Italian family dining, Carmine's is a New York institution that's built a lasting reputation with locals and visitors based on a single gag—size. Everything at Carmine's is colossal—the dining room, the drinks, the crowd, the noise, and even many of the servers. Largest of all are the portions: sized -for-gluttony dishes that are meant to be shared and can serve as many as four. Every night is a bizarre and fun feeding frenzy as groups large and small mob the bar

and wait their turn for a trough. There is no printed menu. Giant scrawls on the wall offer a list of Sicilian-American standards that haven't changed in years. While no single dish is truly outstanding, meals are consistently satisfying. Of pastas—which are hauled to the table on large platters—the best is rigatoni with fennel sausage, broccoli, garlic, and olive oil. Chicken scarpariello, seasoned with fresh rosemary and roasted on the bone, is fragrant and flavorful. Most of the other enormous chicken, seafood, and veal dishes are served with tomato sauce and laden with garlic. There's a surprisingly good wine list and obscenely ginormous desserts that are triumphs of size over finesse. Carmines is a festive, larger-than-life adventure that's best experienced with a large group of friends.

Branch: 2450 Broadway (btw 90th/91st Sts; tel. 1–212/362-2200).

Chow Bar

*230 West 4th St (at Charles St).
Tel. 1–212/633-2212. Reservations
recommended. Kitchen open Sun-Wed 530-
11pm, Thurs-Sat 530pm-midnight.
Main courses $17-$29. AE, MC, V.*

Chef Peter Klein was one of the early creators of the Chino-Latino craze when he cooked at China Grill in the 80s. Now he is doing a reprise here at this jazzy joint in the Village. The up-front bar buzzes with a happy neighborhood crowd, made happier with fine cocktails and specialty sakés. The menu offers an array of alluring small plates—honey plum glazed barbecued spareribs, steamed shrimp dumplings with red pepper miso sauce, and crispy crab spring rolls with red-chile cucumber sauce. You've never tasted the likes of the steak frites served here, bursting with the flavors of cilantro, shallots, garlic, ginger, soy, and chili peppers. Equally seductive are the Shanghai lobster noodles in red Thai coconut sauce. The room has zip too, thanks to the intense lime-green and orange color scheme and glowing lanterns above the bar.

Crudo

*54 Clinton St (at
Rivington St). Tel. 1–
646/654-0116. Open
Tues-Sat 6pm-1am. Main
courses $11-$18. MC.*

There is often an in inverse ratio between menu length and food quality; the shorter the better. With just ten items, all of them fishy, this Lower East Side space proves the rule, serving exemplary dishes that are as delicious as they are well-priced. Look for raw oysters garnished with cilantro-chili, ginger, or ajl panca; salmon sashimi with citrus-ginger relish; market-fresh fish tartares; and a couple of creative cevices. And because Chef Seamus Mullen knows you'll want to sample it all, everything is available is half portions. Singles are catered to with stools fronting the raw bar and a patio out back is perfect in summer. Good Reislings are available by the glass, and there's a full bar too; mojitos are a specialty.

Dawat

210 East 58th St (btw Second/Third Aves).
Tel. 1–212/355-7555. Reservations recommended.
Lunch Mon-Sat noon-3pm; dinner daily 5-11pm.
Main courses $12-$23. AE, MC, V.

Manhattan's best Indian restaurant is as much a curry house as that "restaurant in Central Park" is a tavern. Cookbook author Madhur Jaffrey's exciting menu is packed with food that is at once out of this world and down to earth. The best of Dawat's dishes are original pleasures that haven't been duplicated anywhere else in the city. Mint-infused lamb patties and lightly cooked jumbo shrimp, rubbed with garlic, mustard, and curry are joyous appetizers. Among the entrees, the restaurant is best known for Parsi-style salmon, a hot and sweet delicacy that's steamed in a banana leaf with coriander chutney. The vegetarian platter is a flavorsome mix of okra, carrots, potatoes, green beans, and more, sided with an array of tangy chutneys. More conventional tandoori meals are also available, all of which should be sided with Dawat's great selection of parathas and pooris. Quality has its price at Dawat, but Delhi-belly is definitely not part of the equation. No one—not even Indians, we are certain—go to an Indian restaurant for its desserts, and this place is no exception. There's not much to the Spartan decor either, and Dawat could benefit from a stronger wine list. But they have a good selection of international beers, and a terrific $15 fixed-price lunch that's one of the best deals in the neighborhood.

El Cid

322 West 15th St (btw Eighth/Ninth Aves). Tel. 1–212/929-9332. Reservations recommended. Lunch daily noon-3pm; Sun-Thurs 5-11pm, Fri-Sat 5pm-midnight. Main courses $15-$20. AE.

A hole in the wall but not in your pocket, El Cid is a tiny place verging on dive serving bab tapas at good prices. Rigorously anti-chic, the homey dining room is regularly packed with neighborhood insiders who come to graze or gorge on flavor-packed appetizers. Favorites include squid in garlic sauce, marinated fresh anchovies, piquant chorizo sausage, and chicken stewed in red wine. On weekends, only the earliest birds get the worm.

Ghenet

284 Mulberry St (btw Houston/Prince Sts). Tel. 1–212/343-1888. Kitchen open Tues-Wed and Fri-Sun 1230pm-11pm, Thurs 1230pm-1030pm. Closed Mon. Main courses $10-$19. AE, MC, V.

When Abyssinian/Ethiopian food was first introduced to the United States, diners most often found themselves crouching on uncomfortable stools eating spicy East African equivalents of curry-house fare. At Ghenet this approach is ancient history. The space is sleek and serene. The lime-colored walls are graced with a few stylish artifacts. Throbbing North African music keeps the mixed neighborhood/hipster crowd happy as they gather around the semi-circular bar.

The food has a modest kick, especially those dishes made with berbere sauce, which combines garlic, red pepper, cardamom, and other spices. There are plenty of vegetarian dishes available too. Every dish comes with injera, a delicious bread that's meant for sopping up sauces. And a well-chosen wine list complements the complex flavors of the cuisine.

TAXI

261

Gennaro

665 Amsterdam Ave (btw 92nd/93rd Sts).
Tel. 1-212/665-5348. Reservations not accepted.
Kitchen open Sun-Thurs 5-1030pm, Fri-Sat 5-11pm.
Main courses $10-$13. No cards.

When your stomach starts grumbling on the Upper West Side stop at Gennaro, New York's best affordable Italian place. Physically, it's just a modest storefront on a decrepit block that wouldn't get a second glance if not for the crowds—jostling for one of only 25 seats in a tight, bright dining room that's narrow as a bowling alley and almost as loud. The draw is great southern-ish Italian food, good portions, and closeout prices. A party of four can easily share the huge antipasti platter, a survey of Italian appetizers (prosciutto, grilled shrimp, white beans, bruscetta, lamb shank, and the like) that is best described as Italy on a plate. Among the entrees, regulars rave about the grilled Italian sausage with broccoli rabe and polenta, lemon-scented roast Cornish hen, braised lamb shank in a robust tomato and wine sauce, and tender gnocchi with tomato and basil. Fact is, no matter how you order, it's hard to get a bad meal here. Even the house red is cheap and good. Be sure to ask for the prices of the verbally recited specials, as they are usually more expensive than most menu items. The waiters are friendly, but service tends to go awry when things get ultra-busy, which means weekends can be disastrous. Reservations are not accepted, so be prepared to wait.

The Grange Hall

50 Commerce St (btw Barrow/Bedford Sts). Tel. 1-212/924-5246. Reservations recommended. Lunch Mon-Fri noon-3pm; dinner Sun-Mon 6-11pm, Tues-Thurs 530-1130pm, Fri-Sat 530pm-midnight; brunch Sat-Sun 11am-3pm. Main courses $13-$20. AE.

The Grange Hall earns a listing here for its only-in-New York location, on a wonderfully tiny street in the most beautiful corner of the West Village. Hidden from tourists—and most everybody else—this is a warm, nurturing environment in which to sip strong cosmopolitans and martinis and dine on solid middle-American comfort food. Retro decor includes attractive WPA-style murals, tile floors, a portrait of FDR, and an assortment of deco kitsch. Despite the Depression-era theme, The Grange Hall is a happy and somewhat hip restaurant that's comfortably designed with bare yellow walls, nickel-plated lamps, and wooden booths. And the crowd can be high on the Cool-O-Meter. Herb-breaded organic chicken breast served with fresh corn and sweet pepper salad is the specialty of the house, and the best dish on the menu. Big eaters can pig out on succotash, roasts, and pork chops with cranberry sauce, while grazers might make a meal of side dishes like potato pancakes with fresh scallion sour cream, red rice, rye and barley medley, and yam fries. Many locals come here just for dessert. The selection of American standards—including stellar wild-rice pudding, perfect devil's food cake, and top-notch fruit pies—are made by the owner's mom and have become legendary in the neighborhood. Others come primarily to drink. The bar is an excellent place for cocktails and wine, especially in winter, when the narrow lane outside is a snow-covered fairy tale.

Honmura An

170 Mercer St (btw Houston/Prince Sts). Tel. 1–212/334-5253. Reservations recommended. Lunch Wed-Sat noon-230pm; dinner Tues-Thurs 6-10pm, Fri-Sat 6-1030pm, Sun 6-930pm. Main courses $21-$28. AE, MC. V.

A deep bow to the fine art of noodles, Honmura An is a sleek Japanese pasta parlor specializing in perfectly made udon (thick wheat noodles) and soba (narrow buckwheat linguine). Unless you have spent a lot of time poking around the Shinjuku, these are probably the finest noodles you've ever had. There are several variations, served either dry or in seductively subtle broths. Perfect bento boxes of batter-fried shrimp, sashimi, and sesame-accented squash are also available. Surroundings are oh so Japanese and prices are Tokyo-high. It all appeals to knowledgeable gold-card carriers who fill the dining room nightly with noodle slurps and chopstick clacks.

I Coppi

432 East 9th St (btw First Ave/ Ave A). Tel. 1–212/254-2263. Reservations vital. Open Sun-Thurs 6-11pm, Fri-Sat 6-1130pm. Main courses $13-$25. AE, MC, V.

I Coppi is as close to Tuscany as Manhattan gets. Terracotta brick, rough wood, majolica accents, and rush-back chairs all work their spells, but it's the arias and the flowers that really finish it all off. Far from being just another pretty space, this dining room has a kitchen to match. For starters there's paper-thin tuna carpaccio with a perk-up-your-palate green-peppercorn sauce, and the salad of sliced pears with Gorgonzola and stracchino cheese is a perfect combination we wish we'd thought of. Granted, the pasta is not made on the premises, but it's the best commercial pasta available (Latini and Rustichella) and makes a terrific basis for some fine dishes. And we swear by the creamy polenta which encases layers of sautéed wild mushrooms and ground pork. Most of the *secondi* are packed with flavor too, especially the game and meat dishes like grilled wild-boar tenderloin and beef sirloin grilled with rosemary, which is sliced and served rare. Four or five different pizzas are also available and there's a good predominantly-Italian wine list. In summer, the canopied garden is one of the most enticing in the city.

Il Mulino

86 West 3rd St (btw Sullivan/Thompson Sts). Tel. 1–212/673-3783. Reservations vital. Lunch Mon-Fri noon-230pm; dinner Mon-Sat 5-11pm. Main courses $25-$36. AE, MC, V.

New Yorkers have consistently rated Il Mulino as one of their favorite Italian restaurants for more than 15 years. The draw is awesomely flavorful classic Italian cooking, friendly service, and portions that are far larger than they need to be. Meals begin with gratis garlic bread and plates of marinated eggplant, cold mussels, and Parmesan cheese. Regulars never fail to order an antipasto; indeed, many specifically come here for clams casino (with bacon on top), prosciutto with melon, or any number of sing-in-your-mouth starters. Pastas like fettuccine alfredo,

Iso

175 Second Ave (at 11th St). Tel. 1-212/777-0361. Reservations not accepted. Kitchen open Mon-Sat 530pm-midnight. Main courses $16-$24. AE, MC, V.

"Huge sushi. Small prices." That could be the motto of this good-value fish bar that's always packed to the gills with hungry locals. Tuna, yellowtail, salmon... all the standards are here, along with occasional seasonal delicacies like Kumamoto oysters, abalone, and soft-shell crab. There's not much to the standard Japanese decor of this East Village favorite and seating is not the most comfortable. Big cuts mean big lines so get there early and go solo or in pairs. And insiders never go on Sunday, the one day the fish market fails to deliver.

spaghettini carbonara, and cappelini all'arrabiata are other classic favorites that here taste otherworldly. Signature *secondi* are garlicky osso bucco and chicken with artichokes. Veal chops are reminiscent of *Jurassic Park* and seafood specials really are special. The book of Italian wines is as lengthy as it is expensive. Physically Il Mulino's got no flash, and the wait staff is not particularly attractive. The dark dining room is very noisy and always crowded—even those with reservations have to wait for tables. There is usually a limo or two parked out front but even if it's yours, you'll be treated evenhandedly. Reservations are required at least a week in advance, and if you don't have them, fugetaboutit. You may go through a few phones in your efforts to get beyond the busy signal!

Jean Claude

137 Sullivan St (btw Houston/Prince Sts). Tel. 1-212/475-9232. Reservations accepted. Kitchen open daily 630-11pm. Main courses $17-$20. No cards.

The Left Bank-style bistro that launched Jean Claude Iacovelli's empire is still his best. Tasteful, no-nonsense atmosphere—with food to match—is the secret of its success. The pocket-sized, down-to-earth dining room is all style and elegance, without any of the film-set pretense that characterizes so many lesser restaurants. It's a youth-infected space, packed with attitude-laden beautiful people speaking foreign tongues and pulling on filterless Gitanes. Jean Claude is the kind of place you could enjoy several times a week, and plenty of locals do, drawn by a short, reliable menu of moderately priced bistro fare. Roasted quail is an excellent appetizer, followed by wonderfully herbed roast chicken, competent red snapper with leeks and artichokes, or tender shrimp ravioli.

Joe's Shanghai

9 Pell St (btw Mott St/Bowery). Tel. 1-212/233-8888. Reservations not accepted. Kitchen open daily 11am-1115pm. Main courses $9-$15. No cards.

Soup-filled dumplings—both pork and crabmeat—are the specialty of the house; you will be asked if you want an order before your butt even hits the chair. Using tongs, pluck a dumpling from the steamer and place it on the large plastic spoon, provided. Bite a small corner of the dumpling so the broth oozes into the spoon. Sip the soup, then eat the dumpling. Repeat. Follow these sublime appetizers with a heaping portion of tender braised pork shoulder, rich Shanghai noodles, or wonderful tofu-based mock duck. We've never had anything less than a great meal at this popular Chinatown eatery. The restaurant is busy from morning 'til late, but shared tables and high turnover assure the wait is never impossibly long.

John's Pizzeria

278 Bleecker St (btw Sixth/Seventh Aves). Tel. 1–212/243-1680. Reservations not accepted. Kitchen open Sun–Thurs 1130am–1130pm, Fri–Sat 1130am–1230am. Main courses $6–$20. No cards.

Nothing in New York is more contentious than naming "the best" pizza place, but there can be no doubt about the most popular. It's John's, a West Village institution for over a half-century. Some would argue that John's is not "real" New York pizza. Their perfectly charred, super-thin-crust pies are far closer to the coal-fired pizzas served in Naples than they are to the doughy slices this city made famous. John's doesn't even sell slices. It's a rustic, sit-down restaurant with bullet service and high turnover. Over 50 toppings are available, but tomato-and-cheese is the pie of choice, topped with fresh garlic if you're not on a first date.

Branches: 408 East 64th St (btw First/York Aves; tel. 1–212/935-2895); 260 West 44th St (btw Broadway/Eighth Ave; tel. 1–212/391-7560).

Kang Suh

1250 Broadway (btw 31st/32nd Sts). Tel. 1–212/564-6845. Reservations not accepted. Kitchen open nonstop. Main courses $10–$14. AE, MC, V.

Generous hours, large portions, low prices, and really delicious food make this Korean Midtowner the best of its kind in the city. Kang Suh is a big, bustling, authentic place catering to homesick Koreans and adventurous natives. All the hits are here, including bulgoki (grilled marinated beef, which you spread with bean paste and roll into lettuce leaves) and bi-bimbop (an everything-but-the-kitchen-sink bowl of fried beef and vegetables tossed with rice). The bravest customers are chowing on thin slices of grilled heart (yom tong gui), stewed cows feet (jok moo chim), and fried codfish heads (muh ri jim). The waitresses are famously hurried and charmless, and the dining room is permeated with barbecue smoke so thick it impregnates every fiber of your clothing.

Komodo

186 Avenue A (at 13th St). Tel. 1–212/529-2658. Reservations accepted. Kitchen open Mon–Sat 6–1130pm, Sun 1130am–330pm and 530–1030pm. Main courses $13–$18. AE, MC, V.

Komodo is an excellent storefront restaurant with gray walls and black tablecloths that is just rough enough around the edges to appeal to neighborhood hipsters. Because of it's slightly edgy location, prices are light for what you get: exciting Asian-Latino faves such as tempura oysters with red bean-ancho sauce and sautéed Thai-style shrimp with roasted carrot and chili oil. Similar thrills can be found among chef Maggie Moore's eight or so entrees, which include roasted salmon with blood-orange guava and ginger cream, and chocolate molé chicken.

TAXI

265

WD-50

50 Clinton St (at Stanton St). Tel. 1-212/477-2900. Reservations required. Kitchen open Mon-Sat 6-11pm. Main courses $21-$34.
Chef Wylie Dufresne made a name for himself at 71 Clinton, just down the street. People talked, Dufresne moved, bettered himself, upped his prices, and the hordes arrived. The verdict? A sanctuary of demanding, clever cooking – all of which is still quite shocking for this up-and-coming but still down-at-heels neighborhood. Meals here are routinely like nothing you've ever had. Think foie gras topped with anchovies and dotted with tiny bits of crunchy chocolate. And the revelations continue all the way to dessert, which may include parsnip cake with dreamy coconut-cream cheese sorbet. Wines are offbeat too, and relatively sanely priced. Start with a signature Royal Blush cocktail, made with champagne, vodka, fresh cherry puree, and lime juice. Reservations can be tough, but singles are catered to at the bar.

Lucky Strike

59 Grand St (btw West Broadway/Wooster St). Tel. 1-212/941-0772. Reservations accepted. Kitchen open Sun-Wed noon-3am, Fri-Sat noon-4am. Main courses $9-$20. AE, MC, V.
Keith McNally is the master of creating stylish restaurants that never die. His secret? Doing things right, not just right now. Once the bôite du jour, this aging hipster remains perpetually crowded, and has even improved as it has cooled. Boasting an absurdly loyal fashionista following, Lucky Strike has matured into a cherished SoHo institution with weathered charm that can always be counted on for decent food and a happy, bustling atmosphere. The casual, copper-topped brasserie decor is kept lively with excellent music and an active, multi-culti bar scene that hits its stride between midnight and 2am. The turkey burger, sided with a mound of *frites,* is a sure-fire hit from a menu of Continental pub-grub reliables that always includes choices of fish, fowl, and farm. The wine list is good and the cocktails great.

Mekong

44 Prince St (btw Mott/Mulberry Sts). Tel. 1-212/343-8169. Reservations recommended. Kitchen open Mon-Thurs noon-11pm, Fri-Sat 1pm-midnight, Sun 1-1030pm. Main courses $11-$15. AE, MC, V.
Reasonably priced and very satisfying Viet-American meals are the order of the day at this casual NoLIta neighborhooder. Situated on a serene street and frequented by recognizable local artists and musicians, the simple dining room is dark enough not to see and be seen. Meals are well marinated with hot green peppers and lemongrass galore. A spirited shrimp and papaya salad is mixed with plenty of chili paste and lime. It's spicy stuff, if you want it, with peanut crumbs dusting lots of dishes.

Lupa

170 Thompson St (btw Bleecker/Houston). Tel. 1-212/982-5089. Reservations accepted. Lunch daily noon-245pm; dinner daily 530-1130pm. Main courses $10-$15. AE, MC, V.

Lupa is the latest from Mario Batali, currently one of Manhattan's most lauded chefs. The restaurant was conceived as a casual, lower-priced spot, but there is nothing cut-rate about the quality of the food. From pastas and sausages to oils and wines, almost everything here is custom-made for this kitchen. Once you've tasted the bucatini alla amatriciana loaded with the flavors of bacon, onions, and cilantro, or the orecchiette and spicy broccoli rabe with sweet sausage, you'll never feel good about plopping down $20 bill for a bowl of pasta again. Ditto for main courses like the classic saltimbocca or the pollo all diavola, which has a kick worthy of its name. Sides are great too, including wilted escarole or broccoli rabe soffriti, cooked with a special blend of herbs. Needless to say, this place buzzes and it's tough to get in. Arrive early or expect to wait.

Snackbar

111 West 17th St (btw Sixth/Seventh Aves). Tel. 1-212/627-3700. Reservations suggested. Kitchen open daily noon-midnight. Main courses Main courses $11-$18.

Despite its name, Snackbar is a great place for full meals in vibrant Chelsea surroundings. Having said that, food here is hard to pin down. The Snackbar canapé—brioche with white chocolate, dried apricots, Parmesan cheese, and rosemary—could easily be mistaken for a breakfast treat and tastes something like French toast. Simple grills including seared foie gras, scallops with citrus soy marinade and sweetbreads with anchovy remoulade. Order a "Snackbar Pitcher" with everything. This house-infused orange vodka concoction goes perfectly with the stylish surroundings that include a concrete bar, a lounge with cork walls, and a dining room with white vinyl banquettes. The vibe is both sexy and buzzy, perfect for dates and scensters.

Mexicana Mama's

525 Hudson St (btw Charles/10th Sts). Tel. 1-212/924-4119. Reservations not accepted. Kitchen open Tues-Sun noon-midnight. Main courses $9-$14. MC, V.

This tiny hole in the wall is packed nightly with an eclectic crowd drawn by what is arguably the best, most authentic Mexican in town. There are only a handful of tables and a tiny counter with stools where diners can enjoy the intensely flavored dishes, the best of which are chicken mole burritos that are elegantly cut sushi style, and beef slowly stewed with garlic, oregano, and tequila. Spike with some extra habañero sauce and wash it down with a terrific margaritas from the tequila bar. It's worth the crush.

267

Mi Cocina

Jane St (at Hudson St). Tel. 1–212/627-8273. Reservations suggested. Kitchen open Mon-Thurs 430-1045pm, Fri-Sat 430-1145pm, Sun 430-am-2pm. Main courses $14-$20. AE, MC, V.

Manhattan to offer authentic regional Mexican cuisine, Mi Cocina is a small, down-to-earth place with that takes beef-and-bean *tradicionales* to the next level.

chicken and bathed ... topped with a tomatillo-poblano chile sauce garnished with cream. Other winners include shrimp with roasted tomato, chipotle chile, and white wine, and chicken al agave azul, which is marinated in lime, oregano, and tequila. Powerful margaritas help you get over the fact that chips and salsa are not gratis and you'll probably have to wait for a table, at least until they expand.

Nyonya

194 Grand St (btw Mott/Mulberry Sts). Tel. 1–212/334-3669. Reservations accepted. Kitchen open daily 11am-1130pm. Main courses $8-$17. No cards.

Malaysian cooking combines Chinese, Indian, Thai, and Malay traditions, which results in some of the greatest-tasting Asian cuisine. Top-of-the-line examples are served in this plain, crowded dining room that feels as frenetic as Chinatown itself. While the waitstaff is happy to walk you through the vast menu, don't expect the pace to be leisurely. Particularly delicious appetizers include a riff on sate with crispy tofu stuffed with cucumber and bean sprouts, and Indian pancakes with deep-fried minced shrimp wrapped in bacon. There are innumerable noodle, rice, and soup dishes plus fiery shrimp sambals, extraordinarily rich and pungent chicken curry, and a terrific crab curry cooked with shredded lemongrass.

The Oyster Bar

on the lower level of Grand Central Terminal, 42nd St (btw Madison/Lexington Aves). Tel. 1–212/490-6650. Reservations recommended. Kitchen open Mon-Fri 1130am-930pm. Sat noon-930pm. Main courses $15-$29. AE, MC, V.

The Oyster Bar serves the best bivalves in the Manhattan. Or maybe it just *seems* that way due to its rich history and inimitable cellar setting, on the lower level of the city's busiest train station. Opened in 1913, The Oyster Bar is old-skool New York—a pre-nouveau haven from the highfalutin' dining that's now happening everywhere else. The best seats are for walk-in singles or duos, to the right of the entrance at a long Formica counter where you can watch the famously gruff chefs in action. Others take tables in the tiled main dining room, a comfortable enough space with vaulted ceilings that can get aggressively noisy if a large party is in the house. The emphasis of course is on seafood, and oysters are the specialty. About two dozen varieties are flown in from around the world and are in stock at all times. The pan roast is a forte. It's basically an instant stew made by combining clam juice, cream, Worcestershire sauce, spices, and a handful of fleshy oysters. The rest of the arm's-length menu reads like a survey of mid-Atlantic regional cooking and includes good clam chowders, coquille St. Jacques, crab cakes, Maryland she-crab soup, fried clams, and an extensive fish selection. An equally long wine list attracts plenty of grape nuts. On weekdays, just after offices close, this place can get as crowded as, uh, Grand Central Station.

Pão

*322 Spring St (at Greenwich St).
Tel. 1-212/334-5464. Reservations
recommended. Lunch Mon-Fri noon-
230pm; dinner daily 6-11pm. Main
courses $16-$19. AE, MC, V.*

An exciting mix of surf and turf
(especially surf) simmered in zestful
sauces is the hallmark of Portuguese
cooking, one of Europe's most
interesting and fun cuisines. Pork and
clams stewed in roasted red pepper
sauce—the unofficial Portuguese national
dish—is a lavishly prepared example of
the genre. Cod in a creamy tomato sauce
layered atop garlicky wafers is another
top choice, as is cataplana de marisco,
a spicy sausage and shellfish stew served
as an appetizer. Regulars, who include
an interesting combination of foodies,
fashionistas, and Portuguese expats,
often make a meal entirely of appetizers,
matched with a bottle or three from
the Iberian-only wine list. The space
itself is as funky as it is small, a narrow
and busy room that feels festive most
every night of the week.

Pearl Oyster Bar

*18 Cornelia St (btw Bleecker/West 4th
Sts). Tel. 1-212/691-8211. Lunch
Mon-Fri noon-230pm; dinner Mon-Sat
6-11pm. Main courses $6-$18. MC, V.*

Lots of knowledgeable locals claim that
Pearl is their favorite noshing place.
It's quick and easy to drop into this small
space, grab a stool at the marble bar or
one of the elevated tables, and enjoy up
to-the-minute fresh shellfish and seafood.
The PEI mussels with wine are out of this
world; so too is the bouillabaisse. Look
for us at the bar popping in for clam
chowder, which is made with just a hint
of bacon.

Pink Teacup

*42 Grove St (btw Bedford/Bleecker Sts).
Tel. 1-212/807-6755. Reservations
not accepted. Kitchen open Sun-Thurs
8am-midnight, Fri-Sat 8am-1am.
Main courses $9-$15. No cards.*

It's nice to see that, even in this calorie-conscious age, an unabashed temple to
cholesterol can still draw a crowd. Everyone from street urchins to celebs come to
this divvy joint for a barbecue fix—the real soulful stuff that's hard to find in NYC.
This small restaurant has been lurking behind the same pink façade for years,
turning out the same great breakfasts, delicious barbecue, gutsy pork chops, and
even pig's feet. Nothing's fancy here—just Formica tables, faux stained glass lanterns,
and plenty of extra napkins.

Rosa Mexicano

*1063 First Ave (btw 57th/58th Sts). Tel. 1-212/753-7407.
Reservations recommended. Kitchen open daily 5-
1130pm. Main courses $16-$27. AE, MC, V.*

Rosa's sure ain't no taco stand. This is real Mexican
cuisine—large plates of delicately prepared meats and fishes,
and not a burrito in sight. Most every table begins with
a round of fresh pomegranate margaritas and an order
of guacamole prepared tableside, the avocados peeled
into a large volcanic-stone mortar and blended using
perfect proportions of tomatoes, onions, chilies,

cilantro, and lime juice. Sautéed bay shrimp, marinated in a zesty mustard and chili vinaigrette, is the second most-popular starter, followed by red snapper ceviche flavored with spearmint, basil, parsley, and green olives. Regulars come here for one of two entrees: mixiote de Cordero, an chili-and-garlic-infused lamb shank steamed in parchment hiladas with molé sauce. The lack of decor is surprising, given prices and the Upper East Side location.

Ruby Foo's

1626 Broadway (at 49th St). Tel. 1–212/489-5600. Kitchen open Sun-Thurs 1130am-midnight, Fri-Sat 1130am-1am. Main courses $14-$25 (sushi deluxe, $36). AE, MC, V.
Despite the kitschy glam of the dining room and the mishmash Latin-Asian menu, Ruby Foo's delivers great-tasting food. Foo dogs, huge lanterns, lacquer tables, and a blissful Buddha set a theatrical tone. Slide into a demi-lune booth or, if you're alone, set yourself up at the counter, where you can watch the chefs slice and dice. No matter whether you order green curry chicken or crispy duck with scallion pancakes and pineapple-hoisin sauce, you'll enjoy dishes that are piquant and full of flavor. The 20 or so dim sum are excellent taste treats that, combined, make for a terrific meal. The best? Steamed barbecue pork bao buns with chile mango dipping sauce, and lobster-and-shrimp spring rolls with plum sauce.

Branch: 2182 Broadway (at 77th St; tel. 1–212/724-6700). Kitchen open Mon-Thurs 5-1130pm, Fri-Sat 5pm-1am, Sun 5pm-midnight, AE, MC, V.

Salaam Bombay

317 Greenwich St (btw Duane/Reade Sts). Tel. 1–212/226-9400. Reservations recommended. Lunch Sun-Fri 1130am-3pm; dinner daily 530-11pm. Main courses $13-$27. AE, MC, V.
One of the more elegant and interesting Indian restaurants in New York, Salaam Bombay is an upscale, downtown tandoori room cooking pan-Sub-Continental cuisine with great results. The courtly Raj-style restaurant is designed with luxurious marble floors and an elegant cloth canopy over each table. The gourmet focus is fresh fish, vegetables, and breads, the latter of which are baked in a theatrical glass booth and perfectly speckled with char. All the curry-house traditionals are here, along with biryanis and tandoori dishes. The saag paneer is excellent, made with homemade cheese and fresh spinach and a truly delicious black-bean dal. Knowledgeable and friendly servers can be relied on to guide you through the lengthy menu. Some of the best dishes come from the North and Eastern Gujarat. Undhiyu, a chunky vegetarian medley in a base of lentils, coconut, and spices, is rich and wonderful. And chicken tikka masala—tender tandoori chicken bathed in a spicy, rich cream sauce—is dynamite.

Zenith

888 Eighth Ave (btw 51st/52nd Sts). Tel. 1–212/262-8080. Reservations recommended. Kitchen open Mon-Thurs noon-10pm, Fri-Sat noon-11pm, Sun 1230-930pm. Main courses $11-$15. AE, MC, V.
This friendly, neighborhoody Asian-Vegetarian is a healthist's delight in an otherwise meat-and-potatoes neighborhood. Zestful steamed spring rolls, made with rice crêpes, are followed by excellent dairy-free pastas and wonderfully imaginative vegetable dishes. The hummus and tofu tortellini are excellent—far superior to the strictly functional atmosphere.

Sammy's Roumanian

157 Chrystie St (btw Delancy/Rivington Sts).
Tel. 1-212/673-0330. Reservations recommended.
Kitchen open Sun-Thurs 4-10pm, Fri-Sat 330-11pm.
Main courses $14-$30. AE, MC, V.

Artery-clogging Jewish comfort food and a rollicking, decidedly non-kosher dining room make unlikely bedfellows in this famous, dive-y Lower Eastsider. The crowd can be hit or miss, but when it's on, there's not a more amusing party in the city. On our last visit, there was a strolling fiddler serenading a "birthdaying" Mafia don, a quiet Chinese family, and several large tables of black-clad hipsters who spent most of the night dancing around the room. The resident musicians stir up the crowd enough to take the microphone in a kind of Yiddish version of karaoke. This wouldn't be so odd but for the menu, which is filled with cardiovascular no-no's like kishka (herb-stuffed intestinal casing), sweetbreads (brains), fertilized chicken eggs, and chopped liver mixed with heavy doses of schmaltz (rendered chicken fat). The latter sits on the table in a little pitcher. This is offbeat eating, to say the least. The Romanian hanger tenderloin alone is enough to drop you into an eater's coma. Vodka, frozen in a block of ice, is the drink of choice, along with egg creams.

Second Avenue Deli

156 Second Ave (btw 9th/10th Sts).
Tel. 1-212/677-0606. Reservations not accepted. Kitchen open Sun-Thurs 7am-midnight, Fri-Sat 7am-3am. Main courses $9-$13. AE, MC, V.

A venerable New York institution, Second Avenue Deli is situated in the center of what was once the Yiddish-language-theater district. The sidewalk outside is something of a Jewish walk of fame, etched with the names of bygone stars. Inside is more restaurant than deli, with wisecracking waiters serving an encyclopedic menu of Jewish soul food that includes chicken-in-the-pot (boiled lifeless with vegetables and noodles) and kasha varnishkas (bowtie noodles with buckwheat). Of course, they have matzo ball soup, knishes, chopped liver, and huge sandwiches too.

Sylvia's

328 Lenox Ave (btw 126th/127th Sts). Tel. 1-212/996-0660. Reservations recommended. Kitchen open Mon-Fri 11am-1030pm, Sat 8am-1030pm, Sun 11am-7pm. Main courses $9-$19. AE, MC, V.

On the one hand, Sylvia's is a Harlem cliché—the hackneyed image of Southern soul food that plays primarily to whitey. On the other hand, Sylvia's is legendary for great cooking. It has been open since 1962 and is justifiably famous for tender barbecued ribs, with meat falling off the bone and smothered in the perfect house-made sauce. The collard greens are great too. It's an energetic place, packed with busloads of tourists, slumming downtowners, and a few grandparents from the hood. Reservations are a must, especially on Sundays, when a joyous "Gospel Brunch" is served. At breakfast, go for the Southern fried chicken and grits. It'll pack you off to a good day. If you can't get to the restaurant, stop into a local gourmet food store, where canned and bottled Sylvia's sauces have recently been spotted.

Time Cafe

380 Lafayette St (btw 4th/Great Jones Sts). Tel. 1-212/533-7000. Reservations recommended. Kitchen open Mon-Tues 830am-midnight, Wed-Sun 830am-9pm, Sat 1030am-2am, Sun 1030am-midnight. Main courses $11-$20. AE, MC, V.

Ambiance, food, and location, in equal proportions, draw visitors in droves to this upbeat, organic-oriented scene spot. Depending on the time of day, Time Cafe can be an ultra-casual neighborhood eatery or a slightly edgy spot with heaping portions of scene. On warm summer afternoons, the best seats are out on the sidewalk and hefty challah sandwiches are the meal of choice. When the weather turns, diners head inside to the airy main dining room, where a wood-burning oven churns out Time Pizza, topped with apples, bacon, and Gorgonzola cheese. More substantial dishes like the hoisin-glazed short ribs or the sage-rubbed pork loin with roasted apples, both sided with smashed potatoes, are also soul-warmers. Fez, the Moroccan-flavored bar in back, is filled with comfy couches and Persian rugs and is the perfect place in which to sip Ketel One martinis. And something good is happening most every night in the downstairs performance space (*see* Chapter 9/Cabaret).

Taj

48 West 21st St (at Sixth Ave). Tel. 1-212/620-3033. Reservations recommended. Kitchen open Mon-Wed 6pm-2am, Thurs-Sat 6pm-4am. Main courses $26-$26.

Traditionally named Taj is anything but. Indian fusion is the next frontier of stylish cuisine and Taj is at the forefront of the game. This is due in no small part to the help of chef Jonathan Lindenauer, whose pedigree includes Jean-Georges and Aureole. The result is an ever-changing menu of fancy Frenchish meals with New Indian twists. Witness berry "samosas," wild greens salad spiced up with chaat masala, and tandoori-style red snapper flavored with mushroom ghee. The dining room is sizeable, contemporary and laid-back to the point that some servers even wear sandals. Larger groups can easily be accommodated here, and in such a way that they won't distract from the lovers and starlets secreted in pillow-laden booths. Signature cocktail? Absolute Citron, rosewater and champagne martini.

Virgil's Real Barbecue

152 West 44th St (btw Sixth/Broadway). Tel. 1-212/921-9494. Kitchen open Tues-Sat 1130am-midnight, Sun-Mon 1130am-11pm. Main courses $8-$22. AE, MC, V.

As soon as you step inside Virgil's foyer you're immediately bowled over by wonderful smoky aromas. This is authenticity itself that will practically lift you up and carry you into the cavernous barbecue joint. Sure enough, the flavors are oh so right, generating happy crowds slurping down Memphis-style barbecue platters served with richly flavored barbecue beans, cheese grits, and mashed potatoes. This is a place for raucous eating where, in addition to barbecue, you can pile up on delicious beef brisket, pork shoulder, and Kansas City fried chicken. Lighter eaters might choose a Louisiana-style po'boy (that's a hero down South) or one of the barbecue sandwiches.

Corner Bistro

331 West 4th St (btw Jane St/Eighth Ave). Tel. 1-212/242-9502. Reservations not accepted. Kitchen open Mon-Sat 1130am 4am, Sun noon-4am. Main courses $4-$7. No cards.

Firmly established near the top of most "best burger in NYC" lists, Corner Bistro is well known for fist-sized flame-broiled balls of ground chuck that are juicy and delicious. The sloppy Bistro burger, dripping with smoky bacon and blue cheese, is the best 3am meal in town. And there's decent BLTs, good chili, and great grilled-chicken sandwiches too. Open 'til late and often full 'til close, the "Bistro" is really just a woody dive bar, with hard oak booths, graffiti-carved tabletops, and college hoops on the TV. Draught beer and stiff shots are the drinks of choice. The crowd is an egalitarian mix of tourists, beer guzzlers, trendies, old-timers, frat boys, Wall Streeters, and foodies.

Così Sandwich Bar

165 East 52nd St (btw Lexington/Third Aves). Tel. 1-212/758-7800. Reservations not accepted. Kitchen open Mon-Fri 10am-830pm, Sat noon-5pm, Sun noon-4pm. Main courses $6-$9. AE, MC, V.

The working-class hero turns haute at these upscale sandwich shops, where crusty flat breads are baked in wood-fired ovens then filled with an astounding choice of delicacies that range from smoked meats and fishes to gourmet vegetables and cheeses. Like their sister shop in Paris, these designer lunch spots are especially known for their seasoned breads and flavorful baked fillings.

It's a zoo at the height of lunch hour. After the midday rush, you'll enjoy a fantastic meal surrounded by local office workers pretending they don't have real jobs. Decent wines are served by the glass, and nothing tops $10.

Branches: 60 East 56th St (btw Madison/Park Aves; tel. 1-212/588-1225); 38 East 45th St (btw Madison/Vanderbilt Aves; tel. 1-212/949-7400); 11 West 42nd St (btw Fifth/Sixth Aves; tel. 1-212/398-6662).

Gabriela's

685 Amsterdam Ave (at 93rd St). Tel. 1-212/961-0574. Reservations accepted only for 6 or more. Kitchen open Mon-Thurs 1130am-11pm, Fri-Sat 1130am-midnight, Sun 1130am-10pm. Main courses $7-$13. AE, MC, V.

Really good, authentic Mexican meals, huge portions, and budget prices combine in this wonderful south-of-the-border coffee shop. The best dishes are the almost impossibly juicy Yucatan-style roast chicken, the pungent pork sautéed in orange sauce, and the robust pumpkin-seed stew, chunked out with vegetables. Big crowds, festive mariachi music, and upbeat, lightning service keep Gabriela's buzzing.

273

Golden Unicorn

18 East Broadway (at Catherine St).
Tel. 1–212/941-0911. Reservations
accepted on weekdays. Kitchen open
Mon-Fri 9am-11pm, Sat-Sun 8am-
11pm. Main courses $11-$14;
dim sum $3-$5. AE, MC, V.

Pure and simple, people come here for
the great selection of dim sum, served
daily from 9am to 330pm. Hidden on the
second and third floors of a small building
in the corner of Chinatown, Golden
Unicorn is one of those exotic and
wonderful Hong Kong-style (translation:
crowded, noisy, bullet service, and lazy
susans in the middle of big round tables)
hideaways that you would never find on
your own. A huge variety of dim sum,
piled high on carts, is piloted around the
dining room by middle-aged, no-
nonsense waitresses. Hail one and start
pointing to the little treats you want:
steamed meat-filled dumplings, shrimp
turnovers, rice-noodle rolls, savory pork
triangles, and much more. Other items are
available from a vast Cantonese menu,
but they somehow seem superfluous.

Haveli

100 Second Ave (btw 5th/6th Sts).
Tel. 1–212/982-0533. Reservations
recommended. Kitchen open daily
noon-midnight. Main courses $10-
$18. AE, MC, V.

The best restaurant on Manhattan's Indian-Restaurant Row (6th St, btw
First/Second Aves) is actually located just
around the corner from it. Truth is, menus
at the dozen or so shoulder-to-shoulder
curry houses in this neighborhood are so
similar to one another, people joke
that they share a single kitchen.
But Haveli's more serene

surroundings are just a bit
finer than the competition.
Most people, including many
locals, don't know that these
restaurants are actually
Bangladeshi, specializing in
the creamy North Indian-style
dishes that are common to
both cultures. Ordering could
be as easy as closing your eyes
and pointing: Haveli never
disappoints. Lamb Madras,
vegetarian mattar paneer, and
spiced chicken-in-a-bucket
are tops.

Big Wong

67 Mott St (btw Bayard/
Canal Sts). Tel. 1–212/964-
0540. Reservations not
accepted. Kitchen open daily
9am-830pm. Main courses
$5-$8. No cards.

Of all the dive-y joints in
Chinatown, Big Wong is tops
for terrific Cantonese food at
bargain-basement prices. The
meats hanging in the front
window that is steamed by
boiling broth should tip you
off that barbecue and noodles
are the specialties of this
house. Roast duck, pork, and
spare ribs, all served at room
temperature, are fantastic, as
are the noodles, served hot in
flavorful bouillon, with or
without added meats.
Absolutely packed at lunch,
this linoleum cafeteria is one
of the best budget finds in
Chinatown.

TAXI

275

Goody's

1 East Broadway (at Chatham Sq).
Tel. 1–212/577-2922. Reservations
not accepted. Kitchen open Mon-Fri
1130am-1030pm, Sat-Sun 11am-
1030pm. Main courses $7-$17.
AE, MC, V.

If you don't want to wait for a seat at
Joe's Shanghai, then head over to this
dive-y eatery for equally good pop-in-the-
mouth soup dumplings, excellent noodle
soups, and delicious crab and pork
steamed buns for a little over $5. The best
of a long list of mains are braised spareribs
and sautéed eel served in a hot pot.

Gray's Papaya

402 Sixth Ave (btw 8th/9th Sts).
Tel. 1–212/260-3532. Kitchen open
nonstop. Hot dogs 75¢. No cards.

When your wallet is crying "uncle" and
your stomach is not far behind,
Gray's Papaya comes to the rescue
24/seven with perfectly grilled hot dogs
at prices that can't be beat. These terrific,
skinny pimp steaks are served on warm
buns and topped with sauerkraut or
onions and quality, spicy mustard. The
best part? They're a measly 75 cents
a pop. Now that's "better than filet
mignon."

  Branch: 2090 Broadway (btw
71st/72nd Sts; tel. 1–212/799-0243).

Katz's Deli

205 East Houston St (btw
Ludlow/Orchard Sts). Tel. 1–212/254-
2246. Reservations not accepted.
Kitchen open Mon-Thurs 8am-11pm,
Fri-Sat 8am-3am, Sun 8am-10pm.
Main courses $6-$10. AE, MC, V.

Opened in 1888 and little changed
since, Katz's good food, decent prices,
charmless surroundings, and comically
gruff service make it the quintessential
deli dive. Take a ticket upon entering
and place your order at the counter. Of
the long list of old-skool favorites, the
best meals here are the simplest: plump,
crispy-skinned all-beef Coney Island
hot dogs, hefty knishes, well-marbled
pastrami sandwiches, and golden fat
fries. Wash it all down with Dr.
Brown's celery soda. For a really great
sandwich, regulars suggest you "tip"
the counter person before he assembles
your meal.

Pho Bang

157 Mott St (btw Broome/Grand Sts).
Tel. 1–212/966-3797. Reservations
not accepted. Open daily 10am-10pm.
Main courses $4-$9. No cards.

This Vietnamese noodle house is a step
up from the common Chinatown grunge
spot. It makes a stab at comfort and
décor with its tile floor, classic French
café chairs, and Vietnamese scenics.
And it kills when it comes to food. The
specialties of the house are a dozen or
so versions of rice noodle beef soup and
vermicelli rice dishes studded with
everything from grilled pork and beef
to marinated grilled shrimp.

Menchanko-ti

*131 East 45th St (btw Lexington/
Third Aves). Tel. 1-212/986-6805.
Reservations accepted only for large
parties. Kitchen open daily 1130am-
midnight. Main courses $9-$13.
AE, MC, V.*

This small Japanese eatery has become
extraordinarily popular lunch stops for
neighborhood residents and office
workers alike. A dead ringer for any
number of noodle shops in Tokyo,
Menchanko-ti throws the one-two
punch of delicious and cheap, thereby
beating most competitors in
"lunchmanship." Soba and udon are
served either hot or cold in a variety of
soups and sauces that true aficionados
might find too bland and too thin.
Chicken dishes and a variety of tempuras
are also available and it all seems so
authentically Japanese—except the
reasonable prices.

  Branch: 43 West 55th St (btw
Fifth/Sixth Aves; tel. 1-212/247-1585).

Pommes Frites

*123 Second Ave (btw 7th/8th Sts).
Tel. 1-212/674-1234. Kitchen open
Sun-Thurs 1130am-1am, Fri-Sat
1130am-2am. Fries $4-$7. No cards.*

Specialization is the name of the game
at Pommes Frites, where the single
menu item—ultra-crispy Belgian fries—
is cooked to perfection. Far better than
most in Brussels, these European-style
frites are cut thick by hand, fried to
order, and served in handy paper cones.
Choose from about 30 different dipping
sauces, from mayonnaise and vinegar
to sweet mango chutney and Hawaiian
pineapple.

Rice

*227 Mott St (btw Prince/Spring Sts).
Tel. 1-212/226-5775. Reservations
not accepted. Lunch daily noon-4pm;
dinner daily 6-1145pm. Main courses
$6-$10. No cards.*

One of the busiest restaurants in NoLIta,
Rice is a cheap-and-trendy tip of the
toque to nouvelle Asian cuisine. Small,
dark, and handsome, the restaurant
offers a short menu of simplistic rice-
toppers including vegetarian sushi rolls,
Thai beef salad, and Indian chicken
curry. These can be added to many
different varieties of rice (long-grained
basmati, short-grained Japanese, black
Southeast Asian, or jasmine Thai).
It's a happening place: Cool atmosphere,
good people watching, and competent
food (in that order) translate into long
waits almost every night of the week.

Meals After Midnight

One of the very best things about New York is the dozens of places—in all price ranges—to relieve late-night munchies. Many restaurants listed above keep their kitchens open long after midnight.

Page	Restaurant	Closing Time
257	Blue Ribbon Bakery	2am
282	Cafe Lalo	Sun-Thurs 2am; Fri-Sat 4am
259	Carnegie Deli	4am
273	Corner Bistro	4am
276	Gray's Papaya	Nonstop
265	Kang Suh	Nonstop
276	Katz's Deli	Fri-Sat 3am
266	Lucky Strike	Sun-Wed 3am; Thurs-Sat 4am
254	Odeon	Sun-Fri 2am; Sat 3am
251	Pastis	Sun-Thurs 2am; Fri-Sat 3am
277	Pommes Frites	Sun-Thurs 1am; Fri-Sat 2am
271	Second Avenue Deli	Fri-Sat 3am

Big Nick's

2175 Broadway (btw 77th/78th Sts). Tel. 1–212/362-9238. Kitchen open nonstop. Main courses $5-$10. MC, V.

Think about practically any meal you're hankering for and you can probably get it at Nick's. This diner literally serves everything from chicken cacciatore to cheeseburgers, the latter of which comes with a mound of fries or deliciously crisp onion rings. Grilled fish, feta quesadillas, and meaty breakfasts are also in the house. There are at least five big menus here, and almost every inch of wall space is cluttered with additions. Open since 1962, Nick's is the embodiment of a dive-y luncheonette, with service and surroundings that seem right out of a *Saturday Night Live* sketch. The dining room itself is the only thing small about Big Nick's, one of the best late plates on the Upper West Side.

Cafe Noir

32 Grand St (at Thompson St). Tel. 1–212/431–7910. Kitchen open Sun-Thurs noon-2am, Fri-Sat noon-4am. Main courses $16-$20. AE.

A fixture on the Prada circuit, this French-Moroccan caters to the best-dressed late-nighters with designer sandwiches and tasty tapas. The ultra dim Casablanca interior is one of the sultriest places in town, especially in the loungey back room. The menu ranges from stuffed grape leaves and caviar to paella and foiegras, and there is a good list of hearty French wines. Don't forget to bring a date.

Blue Ribbon

97 Sullivan St (btw Spring/Prince Sts). Tel. 1–212/274-0404. Kitchen open daily 4pm-4am. Main courses $19-$22. AE, MC, V.

Fashionable, fun, and jammed at all hours, Blue Ribbon is the Manhattan restaurant we'd most like to own. It's hard to imagine a more successful scene spot than this polished SoHo dining room. It's just an unpretentious rectangle storefront with tightly spaced tables and a tiny oyster bar by the window. But the wonderful, eclectic menu and bustling atmosphere are like magnets for upscale downtowners. Blue Ribbon is known as the place where chefs from other restaurants go after their own kitchens close. The menu caters to both grazers and gorgers with everything from tofu ravioli and sesame-glazed catfish to fried chicken and sweetbreads. The wonderfully rich and meaty paella is chunked with lots of shellfish and savory sausage. It's a huge dish that you won't want to share. A well-stocked raw bar and decadent desserts round out the offerings.

Coffee Shop

29 Union Sq. West (btw 15th/16th Sts). Tel. 1–212/243–7969. Kitchen open Sun-Mon 8am-2am, Tue-Sat 730am-530am. Main courses $12-$16. AE, MC, V.

The 1980s hotspot that trendies love to hate is actually a great place for vampire dining in those last hours before sunrise. Unlike real coffee shops, this one can always be counted on for decent Brazilian-style food, good music, flattering lighting, and great looking staff. Add the wonderful luncheonette-counter seating of the real McCoy and you have a top late-night pick. Nobody really needs a meaty Rio de Janeiro stew at four in the morning, but it's here if you want it. Sandwiches and breakfasts too. Avoid the kitchen during more mundane hours, when it's a post-work bridge-and-tunnel traffic jam.

Empire Diner

210 Tenth Ave (btw 22nd/23rd Sts). Tel. 1-212/243-2736. Kitchen open nonstop. Main courses $11-$15. AE, MC, V.

A classic, Art Deco-style black lacquer and chrome diner, Empire is club-kid central, tourist trap, and everything in between. This greasy spoon has been the background in dozens of commercials and high prices are the inevitable result of fame. The diner is perfect if you've been partying nearby or are interested in a bout of historical slumming. Otherwise cab it to somewhere where the food is better, the wait staff friendlier, and the prices are anchored to reality.

Florent

69 Gansevoort St (btw Washington/Greenwich Sts). Tel. 1-212/989-5779. Kitchen open Mon-Thurs 9am-5am, Fri-Sun nonstop. Main courses $13-$19. No cards.

No one we know has ever been to Florent during daylight hours. This is one of New York's quintessential late-night fuel stops, often brimming with a coterie of fabulously strange-looking scenesters. One goes to this colorful Meatpacking District bistro for the scene as much as for the food. Well-groomed hipsters and bleary-eyed partiers often make this the last stop in a night of clubbing. Florent is a sophisticated diner that has become something of a downtown landmark. Passable bistro standbys include steak frites, onion soup, and boudin noir (black sausage), along with fantastic bread, budget wines, and breakfast served all night.

L'Express

249 Park Ave South (btw 19th/20th Sts). Tel. 1-212/254-5858. Kitchen open nonstop. Main courses $11-$18. AE, MC, V.

Reliable food, nonstop hours and an easy Gramercy location are the ingredients for the success of this warm and well-styled Provençal bistro. Popular with twenty-somethings looking for moderately priced eats in an otherwise expensive part of town, L'Express serves good roasted chicken, onion tarts, and steak frites in a dark and casual setting. Good wines too.

Breakfast & Brunch

Many of the restaurants listed ab[ove] breakfast and/or brunch, inclu[ding] Green, Balthazar, Rialto, The Grange[,] Golden Unicorn. Many restaurants list[ed under "...] Midnight" are also serving 24/seven. [...] are especially known for morning meals and are highly recommended.

Barney Greengrass

541 Amsterdam Ave (btw 86th/87th Sts). Tel. 1-212/724-4707. Reservations not accepted. Kitchen open Tues-Fri 830am-4pm, Sat-Sun 830am-5pm. Main courses $9-$13. MC, V.

On weekends, the lines at Barney Greengrass are as legendary as their giant fish platters of smoked sturgeon, sable, lox, and salmon. We prefer weekday mornings, when dining is less hurried and there's plenty of room to open a *New York Times*. Open since 1929, the restaurant is physically charmless, featuring wood-paneled walls and linoleum-topped tables. It's an institution, you see?

Sarabeth's

1295 Madison Ave (btw 92nd/93rd Sts). Tel. 1-212/410-7335. Reservations only accepted for dinner. Kitchen open daily 8am-1030pm. Main courses $13-$19. AE, MC, V.

The mini chain of Sarabeth's restaurants is practically synonymous with breakfast. Weekends are zoos, but even then, plenty of people think it's worth an hour's wait for sublime pumpkin waffles with sour cream, cinnamon French toast, raisin scones, and other breakfast items. Sarabeth Levine is widely considered one of the best pastry chefs in the city. For this reason alone, you should pass on the good egg dishes in favor of bakery.

Breakfast is served daily until 330pm.

Branches: 423 Amsterdam Ave (btw 80th/81st Sts; tel. 1-212/496-6280); in the Whitney Museum, 945 Madison Ave (btw 74th/75th Sts; tel. 1-212/570-3670).

Palačinka

28 Grand St (btw Thompson St/Sixth Ave). Tel. 1-212/625-0362. Kitchen open daily 10am-11pm. Main courses $5-$9. No cards.

Palačinka is the perfect place for breakfast or brunch, when you can join the rest of the leather-clad artsy Soho crowd in this tiny retro-industrial-chic diner/cafe. People come for the dozen different sweet crepes, which come in wonderful combinations of lemon and lime, chocolate and Nutella, and other permutations and combinations. Savory crepes are available too, as are soups, sandwiches, and eggy breakfast items. There's a good selection of local brews plus some wines.

Dessert & Cafes

Cafe Lalo

201 West 83rd St (btw Broadway/ Amsterdam Ave). Tel. 1–212/496–6031. Kitchen open Sun-Thurs 9am-2am, Fri-Sat 9am-4am. Main courses $5-$12. MC, V.

Sure, Lalo serves standard cafe fare, including reasonably priced soups, salads, and sandwiches, but this patisserie is famous on the Upper West Side for its desserts—an enormous selection of cakes, pies, and tarts that are divided equally between chocolate- and fruit-based treats. Huge windows facing the street open wide in summer and Lalo serves 'til late.

Caffe Reggio

119 MacDougal St (btw 3rd/Bleecker Sts). Tel. 1–212/475-9557. Kitchen open Sun-Thurs 9am-2am, Fri-Sat 9am-3am. Coffee $4-$6. No cards.

The best of the West Village cafes, Reggio is an Old World Italian coffeehouse thick with bohemian atmosphere. It's a small, rather dark place that feels like a Europe that no longer exists, and perhaps never did. The espresso is good, service is efficient, and they don't mind if you sit all day. Go in the evening and say "hi" to Jack the waiter for us.

Drip

489 Amsterdam Ave (btw 83rd/84th Sts). Tel. 1–212/875-1032. Kitchen open Mon-Thurs 8am-1am, Fri 8am-3am, Sat 9am-3am, Sun 9am-midnight. Main courses $4-$8. MC, V.

Order a *doppio* (the hip way to request a double) and get a date. Drip is a one-stop shop for Upper West Siders in search of a buzz and some action. Great brownies and cakes and mediocre sandwiches and quiches are served in kitschy, comfortable surroundings. The drinks are what sells the place and the fill-out-the-form dating service keeps them coming back.

Krispy Kreme Donuts

265 West 23rd St (btw Seventh/Eighth Aves). Tel. 1–212/620-0111. Open Sun-Thurs 6am-10pm, Fri-Sat 6am-midnight. Donuts about 85¢ each. No cards.

"It's just a donut shop," say the deprived few who have never bitten into one of Krispy Kreme's light-as-air glazed rings. You've got to get them hot off the conveyor belt for the full melt-in-your-mouth experience. That's the secret.
Branches: 280 West 125th St (at Eighth Ave; tel. 1–212/531-0111); 141 West 72nd St (btw Columbus/Amsterdam Aves; tel. 1–212/724-1100); and other locations.

Payard Patisserie & Bistro

1032 Lexington Ave (btw 73rd/74th Sts). Tel. 1–212/717-5252. Reservations recommended. Kitchen open Mon-Sat 7am-11pm. Main courses $15-$25. AE, MC, V.

François Payard, the celebrated pastry chef of Restaurant Daniel (see Celebrity Chefs, above) makes desserts the focus of his own place, a sunset-colored, Parisian-style jewel box filled with cases of sweets. A pastry with hazelnut and chocolate mousse is the specialty of the house, but you could hardly go wrong choosing a perfectly constructed fruit tart, wild-cherry Chinon, designer chocolates, homemade sorbet, or any number of other wonderful confections. Bistro meals—contemporary seasonal interpretations of French classics created by Daniel's former sous chef—are also top-notch. Dining is at petite cafe tables, among casually dressed locals and neighborhood families with kids in tow.

Food Markets

Sure, you can get decent picnic staples at supermarkets like Dagastino's and The Food Emporium, or at any number of Korean grocers all over town. But for something really special, stop into one of the city's gourmet food shops, veritable museums of cuisine that will make you wish you lived nearby. Specialties vary slightly at each of the listings below, but all can be counted on for top-quality produce, meats, cheese, baked goods, and prepared foods. A true foodie can spend hours perusing these incredible selections of imported meats, exotic fruit, fresh olives, and house-baked breads.

Chelsea Market
75 Ninth Ave (btw. 15th/16th Sts). Tel. 1–212/633-9090. Open daily 8am–8pm.
This is a great place to go food shopping because an enormous variety of fine food vendors are all under one roof at this vast warehouse. The scent of freshly baked bread emanates from Amy's Breads, which also offers wonderful brioches and other baked goods; Buon Italia offers olive oils from numerous regions in Italy, along with other superfine Italian products—olives, pastas, sausages, cheeses,—and even majolica serving dishes. There's also an excellent wine store, fine fish and meat vendors, green grocers with good quality (and fairly priced) produce, and even a florist for your table decoration.

Citarella
2135 Broadway (at 75th St). Tel. 1–212/874-0383. Open Mon–Sat 7am–9pm, Sun 9am–7pm.
Fresh seafood and prime meats are the strengths of these East- and West-side siblings. Quality is also tops in their prepared-foods sections. One-stop shopping includes charcuterie, cheese, and pastries too.
   Branch: 1313 Third Ave (at 75th St; tel. 1–212/874-0383).

Dean & DeLuca

560 Broadway (at Prince St). Tel. 1–212/431–1691. Open Mon-Sat 10am-8pm, Sun 10am-7pm.
As big and bright as a SoHo art gallery, D&D is especially known for cheese, chocolates, pastries and fresh produce, at stratospheric prices. A foodie's dream, there's no better place in the city to lick the windows.

Branches: *75 University Place* (tel. 1–212/473–1908); *in the Paramount Hotel, 235 West 46th St* (tel. 1–212/869-6890).

Zabar's

2245 Broadway (btw 80th/81st Sts). Tel. 1–212/787–2000. Open Mon-Fri 9am-730pm, Sat 9am-8pm, Sun 9am-6pm.
The quintessential New York gourmet shop for smoked salmon and other kippered fish. There are at least half a dozen varieties of the first, sliced so thin that it practically takes several slices to register on the scale. Great cheeses and gourmet cookware as well.

Fairway

2127 Broadway (btw 74th/75th Sts). Tel. 1–212/595-1888. Open daily 6am-1am.
Fairway is a huge store known for top produce at low prices plus a great cheese selection. There's lots of exotic fruits and vegetables, and a terrific gourmet grocery too.

TAXI

285

#09 NightLife
Entertaining

TAXI

287

Once home to some of the world's most famous megaclubs, New York City has mellowed considerably—and become even more extravagant in the process.

Clubland is much smaller than it was 10 years ago. Giant "danceterias" have suffered assaults from both sides: The government created the Nightclub Enforcement Task Force, and nightcrawlers seem far less interested in clubbing these days. Contemporary cognoscenti refuse to wait in line at Neanderthal-manned velvet ropes, pay nine bucks for a badly made drink, and sardine themselves into an earsplitting space where conversation is impossible. Today, we're more likely to head to a restaurant, lounge or cozy DJ bar.

Speaking of which, whatever thin line there was between nightclub and restaurant is dissolving, with the former offering full dinner menus and some restaurants devolving into velvet-rope-fronted style scenes. From Harlem and Hell's Kitchen to the Meatpacking District and the Lower East Side, Manhattan is brimming with voguish scene spots pouring expensive cocktails into Y-shaped glasses. Most lounges and wine bars are upscale places distinguished not by clientele, but by their extravagant decor, the common themes being comfy couches, low tables and small plates of food. Often attached to a kitchen, lounges blur the line between restaurant and bar. They are places where you are meant to install yourself and imbibe an expensive roster of retro cocktails—martinis, Manhattans, negronis, cosmopolitans, as well as Latin-style drinks.

When it comes to "serious" music and culture New York is unparalleled. The Metropolitan Opera, New York Philharmonic and New York City Ballet are among the world's finest. And although these venerable cultural

nstituti...s may be centenarians, their
out...re remarkably youthful.

Quantity has always been New York's
strongest suit. Think about anything you
want to do and the city delivers in spades. On
any given night there are literally hundreds of
places to listen to music, get drunk, dance, and
be entertained. In the mainstream or on the
fringe, ...thing's for sure—you'll never get bored.

To find out what's happening before you get to
town check out avantguide.com, where you'll find
inks to everything cultural that's happening in the
city, from theater and music to film, fashion, and food.
Once you arrive, head to the nearest newsstand,
check-out the metropolis' mediascape, and stock up
on the city's listings magazines. *Time Out New York*
s an excellent weekly entertainment guide with art,
theater, film, music and club listings. *PAPER*, a very
cool monthly magazine, is the best publication for
nightlife and Downtown happenings. It's a great read
too. *New York* magazine is a glossy weekly with good
istings and updates on the newest and latest clubs
and restaurants. *The New Yorker* magazine has
extensive listings of highbrow events. Other sources
of entertainment news and listings include the
Village Voice and *New York Press*, both of which
are published on Wednesdays and are available
free from sidewalk boxes. *The New York Times*
has a good Weekend section on Fridays that's
particularly strong on movies, theater, and
special events. *H/X* magazine and *HX for
Her* have good listings of gay and lesbian
happenings. Both are available free at
Downtown clubs, restaurants, music
shops, and clothing stores.

TAXI

289

Style Spots

Bubble Lounge

228 West Broadway (btw White/Franklin Sts).
Tel. 1–212/431-3433. Open Sun-Thurs 5pm-2am,
Fri-Sat 5pm-4am, Sat 6pm-4am.

Deep in the heart of Tribeca there's a place where Wall Street traders and local landowners can toast to each others success over endless glasses of fine champagne and mountains of Petrossian caviar. There are literally hundreds of sparklers to choose from—including more than 20 by the glass—but it will cost a long-bond to get obfuscated. The appealingly rich decor includes overstuffed chairs and sofas, crystal chandeliers, and live jazz on Monday and Tuesday nights—a comfortable environment that appeals to lots of PODs (people on dates).

Lot 61

550 West 21st St (btw Tenth/Eleventh Aves). Tel. 1–212/243-6555. Open Mon-Tues 6pm-2am, Wed-Sat 6pm-3am.

Lot 61 is a stylish, date-ready salon at the edge of the art-gallery district. The cavernous former truck garage is divided by sliding panels that separate a mod bar from cool lounge area set with 1940s cast-rubber sofas said to have been salvaged from Upstate insane asylums. Zebra-patterned banquettes and oversized site-specific artwork by Damien Hirst and Sean Landers round out the funky decor. A delicious menu is restricted to a long list of pricey appetizers like duck spring rolls, crab salad, and honey-lacquered quail with hazelnut vinaigrette to accompany the exquisite raspberry martinis. Reservations are essential to getting in without a hassle, even if you're not actually eating.

Lotus

409 West 14th St (btw Ninth/Tenth Aves). Tel 1–212/243-4420.
Kitchen open Sun-Fri 6-11pm, Sat 6-1130pm; club open Tues-
Sat until 4am.

A small, swanky club for Prada-wearing A-listers, Lotus is a Meatpacking District hotspot with a supper-club ambiance. The space opens into a bar with a few elevated banquettes that simultaneously put diners on stage and let them easily gun across the room. There's a balcony lounge and basement dance club too, each decorated sumptuously with glam silks and satins, painted ceilings, and lush furnishings. Lotus is designed for graying powerbrokers who want to dine

and drink while their twenty-something modelettes prance around on the dance floor (think The Donald). Easiest way to get in? Make dinner reservations and don't forget your Prada Sport loafers.

Morgans Bar

in Morgans Hotel, 237 Madison Ave (btw 37th/38th Sts). Tel. 1–212/726-7600. Open Mon-Fri 5pm-2am, Sat 6pm-315am, Sun 6pm-midnight.

The small bar hidden in the basement of Morgans Hotel is a boisterous spot, popular with fashionistas and business people in search of a quiet drink and some celebrity-watching. Rough brick walls and exposed plumbing contrast with comfortable leather chairs, some choice antiques, and the sexy flicker of candlelight. Morgans peaks after 10pm.

Pravda

281 Lafayette St (btw Prince/Houston Sts). Tel. 1–212/226-4696. Open Mon-Wed 5pm-230am, Thurs 5pm-3am, Fri-Sat 5pm-4am, Sun 6pm-130am.

If, as they say, you can judge the crowd you're with by the condition of the bathrooms, then the people who come here are a seriously stylish crew. Built by Londoners Brian and Keith McNally—the same brothers who brought us Indochine, Odeon, and "44"—Pravda is an ultra-plush post-communist lounge with wonderfully battered leather club chairs, a blini-and-Beluga menu, and a choice of dozens of vodka infusions (ginger, anise, mango...) splashed into oversized glasses.

Royalton Vodka Bar

In the Royalton Hotel, 44 West 44th St (btw Fifth/Sixth Aves). Tel. 1–212/869-4400. Open Mon-Thurs 6pm-1245am, Fri-Sat 6pm-145am. Closed Sun.

Walk into the Royalton's playroom lobby (*see* Chapter 3/Hotels), survey the noisy young scene, and then retreat to the soporific Vodka Bar, concealed on your right, just inside the hotel's front door. Looking very much like the inside of Jeannie's bottle, this tiny, quilted gem is completely filled by a padded circular banquette that only seats a dozen. It's one of the happiest rooms in the city.

TAXI

291

Temple Bar

332 Lafayette St (btw Houston/Bleecker Sts). Tel. 1–212/925-4242. Open Mon–Thurs 5pm-1am, Fri-Sat 5pm-2am, Sun 7pm–midnight.

We love this beautifully designed space. The angles provide an intimate feel, while its concealed entrance gives it a tempting, seductive air. Great bartenders mix generous $10-$13 cocktails for platinum-card-carrying artists, models, and Uptown interlopers. Bar snacks include smoked salmon, oysters, and beluga caviar.

Whiskey Bar

In the Paramount Hotel, 235 West 46th St (btw Broadway/Eighth Ave). Tel. 1–212/764-5500. Open Mon-Sat 4pm-4am, Sun 4pm-3am.

For a short time (when it first opened, of course) this was the most happening place in Midtown. The drinks are still strong, the Spandex-wearing waitresses are still beautiful, and the bar is still extraordinarily dark, which easily allows loungers to imagine they are breathing rarefied air with Hollywood's hippest. Fact is, this place would be on the A-list were it not so far north of SoHo. Its proximity to Times Square and its large clan of single-malts makes the Whiskey a terrific pre-theater or post-theater destination.

Hipster Scenes

Angel's Share

8 Stuyvesant St., 2nd fl (btw Third Ave/9th St). Tel. 1–212/777-5413. Open Sun-Wed 5pm-3am, Thurs-Sat 5pm-4am.

This small upstairs bar takes a bit of finding. You need to climb the stairs to a sushi restaurant and then go through a door to the left that opens into a pint-size room with a long bar and a handful of tables overlooking the street. It's a hidden gem with a great vibe and serious Japanese bartenders mixing good cocktails with scientific precision. Named for the alcohol that's lost to the "angels" during the aging process, this bar is a pleasant spot for conversation, but note the rules—no standing, no shouting, and no groups of more than four.

Bar 89

89 Mercer St (btw Spring/Broome Sts). Tel. 1–212/274-0989. Open daily noon-1am.

A nightly soiree of corporate card-carrying members of G7, Bar 89 is the place to go in SoHo when looking to mingle with what used to be known as the "jet set." That's the bait. The hooks are monster martinis that pack power and cool bathrooms with clear-glass toilet stalls that turn opaque when you latch them.

Ciel Rouge

176 Seventh Ave (btw 20th/21st Sts). Tel. 1–212/929-5542. Open Sun-Thurs 7am-2pm, Fri-Sat 7pm-4am.

With its crimson glow and cheesy sconces, this small Chelsea room looks and feels like a bordello—with less-friendly girls. Still, the caipirinhas here are the real McCoy. One or two of them and the whole scene looks perfectly rosy. Monday and Tuesday there's live jazz, and never a cover.

d.b.a.

41 First Ave (btw Second/Third Sts). Tel. 1–212/475-5097. Open daily 1pm-4am.

In summer, the garden is the draw at this beer-lover's boite. Throughout the year, the bar gets crowded with pseudo-boho East Village locals; that is to say, grungy guys with day jobs. There are about 20 brews on tap, plus 150 or more available in bottles. The single-malt selection is excellent and includes lots of obscure brands.

Drinkland

339 East 10th St (btw Aves A/B). Tel. 1–212/228-2435. Open Sun-Mon 8pm-2am, Tues-Sat 6pm-3am.

While the main room is designed like a hangover—with bull's-eye table tops and a centerpiece ceiling swirl—the low-lit side lounges are the main attractions, seemingly purpose-built for mashing and medicating. Drinkland's bar-meets-club ambiance suits the East Village to a T, attracting local womanizers (and "manizers") with groovy lava-lamp decor, stiff drinks, and danceable DJ tunes that keep customers whirling long into the night.

Grace

114 Franklin St (at West Broadway). Tel. 1–212/343-4200. Open daily 1130am-4am.

Grace is a beautiful Tribeca space that starts early with an after-work crowd from City Hall and Wall Street. Later, it's locals and others who like to hang downtown sipping potent apple martinis and tangerine margaritas. Grace is, well, graceful, with high brushed-metal ceilings and elegant polished-mahogany décor. It's also great for late-night dining.

Hogs & Heifers

859 Washington St (at 13th St). Tel. 1-212 /929-0655. Open Mon-Fri 11am-4am, Sat 1pm-4am, Sun 2pm-4am.

Equal parts *Deliverance* and *Easy Rider*, Hogs & Heifers is a blue-collar Harley bar for keg-bellied bikers that rates high on our pig-o-meter. Despite it's distinctly Southern tone (Confederate flag, country-western music) H&H attracts a crazy mix, a fact that garnishes a lot of press when Julia Roberts,

293

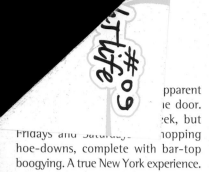

...pparent ...e door. ...ek, but Fridays and Saturdays. ...hopping hoe-downs, complete with bar-top boogying. A true New York experience.

Kemia

630 Ninth Ave (at 44th St). Tel. 1–212/582-3200. Open Tues-Sat 6pm-2am.

Equal parts lounge and martini bar, Kemia is a great place for cocktails in up-and-scummy Hell's Kitchen. The action is in the cellar, down a candlelit stairway that opens into a dreamy North African-inspired place to marinate. Add swoony lighting, sultry nouveau-Arabic tunes and fill your table with kemia, which, not incidentally, means "tapas" in Moroccan. All the hits are here, including chicken tagine, spinach and goat cheese turnovers, and cold citrus soup, which is served a la mascarpone sorbet.

Lansky Lounge

104 Norfolk St (btw Rivington/ Delancey Sts). Tel. 1–212/677-9489. Open Sun-Wed 6pm-2am, Thurs-Sat 6pm-4am.

Named for the 1930s Jewish mob boss, Lansky Lounge is a retro speakeasy run by the son of the owner of Ratner's, the venerable kosher-dairy restaurant

it's hidden behind. There's a distinct aura of cool in this glam and glittery split-level club, where young Hassidic Brooklynites, scenesters from the neighborhood, and good-looking Upper West Siders enjoy fine spirits, stinky cigars, and an array of kosher noshes. The lounge entrance is through a dark alley at 102-106 Norfolk Street. Walk past the hookers and druggies and take the iron stairs to the unmarked door. There's a small cover charge on Saturdays. It's out of the way, but worth the schlep.

B Bar

358 Bowery (at 4th St). Tel. 1–212/475-2220. Open Sun-Thurs 1130am-midnight, Fri-Sat 1130am-330am.

It's a wonderful thing when a formerly sizzling scene-bar cools down and actually improves. That's exactly what happened to the Bowery Bar (now just B Bar). Once the hottest ticket in town, it's now turned into a chic-simple saloon. It's best on Tuesdays, when this former filling station attracts a Downtown, predominantly gay crowd for "Beige." And almost any warm night in summer the outdoor patio is hard to beat. The menu features American bistro fare with Asian influences, but insiders don't even think of eating here, except maybe on weekends for the all-you-can-drink champagne brunch.

TAXI
295

Luna Park

In Union Square Park (Broadway/17th St). Tel. 1–212/475-8464. Open May-Sept only, Mon-Fri noon-midnight, Sat noon-1am, Sun noon-11pm.

From May through early September this open-air bar/restaurant at the north end of Union Square Park bustles with fashionable locals quaffing draft beers and cocktails. Warm nights draw big crowds, many of whom also come to eat a decent Mediterranean meal. Owned by the nearby Coffee Shop (but way more cool), this is a great space—one of those unusual New York spots that make this city so wonderful.

Opium Den

29 East 3rd St (btw Second Ave/Bowery). Tel. 1–212/505-7344. Open daily 8pm-4am.

We love this relaxed techno lounge, lit entirely by candlepower and enveloped in the sounds of ambient, groove, and trance. The exposed-brick living room has a couple of cozy nooks and crannies, but there's no privacy on weekends, when it seems like the whole neighborhood drops by for a drink. Try a lychee martini and toast the wee hours.

K

30 West 52nd St (bet Fifth/Sixth Aves). Tel. 1–212/265-6665. Open Mon-Sat 5pm-4am.

We can think of worse themes for a bar than the Kama Sutra. Situated above Bombay Palace restaurant, K is an epically imaginative red velvet womb in which wonderful cocktails are served in a fun and sexy setting. It's a romantic space, set with silver chairs and comfortable chaise loungers, along with a 3-D skyline of Jaipur, Kama Sutra wall carvings and Bollywood flicks on flat screens. In short, K is a style spot, co-owned by the Time Hotel's Vikram Chatwal and Mallika and Gotham Chopra (daughter and son of Deepak Chopra). DJs sometimes spin here and the nosh-sized kebabs and tikkas are good too. Head for the pillow room in back for the sexiest time.

Passerby

436 West 15th St (btw Ninth/Tenth Aves). Tel. 1–212/ 206-7321. Open daily 6pm-2am.

Gallery owner Gavin Brown's tiny mirrored bar attracts fashion designers, artists, and e-types (as in "electronic," not "ecstasy") from the surrounding neighborhood. It's best on weekends, when the uncomfortable and minimalist stools at the trio of tables are folded away and the bar becomes standing-room-only. The floor is the most dramatic aspect of the décor—flashing illuminated colored squares that change from red and yellow to green and purple and remind us of a postmodern *Saturday Night Fever.*

A Night You'll Never Remember

Bargain-shopping district by day, the Lower East Side transforms nightly into one of the most active bar scenes in the city. Ludlow and Orchard streets just south of Houston is the epicenter of this trendy "LoHo," where you can easily floss in and out of almost a dozen bars in the course of a single night. Most of the revelers tend towards career-oriented youngsters wrestling with rebellion-postponement. There's rarely a cover, and the off-center location ensures the crowd is never too *haute*—a plus in this gilded age of the velvet rope. Below are some of the best.

Adultworld

116 Suffolk St (btw Rivington/Delancey Sts). Tel. 1–212/253-0035. Open Tue-Sun 9pm-late.

Encouraged by a stipclub that owner Eric Raz loved as a young man, Adultworld is a straightforward and snazzy space hiding behind an unmarked door on a quiet residential street. The kind if place that you have to know about to find, it's a hit with black-clad hipsters who drink colored drinks from Y-shaped glasses. There's usually a DJ on hand and the going can get wild as the night wears on.

Kush

183 Orchard St (btw Houston/Stanton Sts). Tel. 1–212/677-7328. Open Tues-Sat 6pm-4am, Sun-Mon 8pm-4am.

Bring your harem to this Moroccan-inspired lounge. It's an incredibly atmospheric and romantic place built with concrete walls, richly colored tiles, and kasbah lanterns. You know, the kind of place where oranges, not pretzels, adorn the bar. Besides good cocktails, there's a particularly fine selection of wines by the glass.

Ludlow Bar

165 Ludlow St (btw Houston/Stanton Sts). Tel. 1–212/353-0536. Open Mon-Fri 6pm-4am, Sat-Sun 7pm-4am.

Nobody comes to the neighborhood specifically to visit Ludlow Bar, but everyone, it seems, floats through here sometime during the night. It's a fine cellar space with a true underground feel and good selection of draft beer. Good DJs keep shoe-gazing to a minimum.

297

Orchard Bar

200 Orchard St (btw Houston/ Stanton Sts). Tel. 1–212/673- 5350. Open Tues-Sat 8pm-4am, Sun-Mon 8pm-2am.

This postmodern attitude bar epitomizes the newly gentrified Lower East Side. Here, would-be clubbers slip by stone-faced door jockeys to groove to deejayed ambient music (including world-famous Spooky on Tuesdays). The pseudo cyber shrub decor—floral-theme video installations and Hockney-esque photo collages—attracts good-looking Oasis-loving guys and plenty of YATCH (Young Attractive, Tantalizing, Cute Hoes).

Tonic

107 Norfolk St (btw Delancey/ Rivington Sts). Tel. 1–212/358-7501. Shows usually Thurs-Sun at 8pm, 10pm and midnight.

Contemporary musicians love Tonic; indeed, it's considered by many to be the locus of today's downtown music scene. It's a quirky lounge/cafe/theater space catering to scenesters and avant-performance addicts. Most of the action is upstairs, where edgy jazz, world-beat, and electronica artists entertain. The cellar, which is open only on weekends, offers a snug chill-out room blessed with comfortable, candlelit seating, a DJ booth, and ginormous wine casks left over from the previous tenant, Kedem kosher winery! Expect rock or techno, depending on the mood.

Sapphire Lounge

249 Eldridge St (btw Houston/Rivington Sts). Tel. 1–212/777-5153. Open daily 7pm-4am.

A lounge in name only, Sapphire is a downscale concrete-and-brick bar that looks something like a basement, despite the fact that it's situated on street level. Come the weekend, the place packs out with good-looking people who come here to kick back, dance to techno, hip-hop, and reggae and have a few drinks before heading to the next place.

Welcome to the Johnsons

123 Rivington St (btw Essex/Norfolk Sts). Tel. 1–212/420-9911. Open Daily 11am-5pm and 6pm- 4am.

Johnsons is a throwback to the 1970s-era suburbs that never were. Not for us, anyhow. But if a suburban rec room is what you crave, complete with wood-paneled walls, plastic-covered sofas, and ugly wall art, you've found your nirvana. And what other bar in the city serves orange soda and root beer on draft?

Slipper Room

167 Orchard St (at Stanton St).
Tel. 1-212/253-7246. Open Tues 8pm-
2am, Wed-Sat 8pm-2am.

One of the trendiest hotspots in the neighborhood, this retro-vaudeville act often inspires some clubby customers to do a partial monty. Velvet and gilt set the scene for the cabaret artists who range from the campy Murray and Penny show to aspiring torch singers. All the the latest martinis and cocktails are on tap along with some ritzy dishes that would not be out of place in finer neighborhoods.

Cultivated Classics

Bemelman's Bar

In the Carlyle Hotel, 980 Madison Ave (btw 76th/77th Sts).
Tel. 1-212/744-1600. Open Mon-Sat 11am-130am, Sun noon-midnight.
Featuring murals by Ludwig Bemelman, author of the *Madeleine* series of children's books, Bemelman's Bar is a club-room classic in one of the city's most prestigious hotels. Luxurious leather chairs and a grand piano appeal to the hotel's older guests and WASPy neighbors.

Club Macanudo

26 East 63rd St (btw Madison/Park Aves). Tel. 1-212/752-8200.
Open Mon-Tues 5pm-1230am, Wed-Fri 5pm-130am, Sat 6pm-2am.
Of all the stinky cigar bars to open in the late 1990s, Club Mac is not only still open, but is routinely voted "best" by in-the-know SINK SCUM (Single, Independent, No Kids, Self-Centered Urban Males). It's a plush place, designed with deep leather chairs, a brass bar, Raj-style paintings, handsome humidors, and lots of clubby accessories. A good selection of single-malt whiskies, single-barrel bourbons, and vintage wines compliment a lobster-and-caviar menu. Although women have been spotted here, the club is mainly for men unencumbered by wives.

Elaine's

1703 Second Ave (btw 88th/89h Sts). Tel. 1-212/534-8103. Open daily 6pm-2am.
Elaine's is a neighborhood place in one of New York's most expensive neighborhoods. If it weren't the regular watering hole for lots of well-heeled sixty-something celebs and socialites, this place wouldn't even be on our radar screens. As it happens, Elaine's is frequented by the likes of Barbara Walters, George Plimpton, Norman Mailer, Gay Talese, Woody Allen, and a plethora of other Upper East Side regulars, not to

mention all the journalists and gossip columnists who nurse drinks here while collecting grist for their mills. Even loyalists agree that the hearty Italian food is just OK, but portions are huge and the atmosphere is terrific.

Fifty-Seven Fifty-Seven

In the Four Seasons Hotel, 57 East 57th St (btw Madison/Park Aves). Tel. 1–212/758-5700. Open Mon-Sat 3pm-1am, Sun 3pm-midnight.
While the cost/benefit ratio of the 57/57 restaurant is too low to earn it a listing in this guide, the terrific bar offers the best of all worlds, at prices that even non-platinum card holders can afford. Designed by IM Pei, with soaring ceilings and a geometric minimalism that's reminiscent of a futuristic-film set, this is a stunning place in which to sip the perfect cocktail. Fifty-Seven 57 is the ultimate see-and-be-seen stage for billionaire barflies, wannabe-hip power-brokers, and the more-than-occasional Hollywood celeb, many of whom are sleeping upstairs (*see* Chapter 3/Hotels). Nowhere else has a $17 martini tasted so crisp, served on a silver tray, sided with a dish of dried cherries, and accompanied by live piano jazz six nights a week.

FireBird

365 West 46th St (btw Eighth/Ninth Aves). Tel. 1–212/586-0244. Open Sun-Thurs 5-11pm, Fri-Sat 5-1130pm.
It's hard not to be bowledover by the sheer opulence of this ultra-upscale Russian restaurant, designed in the style of a pre-Revolutionary mansion inside twin townhouses on Restaurant Row. Lavishly deckedout with antique furnishings, elegant oil paintings, regal statuary, gold-painted ceilings, and fresh flowers, these Old World rooms are the closest we'll ever get to lounging inside a Fabergé egg. The food—braised artichokes with potatoes, marinated smoked salmon, blinis, roasted chicken with apricots, and the like—is forgettable and expensive, a bad combination if ever there was one. But there are few better places to relish such plush surroundings over some cold vodka and toast the czars.

King Cole Bar

In the St. Regis Hotel, 2 East 55th St (btw Fifth/Madison Aves). Tel. 1–212/753-4500. Open Mon-Thurs 1130am-1am, Fri-Sat 1130am-2am, Sun noon-midnight. May close earlier in summer.
As famous for its Bloody Marys as it is for its Maxfield Parrish mural, this former Establishment drinkery now pours it out for post-work execs and foreign visitors who are staying in the neighborhood.

Monkey Bar

In the Hotel Elysée, 60 East 54th St (btw Madison/Park Aves). Tel. 1-212/838-2600. Open Mon-Thurs noon-2am, Fri noon-3am, Sat 5pm-3am, Sun 5pm-midnight.

Once a favorite watering hole of hoi-polloi like Tallulah Bankhead, Humphrey Bogart, Marlene Dietrich, Joan Crawford, and Tennessee Williams, this revered hotel bar remains gloriously anchored in its Golden Age with trademark frolicking-monkey decor and olive-shaped barstools. Today's crowd is young, creative, and ambitious—think suspender-wearing hep cats from the publishing industry. Decent food is served in the attached dining room and jackets are required.

The Rainbow Grill Bar

30 Rockefeller Plaza (49th St, btw Fifth/Sixth Aves). Tel. 1-212/632-5000. Open Sun-Mon 4-1030pm, Tues-Thurs 4-1130pm, Fri-Sat 4pm-1am.

Wow! is the only appropriate response when you enter this bar, so exquisitely sexy and seductive, it practically breathes "cocktail" while whispering in your ear that you've arrived. The bar has "romantic date" written all over it and is also the ideal place to take out-of-towners for a drink and dazzle them with the lights of New York—an awesome panorama. Now under the aegis of the famous Cipriani family, the Grill's cocktail of choice is the Bellini, although gimlets, martinis, and Manhattans are all shaken or stirred by experienced hands. The bar food is upscale and good. Jackets are required.

The View

In the Marriott Marquis Hotel, 1535 Broadway (btw 45th/46th Sts). Tel. 1-212/704-8900. Open Sun-Thurs 530pm-1am, Fri-Sat 430pm-2am.

Our most unlikely recommendation is the revolving bar 48 floors above Times Square, in the hotel that just might be Manhattan's greatest architectural disaster. In-the-know locals join the Wisconsin tourists in hardy drinks at Herculean prices. The view is spectacular in all directions. There's a cocktail-hour buffet, forgettable on-hold music, and a small cover charge after 9pm.

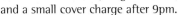

TAXI

301

Downscale Classics

The Blue Bar

In the Algonquin Hotel, 59 West 44th St (btw Fifth/Sixth Aves). Tel. 1–212/840-6800. Open Mon-Thurs 1130am-1245am, Fri-Sat 1130am-115am, Sun noon-1245am.

The drinkery adjacent to the Algonquin's legendary Round Table is a low-lit, moldy geezer bar that hasn't changed one iota since the 1920s, when the literary elite pranced through on their way from the nearby offices of *Vanity Fair* and *The New Yorker*. It's an easy stumble from most Broadway theaters.

Chumley's

86 Bedford St (btw Barrow/Grove Sts). Tel. 1–212/675-4449. Open Mon-Thurs 4pm-midnight, Fri-Sat 4pm-2am, Sun noon-midnight.

Walk under a brick portal on Bedford Street and through a small courtyard to an unmarked door that is lit at night. The concealed entrance hasn't changed since this was a speakeasy during Prohibition, and to this day kegs of beer still come up from the cellar via trick floorboards. There's little more to the casual rustic decor than a small brick fireplace and sawdust-covered floors. Chumley's attracts college-aged slackademics who carve their names in the tables and outerborough kids looking to impress friends with their intimate knowledge of the Big City. The place is packed after 9pm on weekends and, although they serve food, eating remains an afterthought.

Ginger Man

11 East 36th St (btw Fifth/Madison Aves). Tel. 1–212/532-3740. Open Mon-Wed 1130am-2am, Thurs-Fri 1130am-4am, Sat 1230pm-4am, Sun 3pm-midnight.

It's good to know about this old-fashioned, beery Midtowner, where some serious partying occurs most weekdays just after the surrounding offices close. The bar attracts a mixed crowd that includes suits, garmentos, and rowdy frat-types, all of whom are drawn by the dozens of beers on tap.

McSorley's Old Ale House

15 East 7th St (btw Second/Third Aves). Tel. 1–212/473-9148. Open Mon-Sat 11am-1am, Sun 1pm-1am.

Opened in 1854, McSorley's is one of the oldest taverns in New York, second only to Fraunces Tavern (54 Pearl St) in Lower Manhattan, which dates from 1763. It's a hip-resistant institution with sawdust on the floor, a turkey-wishbone collection above the bar, a century of history on the walls, and urinals that should be landmarked. Women weren't allowed in until the 1970s, and then only by court order. Only two kinds of beer are served—house-brand light and dark—in glasses so small you can only order them in pairs. The crowd oscillates between older locals, college biftads, and Jerseyites who line up around the block on weekends.

Old Town Bar

45 East 18th St (btw Broadway/Park Ave South). Tel. 1-212/529-6732. Open Mon-Thurs 1130am-midnight. Fri 1130am-2am, Sat noon-1am, Sun noon-11pm. Old Town Bar is another great neighborhood saloon with an authentically retro turn-of-the-century atmosphere. A long oak bar backed by an equally lengthy mirror sits opposite tight, private wooden booths where local PR and publishing workers and fashion-unconscious neighborhood types tuck into cheap and tasty burgers, sandwiches, and fried calamari.

White Horse Tavern

567 Hudson St (at 11th St). Tel. 1-212/243-9260. Open Sun-Thurs 11am-130am, Fri-Sat 11am-330am. Open since 1880, this West Village Colonial landmark is a bona fide "olde" pub with an ancient-feeling interior and a terrific neighborhood vibe. The White Horse is most famous for being the place in which writer Dylan Thomas drank himself to death. It's best in summer, when picnic tables pack out the sidewalk corral and you can raise your pint to passersby. There's a decent, inexpensive bar menu too.

Wine & Speciality-Drinks Bars

Burp Castle

41 East 7th St (btw Second/Third Aves). Tel. 1-212/982-4576. Open Sun-Thurs noon-midnight, Fri-Sat noon-2am.
If you're serious about beer, head to New York's kings of Belgian ale, where waiters in monks' habits speak in soft tones and serve 250 varieties of gourmet brew to the sound of Gregorian chants. Despite its name, the "Castle" is a small East Village dive that vigorously enforces its unusual "No Loud Talking" policy. No loud belching either.

Enoteca I Trulli

122 East 27th St (btw Park Ave South/Lexington Ave). Tel. 1-212/481-7372. Open Mon-Thurs noon-1030pm, Fri noon-11pm, Sat 5-11pm.
There's plenty of room to expand your knowledge of Italian wines in this bright and airy classic enoteca. Take a seat at the marble bar and enjoy a selection of some 40 varieties offered by the glass, accompanied by some top-quality cured meats, cheeses, and olives courtesy of I Trulli next door.

TAXI

303

#09
Bars

Flute

205 West 54th St (btw Seventh Ave/Broadway). Tel. 1–212/265-5169. Open Mon-Sat 5pm-4am, Sat 7pm-4am, Sun 7pm-2am.

It's easy to miss the stairs that lead down to this former speakeasy basement bar. Step past the velvet-curtained entrance into a room that is graced with gilt mirrors and glam alcoves that can be curtained off for a romantic tête-à-tête. The zinc bar stocks more than 20 champagnes by the glass and about 100 on the wine card. To hell with the prices, toast to your success.

Branch: 40 East 20th St (btw Park Ave/Broadway; Tel. 1–212/529-7870)

Il Posto Accanto

192 East 2nd St (btw Aves A/B). Tel. 1–212/228-3562. Open Tues-Sun 6pm-2am.

Built with blond wood, tile floors, and lace curtains, this comfortable, traditional Italian-style wine bar was one of the first of its kind in the East Village. There's about 100 wines to choose from, available by the bottle and carafe. Small plates of Italian appetizers are also on hand since, like the name says, the bar is owned by the trattoria next door.

Markt

401 West 14th St (at Ninth Ave). Tel. 1–212/727-3314. Open Mon-Fri 1130am-430pm and 530pm-1am, Sat-Sun 9am-430pm and 530pm-1am.

Wildly popular in summer, when the outdoor tables are some of the most coveted real estate in the Meatpacking District, Markt was a pioneer in this newly-hip westside neighborhood. It's a Belgian-style bar/restaurant, which means there are numerous Belgian brews (along with a fine selection of other liquors) served in a good looking wood-and-brass interior. And where there's Belgian beer there's mussels, steamed in garlic and wine, along with very good steaks, fries, and other traditionals.

Morrell Wine Bar & Cafe

1 Rockefeller Plaza (49th St, btw Fifth/Sixth Aves). Tel. 1–212/262-7700. Open Mon-Thurs 1130am-10pm, Fri-Sat 1130am-midnight.

An incredible selection of wines by the glass (about 120, ranging from $5 to $60) is what draws the local office crowd to Morrell's small, curvaceous bar. The list has to be great, considering this place is owned by one of the most prestigious wine vendors in Manhattan. There's great, if pricey, food too, served in a modern minimalist dining room.

Russian Vodka Room

265 West 52nd St (btw Broadway/ Eighth Ave). Tel. 1–212/307-5835. Open Sun-Mon 4pm-2am, Tues-Sat 4pm-3am.

There's something about this basement Russian-mafia bar that suggests some serious drinking is going on. Perhaps it's because it's old fashioned and smoke-filled. Or maybe it's just the vast stock of vodkas, including dozens of flavored varieties, behind the bar (sweet cranberry, apple cinnamon), all of which goes into martinis that are served by the carafe. There's a terrific and inexpensive caviar-and-blini menu. And the beautiful straight-out-of-Kiev waitresses are terrific.

St Andrew's

120 West 44th St (btw Sixth/Seventh Aves). Tel. 1–212/ 840-8413. Open Sun-Mon noon-10pm, Tues-Wed noon-11pm, Thurs-Sat noon-midnight.

A wee bit of Scotland set in the middle of Midtown, St Andrews is a clubby traditional restaurant with one of the finest selections of single malts anywhere. There are many singular bottles behind the bar and new arrivals are chalked up on the blackboard so that you can keep track of your tastings. Scottish and other international beers are also on tap (Tennent's and John Courage, for instance). St Andrew's is the real deal, drawing lots of middle-aged suits from the Old Country.

Sakagura

211 East 43rd St (btw Second/Third Aves). Tel. 1–212/953-7253. Open Mon-Thurs 5pm-2am, Fri 5pm-3am, Sat 6pm-2am, Sun 6pm-1am.

Early evenings this hard-to-find bar/restaurant in the basement of a nondescript high-rise is jammed like a Tokyo subway car with Japanese "biznismen" snacking on sushi and pounding saké. More brands of saké than we've ever seen (200+) are lined up behind the bar, proving that there is life beyond Sho-chi-kubai. And you can sample them all with flights of four starting at $14. Best of all, rather than being a kitschy theme bar, Sakagura is a true cultural adventure.

Xunta

174 First Ave (btw 10th/11th Sts). Tel. 1–212/614-0620. Open Sun-Thurs 5pm-midnight, Fri-Sat 5pm-2am.

A Spanish tapas bar that could have been transferred here wholesale from Barcelona or Madrid, Xunta attracts a sophisticated neighborhood crowd. Earthenware pitchers of sangria atop elevated barrel bar tables are complimented by a long list of tapas that are heavy on mussels, garlic, and shrimp. There's a good list of Spanish wines and a full range of sherries. And entertainment often includes flamenco and sultry guitar.

TAXI

#09 Gay

Gay/Lesbian Bars & Clubs

The city's Nightclub Enforcement Task Force has been especially tough on the pink-triangle set, but there's still plenty of places to get up and dance (though not necessarily in that order). Most of Manhattan's megaclubs have dedicated gay nights (*see* Dance Clubs, below), if they're not already catering to boys almost exclusively.

The scene is decidedly less exciting for lesbians - there are only about a half-dozen girl clubs in Manhattan and most are only a heartbeat away from dead during the week. Some of the best events are one-time parties at various venues around town. *PAPER* magazine and *H/X for Her*, distributed free in Chelsea and Greenwich Village bars, cafes, and clubs, contains the latest.

Barracuda

275 West 22nd St (btw Seventh/ Eighth Aves). Tel. 1–212/645-8613. Open daily 4am-4pm.

This neighborhoody bar is comfortable and the music is just low enough to allow for conversation, at least early in the evening. A few raised bar tables are upfront and there's a pool table in back. The TV plays campy drag films early in the evening but cranks up to porn after 9pm. Fun drag shows often go on in the back.

Hannah's Lava Lounge

923 8th Ave (btw 54th/55th Sts). Tel. 1–212/974-9087. Open daily noon-4am.

Straight-man's dive turned omnisexual marketplace, Hannah's is a lesbian-owned drinking hole that plays to both 30-something gays and the metrosexuals who love them. Women are also in abundance. High-backed wicker chairs, found couches, Christmas lights and a danceable jukebox make up the entire decor. Regular fun and game nights include bingo on Sundays, tarot readings, and mid-week performances by the Lounge-o-Leers.

Don Hill's

511 Greenwich St (btw Spring/ Greenwich Sts). Tel. 1-212/219-2850. Open Wed-Sun 8pm-4am.

Although gay rock is hardly new to New York, Don Hill's is the first city club to trade exclusively on the queer-core scene. The result is a very happening venue, consistently peopled with one of the most gender-inclusive crowds we've seen. There's hardcore gay porn on the video screens, but the club is decidedly egalitarian and "metrosexual"—brimming with gays, straights, and those who butter their bread on both sides. A sort of latter-day CBGBs, Don Hill's is grungy and loud, power-popped with deejayed tunes and quirky live bands that are often so bad they're good.

G

223 West 19th St (btw Seventh/Eighth Aves). Tel. 1-212/929-1085. Open daily 4pm-4am.

One of the few boy bars in the city completely devoid of any apparent element of sleaze, G is a thoroughly upscale and sophisticated hangout for the most stylish members of the rainbow-flag coalition, who come here to eye and cruise one another. There's nowhere really to sit except for a handful of chairs/ottomans upfront, so people mingle around the circular bar. It attracts a democratically mixed crowd after work and an avalanche of good-looking guys on weekends. It's a fashionable place, right down to the rear juice bar, frozen cosmopolitans, and unisex bathrooms.

Hell

59 Gansevoort St (btw Washington/Greenwich Sts). Tel. 1-212/727-1666. Open Sat-Thurs 7pm-4am, Fri 5pm-4am.

Gay bars near the West Side Highway have always been the sleaziest in town. But the so-called Meatpacking District is slowly becoming a more stylish place to hang. Hell, one of the first lounges in the area, was created by the owner's of the popular Chelsea cafe Big Cup (228 Eighth Ave; tel. 1-212/206-0059). The phallocentric, thirty-something crowd is a mix of gays and straights enjoying spicy martinis, 80s pop music, and low couches. It's a relaxed space that's best during happy hours, from 7 to 10pm.

TAXI

307

Meow Mix

269 East Houston St (at Suffolk St). Tel. 1–212/254-0688. Open daily 530pm-4am.
Although competition is thin, Meow Mix is currently the best lesbian scene in the city. There's not much to the basic bar decor except grunge, but the crowd's the thing—encouraged by good music and a different distraction every night, ranging from live bands and loud DJs to poetry readings and performance art. A bastion of dykedom of the lipstick variety, along with plenty of LUGs (lesbians until graduation), the club is very girl-oriented, but not exclusively so.

View Bar

232 Eighth Ave (at 22nd St). Tel. 1–212/929-2243. Open daily 4pm-4am.
This sleek and minimalist spot is a contemporary Chelsea DJ bar par excellence with a full dose of the muscle-boy ethos that reigns in the hood (The View, get it?) The bar is elegant, there's a pool table in back, and cosmos are the drink of choice. Beauties come to cruise and party and dance to house music.

Roxy

515 West 18th St (btw Tenth/Eleventh Aves). Tel. 1–212/645-5156. Open Tues-Sat 8pm-4am.
This vast party space, which began as a roller rink, has been making a comeback. It's one of the hottest gay parties in town on Saturday nights when Victor Calderone spins for the Chelsea boys, after which, it seems, everyone moves to Twilo. Tuesday and Wednesday are roller-boogie nights.

Code Bar

255 West 55th St (btw Eighth Ave/Broadway). Tel. 212/333-3400. Open daily 4pm-4am.

An all-around great bar, Code is a chic-simple bi-level Hell's Kitchen hangout that's stylishly designed and draws a smashing crowd. Beautiful bartenders and an approachable clientele conspire to make this attitude-free place one of the best of its kind. Weekends can be a crush, but the crowd is always amusing.

Splash

50 West 17th St (btw Fifth/Sixth Aves). Tel. 1-212/691-0073. Open daily 4pm-4am.

Tom Hanks and Darryl Hannah inspired this scene, and it's one of the most happening gay bars going. On weekends Splash is filled with a sea of beautiful men flaunting their muscles and strutting their egos. Numerous large screens flicker with erotica and go-go boys indulge in water sports. Check out the monitors in the urinals too. In short: a scene. Unescorted women, and men who are not buff, may feel like fish out of water.

Dance Clubs

Physically, Manhattan's megaclubs are some of the most attractive in the world. The sound and light systems are generally top-of-the-line, and most places have two or more dance floors grooving simultaneously. Even drug use has become elaborate. The trend is multi-substance usage rather than one signature high; CK One (a cocaine and ketamine mix) is a popular combination. When it comes to special events, some of

the best club parties (along with the occasional rave) are happening in the Meatpacking District, around Gansevoort Street on the far West Side. Check avantguide.com or the listings magazines *PAPER* and *Time Out New York* before traipsing across town in your dancing shoes.

Centro Fly

45 West 21st St (btw Fifth/Sixth Aves). Tel. 1-212/627-7770. Open Thurs-Sat 10pm-6am.

With its black-and-white decor, Op Art spirals, Plexiglas, and white banquettes and sunken lounges Centro Fly has been dubbed "shagadelic," much to the consternation of the owners. A true dance emporium, with multi-level floors and a full DJ roster, this is club-kid central, with lots of Wall Streeters and B&Ters thrown into the mix. The climax of each month is the last Saturday, when everyone turns out for superstar spinner Roger Sanchez. Dinner reservations (entrées $13-$19) are the back door into what can otherwise be a bad velvet-rope experience.

Coral Room

512 West 29th St (at Eleventh Ave). Tel. 1-212/244-1965. Open daily 10pm-4am.

Glam dance club meets romantic club, the Coral Room is a scuba-theme DJ space in which all things fishy are brought to the fore. A faux-coral-wrapped dance floor and fantastic aquarium behind the bar is augmented by the occasional live bikini-clad swimmer, stroking to the latest house beat. It's a spacious and sumptuous spot that seems to attract a little of everyone; which in our book is quite a good thing. You'll need to cab it since the Coral Room is in the middle of a very desolate ocean.

Cielo

18 Little West 12th St (btw Hudson/Washington Sts). Tel. 1-212/941-1540.

Great design and great music merge in this fabulous Stephane Dupoux (of Miami's Pearl) space. Well, the music is not always of our liking, of course, but when it's deep it is way deep. The crowd is your average actress-model wafer-thin variety. But if this is your scene than you're in for a great time.

Club MK

431 W. 16th St (btw Ninth/Tenth Aves).
Tel. 1-212/414-4282.
This Chelsea club is full-size and dazzling in intensity, yet it remains a relatively egalitarian and humanist place. It can be good any night of the week, but weekends rule because they play mainly to Koreans, who get sloshed at tables with bottle service and hit on each other at a handful of lounges. Music is all over the place, but Thursdays can bring some of the best with Body and Soul from Vinyl. A great venue.

Float

240 West 52nd St (btw 8th Ave/Broadway). Tel. 212/581-0055.
A grand venue that can stun even the most jaded club-goer, Float offers a trio of dance floors that play to some of New York's most moneyed denizens (and the boys and girls who dig them). A starlet or two is often in attendance, drinks are expensive and the door policy can be brutal. But if you want to peak at how the top five-percent live, this is the place to go.

Webster Hall

125 East 11th St (btw Third/Fourth Aves).
Tel. 1-212/353-1600. Open Thurs-Sat 10pm-4am.
A four-story disco theme park, Webster Hall is a welcoming venue with something for everyone, from reggae and rock to acid-jazz, hip-hop, and techno. There are plenty of nooks and crannies to explore and, on any given night, the club attracts the entire spectrum of clubbers, from frat boys to homeboys.

Cheek To Cheek

The Rainbow Room

30 Rockefeller Plaza (49th St, btw Fifth/Sixth Aves). Tel. 1–212/632-5000. Open daily. This fabled skyscraper supper club with revolving dance floor has been the supreme venue for the big-band sound since 1934. Today there's usually big band on Fridays only. The schedule is set four to six weeks in advance. Phone for reservations.

Live Rock, Rap, Funk & Reggae

NYCs rock 'n roll heyday was in the mid-1970s, when CBGBs was the genre's mecca, the Talking Heads and Blondie were regular performers, and Debbie Harry and Joey Ramone lived within a couple of blocks of the bar. Things have gotten a lot more corporate since then, and the music's center of gravity has moved L.A.-ward. That leaves this city with a handful of grungy spaces for unknown local alt rockers and alterna-poppers whose short sets are usually served up by the half-dozen.

Arlene Grocery

95 Stanton St (btw Ludlow/Orchard Sts).
Tel. 1–212/358-1633. Open daily 6pm-4am.
Still one of the edgiest live-rock venues in town, Arlene Grocery is a small post-punk dive with no-name thrasher bands served up nightly. It's a good place to hear up-and-comers, along with an occasional came-and-wenter debuting a new project. Few audience members stay an entire night, unless they're "with the band." But, because there's no cover during the week and it's only a few bucks on weekends, you can easily add this former bodega to your Lower East Side crawl.

Bowery Ballroom

6 Delancey St (btw Chrystie St/Bowery). Tel.
1–212/533-2111. Phone for showtimes.
This indie dance hall books a wide variety of acts from rock and folk to jazz. It's a reclaimed vaudeville theater with all the extravagant accents, from balcony to handsome proscenium stage. There's plenty of dance space and bars on all three floors.

Avant-New Yorker: Peter Gatien

The enigmatic, eyepatch-wearing czar of New York nightlife began his club career at age 19 when he took over a dilapidated tavern and booked the fledgling band Rush as the first act. Gatien opened the first Limelight club in Florida, followed by other Limelights in Atlanta, Chicago, London, and New York. Situated in a former Episcopal church (which, ironically, was also a former drug rehab center), the NYC Limelight—along with his other club, Tunnel—became ground zero for club kids in the early 1990s. Subsequent police raids led to federal racketeering charges that Gatien was operating "massive drug supermarkets." He was acquitted in 1998.

Avant*Guide_Is New York nightlife different from other cities?

Peter Gatien_New York nightlife is by far the most active in America and the only place in the country where you can go out seven days a week. It's also a very demanding, competitive, and intelligent market where every industry—including fashion, art, and music—is really well represented so you can draw a very diverse clientele. You have to be a lot more conscious of music trends and, because music has splintered a lot, you have to offer more than one dance floor. In the end, your club can be gilded in gold, but it's really the crowd that makes your club exciting or not.

A*G_What is the future of megaclubs in New York?

P.G._People have been dancing for thousands of years and they're not about to stop. Right now the nightclubs are busy, but I just don't understand the conservative mentality [of the government].... Most of the people who are in power grew up in the 60s, but their mentality is to deny others of their rite of passage. It's like this administration in New York doesn't want people to enjoy themselves. More now than ever, people need a good place to unwind, have a good time, forget about their daytime job, and go a little wild.

A*G_Are you happy?

P.G._Since my legal problems are behind me, I've really learned to appreciate things that I took for granted before. After facing the Feds there's nothing you can't handle.

Brownies

169 Ave A (btw 10th/11th Sts). Tel. 1-212/420-8392. Open daily 6pm-4am.

Decent double bills, cheap beer, and high volume are the secrets of success for this bastion of indie rock. Youthquakers are drawn by a talent they've vaguely heard of—a one-hit-wonder guitar band, perhaps—that usually takes the stage after a local garage band does a set.

CBGBs

315 Bowery (btw 1st/2nd Sts). Tel. 1-212/982-4052. Open daily 830pm-4am.

Looking something like an alley with a roof, this king of scum rock is the New York institution that launched the Patti Smith, the Talking Heads, and a host of loud and angry punk rockers. Few places would appreciate being described as "scummy," but that moniker is cherished in this hole, in which the mystique survives and a single paint job would destroy decades of credibility. Tonight's bands are mostly post-grungers, but in a rare retro performance you might still find bands and fans gobbing each other. A half-dozen bands usually play back-to-back and Monday is Open Mike night.

Mercury Lounge

217 East Houston (btw Ave A/Ludlow St). Tel. 1-212/260-4700. Open daily 730pm-4am.

This dark Lower East Sider features good local alternateen bands in a plusher-then-usual environment. It's an intimate venue with decent sound and unobstructed sight lines, even from the back bar.

TAXI

317

Live Folk, Country & Lite Rock

The Bitter End

147 Bleecker St (btw Thompson/LaGuardia Sts). Tel. 1–212/673-7030. Open Sun-Thurs 6pm-2am, Fri-Sat 8pm-4am.

Billy Joel, Carly Simon, Stevie Wonder, Arlo Guthrie, and other musical icons played at this Greenwich Village landmark before fame visited them. Today, nobody you've ever heard of can still be found strumming here seven nights a week. It's a casual space that never lost its Village-in-the-60s atmosphere (see Kenny's Castaways, below), though it can be a bridge-and-tunnel traffic jam on weekends. Cover is usually $5.

CBs 313 Gallery

313 Bowery (btw Bleecker/2nd Sts). Tel. 1–212/677-0455. Open Sun-Thurs noon-2am, Fri-Sat noon-4am.

Art gallery by day, unplugged singer/songwriter venue by night, this fashion-forward club is the antithesis of CBGBs, the furious and loud sister stage next door. For folk and experimental rock, 313 has become a top place to hear up-and-coming musicians. A bar in back and chairs in front let you choose between talking and listening. There's a good lineup of lots of bands nightly, interspersed with more than occasional improv theater and club nights. The first band usually takes the stage around 8pm.

Kenny's Castaways

157 Bleecker St (btw Thompson/Sullivan Sts). Tel. 1–212/979-9762. Open Sun-Thurs 8pm-2am, Fri-Sat 8pm-4am.

Showcasing live rock and blues nightly, Kenny's is a holdout from a previous era, when the Village was the bohemian vanguard attracting the nation's musical wannabes. Though the world has changed around it, Kenny's remains wonderfully and steadfastly attached to 1968.

Copacabana

560 West 34th St (at Eleventh Ave). Tel. 1-212/ 239-2672. Open Tues & Fri 6pm-4am, Sat 10pm-5am.
For live Latin music, it's the Copa Tuesday, Friday, and Saturday. Live meringue and salsa in one room and a disco in another, where DJs spin classic and contemporary club music in a plush red interior recalling the original 1940s "Copa."

SOBs (Sounds of Brazil)

200 Varick St (btw Houston St/Seventh Ave). Tel. 1-212/243-4940. Open daily 6pm-4am.
SOBs has carried through the decades with a tropical motif and Carmen Miranda atmosphere that dishes out daily doses of contemporary African, Caribbean, and world-beat music that traverses the Southern Hemisphere. Mondays are given over to salsa, and the price of admission includes a group dance lesson. Fridays sometimes see classic rhythm and blues bands, and, of late, live hip-hop and jungle has been added to the lineup. Phone for events and show times.

TAXI

Live Jazz & Blues

Jazz and blues clubs usually start sets at 9pm and 11pm, with an additional show on weekends after midnight. Most serve dinner, but as long as you down the usual two-drink minimum, no food is required and is usually best avoided. Phone for show times, reservations, and prices before heading out.

Lenox Lounge

288 Lenox Ave, a.k.a. Malcolm X Blvd (btw 124th/125th Sts). Tel. 1–212/427-0253. Open daily noon–4am.

Lenox Lounge was at the center of the Harlem Renaissance when artists like Billie Holiday and other jazz greats performed at this temple of jazz and Art Deco club. A Harlem dive bar by day, Lenox Lounge transforms into a great neighborhood jazz joint at night, when some of the best local musicians perform here for love, not money. It may not be the friendliest place in the world (i.e., don't get caught doing any reckless eyeballing), but when this place is hot, it's the sizzlingest space in the city. If you're not a nightfly then go and get riled up at the gospel/jazz performances on Sundays at 4pm. There's no entertainment Tuesday and Wednesday.

The Blue Note

131 West 3rd St (btw Sixth Ave/ MacDougal St). Tel. 1–212/475-8592. Open Sun-Thurs 7pm-2am, Fri-Sat 7pm-4am.

The most prestigious (and most expensive) club of them all regularly presents the biggest names in jazz, blues, R&B, and even soul, like B.B. King and Oscar Peterson, to name two. Blockbuster double bills are commonplace. Mondays showcase newer talent, and brunch with entertainment has been a great Sunday tradition for years. The space itself is as tight as a gnat's chuff, and an evening here will set you back about $30 an hour.

Iridium

1650 Broadway (at 51st St). Tel. 1–212/582-2121. Open daily 7pm-midnight.

The best jazz bar north of the Village, Iridium is a swanky, first-rate jive room with a terrific booking policy, great sound system, and fine sight lines. Players include both mainstream giants and adventurous newcomers. Guitar legend Les Paul is in the house most Monday nights.

The Jazz Standard

116 East 27th St (btw Madison/Park Aves). Tel 1–212/576-2232. Open daily 6pm-3am.

This spacious and good-looking club offers a fabulous mix of stars and up and comers and attracts serious jazz lovers. The place is swanky—a far cry from the old grungy, smoke-filled jazz joint. You can even get some good food here too.

Fat Cat

75 Christopher St (at 7th Avenue South). Tel. 212/675-7369. Open Thurs-Sat 10pm-4am.

Since the legendary Smalls closed a couple of years ago, this divvy billiards parlor has been taking up the slack, serving 6 hours of music several nights a week for a measly $10. It's really a great place to hang out, suck some beers, and hear some top-notch musicians work out their chops. And if you ever get tired you can always rack up a game.

Village Vanguard

178 Seventh Ave South (btw 11th/Perry Sts). Tel. 1-212/255-4037. Open Sun-Thurs 830pm-1245am, Sat-Sun 830pm-215am.

The Vanguard represents the top of the food chain for successful boppers. Open since 1935 and still going strong, this legendary place is the jazz world's equivalent of Yankee Stadium—the house that Miles built; or Monk or Coltrane or the Colemans (Ornette and Hawkins). Prices are enormous and sight lines are horrible, so get there early to snare a table in front, and bring your gold card.

Zinc Bar

90 West Houston St (btw Thompson St/La Guardia Pl). Tel. 1-212/477-8337. Open daily 6pm-330am.

This small jazzery is hidden in plain sight, downstairs at the southern end of the Village. Cheap and friendly, it's full of locals enjoying good jazz jams in a lighthearted environment. Arrive early, or just be plain lucky if you want a table. Otherwise, you'll probably be bopping by the bar—which is actually the best place to be on Saturdays and Sundays when Brazilian bands are in the house. Cover is low and reservations are not accepted.

TAXI

321

#09
Classical

Classical Music, Opera & Dance

Nightlife #09

Lincoln Center for the Performing Arts, 64th St and Broadway (btw Columbus/Amsterdam Aves; tel. 1-212/875-5400), incorporating Avery Fisher Hall, the Metropolitan Opera House, Alice Tully Hall, the New York State Theater, the Vivian Beaumont Theater, Julliard School of Music, the Guggenheim Bandshell, and a public library for the performing arts, is New York's one-stop shop for top-rated "serious music," opera, and dance.

The Center's Avery Fisher Hall is home to the **New York Philharmonic** (tel. 1-212/875-5030), the oldest symphony orchestra in the United States. Founded in 1842, this is one of the world's great orchestras, performing a broad repertoire which includes Tchaikovsky, Mahler, Rachmaninoff, Strauss, Toscanini, Stravinsky, Boulez, and Bernstein. Musical Director Kurt Masur worked hard to broaden the orchestra's audience and make it more accessible to lay listeners by peppering each season with contemporary works and creating programs like "American Classics," which featured vocal and orchestral works by the likes of Barber, Bernstein, and Copland. Even those with untrained ears can notice that the acoustics in Avery Fisher Hall are less than perfect. Renovations have improved the place, but it's still hard for a conductor to tease the subtle notes here. The hard-working Philharmonic plays the majority of their 200 concerts a year here, in a season that runs from September through June. Ticket prices range from about $15 to $80 for the best seats on the first tier.

TAXI

323

Opera

In addition to the Met and the NYC Opera, there are literally dozens of small opera companies in the city offering stages to younger singers. Lots of big-time divas are alumni of the city's lesser-known companies, and smaller shows are especially good for hearing lesser-known works. Companies to look out for include **The Amato Opera**, *319 Bowery (at 2nd St; tel. 1–212/228-8200)*; **Opera Orchestra of New York**, *Carnegie Hall (tel. 1–212/799-1982)*; and **New York Grand Opera** *(tel. 1–212/245-8837)*. Many critics scoff that pygmy operas are created for the benefit of junior singers and composers rather than the audiences they perform for. So unless you are a die-hard opera fan, or you spot a show in the listings magazines that really piques your interest, it's probably best to spend your time at Lincoln Center.

Metropolitan Opera

At Lincoln Center, 64th St and Broadway. Tel. 1–212/362-6000.
The Metropolitan Opera has been one of the world's leading companies since its inception in 1883. In any one season the company usually performs 25 or so operas, including about six new productions. They range from the popular Verdi and Puccini repertoire to less-familiar works by Busoni, Prokofiev, and others. More than two dozen world premieres have been held at the Met, including John Harbison's *The Great Gatsby* in December 1999, a performance that irked some traditionalists in their $250 boxes, who have been known to boo directors mounting productions deemed too avant.

The Metropolitan Opera House itself might be the best theater for grand opera anywhere, and it's absolutely worth visiting. Behind two huge Marc Chagall paintings and a sweeping white-and-crimson grand staircase is an enormous, horseshoe-shaped auditorium filled with comfortable seats. It's decorated in red velvet and gold leaf and lit by dramatic mobile crystal chandeliers. Each guest—even those standing at the railings—has an individual "Met Titles" screen, which provides instant English translations of the action on the stage. Artistic Director James Levine presides over the cavernous orchestra pit, and directs performances that make full use of stage turntables, elevators, and some of the world's best set and costume designers.

Seats range from $25 to $250. Standing room at the Met is one of New York's best bargains. Tickets are available at the box office one hour before curtain, and you can usually find an empty seat after the lights go down.

New York City Opera

at Lincoln Center's New York State Theater, 64th St and Broadway. Tel. 1–212/870-5570.
While conventionalists rule at the Met, unorthodoxy is the religion of the NYC Opera. Here they might perform *Faust* one night and a vintage Broadway musical the next. All types of musical theater are performed here, with an emphasis on English-language productions and contemporary classics from around the world. Artistic Director Paul Kellogg does not shrink from controversy in his quest for fresh talent. Don't expect opera as usual at this company. Seats range from $25 to $98.

When it comes to dance, New York has long been the center of the world. From George Balanchine and Martha Graham to Mikhail Baryshnikov and Jerome Robbins, almost all the biggest names from the classical and modern schools have based themselves here. In addition to Mark Morris, Paul Taylor, Alvin Ailey, the Joffrey, and Dance Theater of Harlem—all of which perform here on an irregular basis—keep an eye out for the Seán Curran Company, directed by the choreographer of the hit East Village show *Stomp*.

The New York City Ballet

At Lincoln Center's New York State Theater, 64th St and Broadway. Tel. 1–212/870-5570.

The NYC Ballet was born in 1948 out of a desire to train talented American dancers, instead of importing artists from abroad. George Balanchine was the troupe's first great teacher. Both he and choreographer Jerome Robbins fashioned the City Ballet into one of the most respected companies anywhere. The Ballet remains unique in that it trains its own artists (over 350 aspiring dancers are being schooled in the adjacent Rose Building), creates its own works, and performs in its own homes, at Lincoln Center and the Saratoga Performing Arts Center in upstate New York (during summer). The 90-dancer company is also the dance world's best-dressed, outfitted with more than 9000 costumes created by the late Madame Karinska, who was famous for her use of luxurious fabrics and exquisite workmanship. The Ballet is on-stage 23 weeks a year performing an active repertory of over 100 works. The most famous of these is Balanchine's Christmas spectacular, "Nutcracker Suite," which runs each year from November through January.

American Ballet Theatre

At the Lincoln Center Opera House, 64th St and Broadway; and City Center, 131 West 55th St (btw Sixth/Seventh Aves). Tel. 1–212/477-3030.

Since its launch in 1939 the American Ballet Theatre (ABT) has pursued the dual goals of dancing all the great 19th-century classical ballets, such as *Swan Lake*, *Sleeping Beauty,* and *Giselle*, while encouraging the creation of new works by contemporary choreographers. Under Mikhail Baryshnikov's artistic direction in the 1980s, the company's classical tradition was strengthened and refined. Over the years, ABT has commissioned works by all the choreographic geniuses of the 20th century, including George Balanchine, Jerome Robbins, and Agnes de Mille. Twyla Tharp's memorable *Push Comes to Shove* was created for the company in 1976 and provided Mikhail Baryshnikov with one of his most defining moments. Her newer works have premiered at ABT.

TAXI

325

Theater

The heart of the Broadway Theater District, between Broadway and Eighth Avenue from West 44th to 48th streets, is clogged with tour buses filled with Midwestern school groups heading to see *Les Misérables, Miss Saigon, The Phantom of the Opera, Rent,* and *Titanic*. Happily, the best shows are usually less popular than the hit musicals, and off-Broadway productions are practically unknown to the masses. Most shows begin at 8pm, and the majority of theaters are dark Mondays.

Information

Getting info on what's happening in the theaters is not a difficult feat. *New York* magazine, *Time Out New York* and the Friday and Sunday editions of *The New York Times* all have excellent, comprehensive theater listings.

You can also get the latest info on Broadway and Off-Broadway shows by calling **The League of American Theatres and Producers' Broadway Line** (tel. 1–212/302-4111).

Recent reviews of theater, music, dance, and art are available on the Internet from **The New York Times on the Web** (www.nytimes.com), the **New York Theatre Wire** (www.nytheatre-wire.com), and the **League of American Theatres and Producers** (www.broadway.org).

Getting Tickets

Theater tickets can be purchased in advance or on the day of performance at theater box offices. For a service charge ranging from $3 to $6, you can purchase tickets by phone through **Tele-Charge** (tel. 1–212/239-6200) or **TicketMaster** (tel. 1–212/307-4100).

TKTS (tel. 1–212/768-1818) booths in Times Square (Broadway at 47th St) and downtown at South Street Seaport (at Front/John Sts) sell same-day theater tickets to on- and off-Broadway productions for up to 50% off box-office prices, plus a $2.50 service charge. Situated outdoors on a traffic island, the Times Square location opens at noon for matinees and 3pm for evening shows. It's not unwise to show up late, as additional tickets often go on sale immediately before curtain time. Because it's

NO STANDING
ANYTIME
→

DEPT. OF TRANSPORTATION

#09
Stag

far less
Dow
c

ABSO

"BROADWAY HAS A
LOVELY NEW MUSICAL."

TAXI

327

convenient for most people, the ...ntown booth is consistently less ...owded than the Midtown one. It's also ▮ doors and sells matinee tickets a da▮ n advance. Both locations only acce▮ cash and traveler's cheques.

Ju▮ because the show you want to see ▮ d out doesn't mean you're SOL. When no VIPs appear to claim them, theaters offer their best **"house" seats** to the general public on the day of the show. Ask about these when you belly up to the box office.

Broadway Cares/Equity Fights AIDS (tel. 1–212/840-0770, ext. 230) and **The Actor's Fund** (tel. 1–212/221-730▮ ext. 133) are both non-profit charities that sell great seats to top shows for twice their face value. Tickets are released 48 hours before each performance, and half of what you pay is tax-deductible.

Some theaters offer low-priced **standing-room-only** tickets on the day o▮ how, and, once you're in, it's rare ▮▮ to find an empty seat. Many prod▮ ions also offer discounted **"rush" tickets** for students, usually available 30 minutes prior to show time.

When all else fails, take a deep breath and talk to a hotel concierge or a legal scalper like **Ticket Box** (tel. 1–800/842-5440), **Prestige Entertainment** (tel. 1–800/243-8849), and **East Coast Ticket Exchange** (tel. 1 ▮ 800/565-8499). **Continental Gues▮ Services** delivers instant seat availability and confirmations on the internet (www.intercharge.com).

Off-Broadway Performance Spaces

Most off-Broadway productions are mounted in the East Village or the Lower East Side where rents are cheap and audiences are more forgiving. Check the listings magazines for program information and show times.

PS 122

150 First Ave (at 9th St). Tel. 1–212/477-5829.
Because it consistently hosts great shows, this former elementary school is our candidate for best off-Broadway theater. There's always something cool happening here. PS 122 gave a stage to Spalding Gray, Karen Finley, and lots of others who played here before fame visited them. And these alums keep coming back long after they can fill larger and pricier spaces elsewhere. There are two theaters. The best seats in the larger upstairs venue are right in the middle.

The Kitchen

512 West 19th St (btw Tenth/Eleventh Aves). Tel. 1-212/255-5793.

The Kitchen has been NYC's premiere avant music, dance, and performance space for over 25 years. Its specialty is esoteric presentations of New Art that is largely inaccessible to most mortals. If you have a passion for the strange and extraordinary, there's something here for you most every night of the week.

La Mama, E.T.C.

74-A East 4th St (btw Second Ave/Bowery). Tel. 1-212/475-7710.

For almost 40 years La Mama has been producing some of the city's best off-off-Broadway theater. Look for everything from the first staging of new comedies to offbeat classics like Brecht's *The Caucasian Chalk Circle*.

Here

145 Sixth Ave (btw Spring/Dominick Sts). Tel. 1-212/647-0202.

A fantastic multi-disciplinary studio in SoHo, Here comprises a cafe, art gallery, and three performance spaces that sometimes operate simultaneously. Productions run the gamut from dance and "dramedy" to underwater puppet theater.

Knitting Factory

74 Leonard St (btw Church St/Broadway). Tel. 1-212/219-3055.

This multi-story, double-staged complex is Manhattan's king of alternative productions. Any given night you'll find folk rock, drama, spoken word, and very avant jazz. Two well-stocked bars specialize in microbrews.

Cabaret

Bar d'O

29 Bedford St (at Downing St). Tel. 1-212/627-1580. Open Sun-Thurs 7pm-2am, Fri-Sat 7pm-4am.

Each Tuesday, Saturday, and Sunday, this sleepy West Village lounge is brought to life by Joey Arias, Raven-O, and Sherry Vine—New York's hardest-working transgenderists. Bar d'O is little more than a small room with plushly pillowed couches and a wooden bar at one end. But thrice weekly it explodes with fun as Arias "channels" Billie Holiday, Vine belts out jazz standards, and Raven-O chirps sweet originals. Most members of the crowd are gay but the vibe is gender-inclusive.

TAXI

329

#09 Stage

Cafe Carlyle

In the Carlyle Hotel, 35 East 76th St (btw Madison/Park Aves). Tel. 1–212/744–1600.
The classic cabaret room of the posh Carlyle Hotel gives a regular stage to velvety smile-addicted Bobby Short and director/clarinetist Woody Allen, who performs with Eddy Davis and his New Orleans Jazz Band on Monday nights. Other worthy stylists to look out for are Andrea Marcovicci, Amanda McBroom, and Julie Wilson.

Don't Tell Mama

343 West 46th St (btw 8th/9th Aves). Tel. 1–212/757–0788.
The hardest-working nightclub in town has two busy cabaret rooms and a popular sing-along piano bar. It's not hype or hyperbole to say that there's always something good going on here. There are sometimes as many as a half-dozen different happenings in a single night, ranging from show-tune and torch-song crooners to small-scale improv shows. The action usually gets underway around 9pm.

Duplex

61 Christopher St (at Seventh Ave). Tel. 1–212/255–5438. Open Mon-Fri 4pm-4am, Sat-Sun 3pm-4am.
The West Village's synagogue of high camp is a multi-level space brimming with comedy, cabaret, and musical theater, much of which seems to be performed by gender illusionists with tongue firmly in cheek. The main room is set with small cocktail tables facing the main stage, but with so many characters in the audience, it's often hard to distinguish spectators from performers.

Fez

At Time Cafe, 380 Lafayette St (btw 4th/Great Jones Sts). Tel. 1–212/533–7000.
This neo-Moroccan is the pre-SoHo crowd's preferred spot to hear the sounds of world beat, cabaret, pop, poetry, and jazz. Beneath an exotically styled bar-lounge filled with comfy couches and Persian rugs is a dimly lit, sexy showroom designed with candlelit tables and gold lamé curtains. The raised back booths are best but tough to snag unless you make a reservation and arrive early. Something is happening every night of the week. The 14-piece Mingus Big Band holds down the house every Thursday for two perfor-mances; shows usually begin between 7 and 9 pm. The crowd is good-looking, young, and employed, and the full menu from the upstairs Time Café is available (*see* Chapter 8/Dining).

Comedy

It seems like every comedy club advertises that theirs is the place where Jerry Seinfeld, David Letterman, Billy Crystal, and every other funny bone got their starts. None of them is lying: When you're a struggling comedian you play everywhere. All of the clubs below offer essentially the same acts: Comedians are served up by the half-dozen and, despite the occasional "sarcastrophe," quality is tops. Most clubs charge about $10 on weeknights and $20 on weekends, and there's usually a two-drink minimum. Phone for show times and reservations.

Boston Comedy Club
    82 West 3rd St (btw Thompson/Sullivan Sts). Tel. 1–212/477-1000.
Caroline's Comedy Club
    1626 Broadway (btw 49th/50th Sts). Tel. 1–212/956-0101.
Comedy Cellar
    117 MacDougal St (btw West 3rd/Bleecker Sts). Tel. 1–212/254-3480.
Comic Strip
    1568 Second Ave (btw 81st/82nd Sts). Tel. 1–212/861-9386.
Dangerfield's
    1110 First Ave (btw 61st/62nd Sts). Tel. 1–212/593-1650.
Gotham Comedy Club
    34 West 22nd St (btw Fifth/Sixth Aves). Tel. 1–212/367-9000.

Film

New York is a city of cinemaniacs. Big films often open on New York screens before they're unveiled anywhere else, and even where ticket prices approach $10, evening shows constantly sell out. Most theaters show Hollywood flash and trash exclusively, but there are still a handful of alternative houses.

The **Walter Reade Theater** (see below) is the best in the city. Built in 1991 by the Lincoln Center Film Society, it features a huge screen, great sound, thickly padded seats, and great lines of vision from every seat in the house.

Cineplex Odeon's Worldwide Plaza, 50th St (btw Eighth/Ninth Aves; tel. 1–212/777-3456) is good to know about because it shows movies for about a third the price of most other theaters. Films seem to arrive here about the same time they're released on video.

There are two **IMAX theaters** in the city—Loews Lincoln Square, 1998 Broadway (at 68th St; tel. 1–212/336-5000); and the IMAX Theater at the

TAXI

331

Museum of Natural History, Central Park West (btw 77th/81st Sts; tel. 1-212/769-5034). Programs on these eight-story-high screens usually change every few months. All the listings magazines and most newspapers have comprehensive movie listings. MoviePhone (tel. 1-212/777-3456) is the number to call for automated information on what's playing at every major cinema in the city. The line doesn't cost any money, but you pay for the service by having to listen to horrible advertisements for films. Using your credit card, you can purchase tickets by phone too, for a small service charge per ticket.

New York's Non-Hollywood Screens

Angelika Film Center
18 West Houston St (at Mercer St).Tel. 1-212/995-2000.

Anthology Film Archives
32 Second Ave (at 2nd St). Tel. 1-212/505-5181.

Cinema Village
22 East 12th St (btw University Place/
Fifth Ave). Tel. 1-212/924-3363.

Film Forum
209 West Houston St (btw 6th Ave/Varick St).
Tel. 1-212/727-8110.

Lincoln Plaza Cinemas
1886 Broadway (btw 62nd/63rd Sts). Tel. 1-212/757-2280.

Museum of Modern Art Gramercy Theater
127 East 23rd St (at Lexington Ave). Tel. 1-212/708-9480.

Quad Cinema
34 West 13th St (btw Fifth/Sixth Aves). Tel. 1-212/255-8800.

Paris Theater
4 West 58th St (btw Fifth/Sixth Aves). Tel. 1-212/688-3800.

Walter Reade at Lincoln Center
165 West 65th St (btw Broadway/Columbus Ave).
Tel. 1-212/875-5600.

Film Festivals

The **New York Film Festival** (tel. 1-212/875-5600), held in late September or early October, features about 20 films from studios and independents both big and small. The year's best documentaries are screened at the **Margaret Meade Film Festival** (tel. 1-212/769-5650), held each November at the Museum of Natural History. NYU film school students screen their best at the annual **First Run Festival** each April. And the **Lesbian and Gay Film Festival** hits New York in June at the Public Theater in the East Village.

These are bad times for sex in New York. After former Mayor Giuliani aimed his so-called "Quality of Life" reforms at the city's dens of iniquity, several strip clubs, sex parlors, and peep shops were forcibly shuttered. It's a far cry from 1977, when, despite torrential rain, the line stretched around the block for the opening night of the swingers club Plato's Retreat. We're certainly not saying that consensual non-monogamy is completely dead in NYC—The Bell Atlantic Manhattan Yellow Pages contains 40 pages of ads and listings for personal companions under the heading "Escorts" (most are open nonstop and accept credit cards)—but, most of the city's existing sex clubs are musky, men-only affairs. At the moment, there are still several venues in which to see stripping cleavage-wielders, and many of the Eighth Avenue video shops (btw 34th/48th Sts) are skirting around anti-X laws by also offering T-shirts and other tourist junk.

The best guide to everything lascivious in the city is *Sexy New York,* a pocket-size primer that's sold in most bookstores and magazine shops.

Le Trapeze

17 East 27th St (btw Fifth/Madison Aves). Tel. 1-212/532-0298. *Open by appointment.* Le Trapeze can be great, or not. It's really hit or miss. Either way, the club is best on Fridays and Saturdays, when it gets filled with board suburbanites. Mid-week is usually dead. There are a lot of older (read: 40-something) couples, but babes do make this scene. It costs $135 per couple (no single men allowed), but towels and condoms are free.

Checkmates

East 58th St. Tel. 1-212/686-5477. *Open by appointment.* This Upper East Sider is our friend Gary's favorite New York City club, hands down. Or hands pretty much anywhere for that matter. That said, this place doesn't hold a candle to those that we have been to in Europe, on the West Coast, or practically everywhere else for that matter. Still, for a man like Gary to be a regular at this place, it must have something special going for it.

The Lure

409 West 13th St (btw Ninth/Tenth Aves). Tel. 1-212/741-3919. *Open daily 8pm-4am.* This leather fetish house with a strict dress code (on Friday and Saturday) lures a hard-core crowd of rubber-clad musclemen who do the "five knuckle shuffle" and act out their most warped fantasies. Cover ranges from $10 to $20.

#10 Planning
Before You Go Essentials

Planning Information

The www.avantguide.com CyberSupplement™ is the best source for happenings in New York during your stay. Visit us for up-to-date info on cultural events, restaurant openings, and more.

For specific questions, contact the **New York Convention & Visitors Bureau** (tel. 1–212/484–1200; www.nycvisit.com). The Bureau's free *Official NYC Guide* contains about 30 discount coupons to stores, attractions, sightseeing companies, and more. It's published quarterly and is available by mail.

For information about trade shows and conventions happening at the **Javits Convention Center,** check out their Web site (www.javitscenter.com).

NYC Weather Averages

Month	Temperature Ranges	
January	26-38F	-03-03C
February	27-40F	-03-04C
March	34-49F	01-09C
April	44-61F	07-16C
May	53-72F	12-22C
June	63-80F	17-27C
July	68-85F	20-29C
August	67-84F	19-29C
September	60-77F	16-25C
October	50-66F	10-19C
November	41-54F	05-12C
December	31-42F	-01-06C

Braille and large-print information about New York City are available from The Lighthouse (tel. 1–212/821-9200). **Big Apple Greeter** (tel. 1–212/669-8159; fax 1–212/669-4900; TTY 1–212/669-8273; www.bigapplegreeter .org), a free public service that connects visitors with knowledgeable volunteer guides, is especially well-suited to disabled travelers. Greeters are not professional tour guides, but ordinary New Yorkers who volunteer to pass on their love of the city to visitors from around the world. Many Greeters are disabled themselves and are particularly sensitive to the needs of special travelers. Ask them to send you the Mayor's Office for People with Disabilities' free *Access Guide for People with Disabilities*, a guide to the accessibility of the city's cultural institutions, restaurants, and hotels.

MTA-New York City Transit offers a wide range of services and programs for people with disabilities, ranging from Access-a-Ride (a call-ahead van service for those unable to use city bus or subway service) to Braille subway maps and reduced-fare programs. Call the MTA (tel. 718/330-1234) for their free booklet *Accessible Travel*.

Wheelchair users and one companion can get discounts at some Broadway theaters, subject to availability. Phone theater box offices or Telecharge for information.

For Travelers with Disabilities

New York City is very hospitable to wheelchair-bound and other disabled travelers. The terrain is relatively flat and every curb and public building is ramped, although some may need some smoothing.

Access for All, published by Hospital Audiences, Inc. (tel. 1–212/575-7676; fax 1–212/575-7669; TTY 1–212/575-7673), is an excellent guide to New York City's cultural institutions for people with disabilities. The book includes comprehensive information on elevators, ramps, Braille signage, services for people who are hearing impaired, restroom facilities, and more. This guide allows you to evaluate the accessibility of cultural institutions from museums and art galleries to Broadway theaters and top sights.

Saving Money Getting There

Frankly, we don't trust most travel agents to really dig for the lowest fare. They get paid a percentage of the price of each ticket, so it doesn't benefit them to spend more time trying to make less money. We usually make reservations ourselves, directly with the airlines, then visit our travel agent for ticketing. Here's the secret to getting the best deal: If you don't know airline jargon, don't use it. Just ask for the lowest fare. If you're flexible with dates and times, tell the sales agent. Ask him or her to hunt a bit.

When it comes right down to it, it doesn't really matter which of New York's three airports you fly into. They are all more or less close to Manhattan, and each has its drawbacks and advantages. John F. Kennedy (JFK) and La Guardia are closer to Manhattan's east side, while Newark is more convenient for those staying on the west. More importantly, choose an airport you can fly in and out of while avoiding rush hours (7-10am inbound; 4-8pm outbound). This will save you a lot of frustration and drive time. See Chapter 2/Arriving for complete information regarding transportation to and from New York's airports.

Airlines on the Web

Recently, we've been finding the best fares on www.orbitz.com, a comprehensive ticketing site owned by a consortium of airlines. Other booking sites that rate high on our list are www.travelocity.com (which taps into professional travel agents' Sabre reservations system), www.expedia.com (which negotiates special fares with airlines), and www.lowestfare.com and www.cheaptickets.com, both of which are consolidators that buy airline seats in bulk in return for deep discounts.

Airline	US Telephone	UK Telephone
Air Canada	1-888/247-2262	0990/247226
Air France	1-800/237-2747	0345/581393
Air India	1-212/751-6200	01753/684828
Air New Zealand	1-800/262-1234	0208/741-2299
Alaska Airlines	1-800/252-7522	---------
Alitalia	1-800/223-5730	0870/544-8259
American Airlines	1-800/433-7300	0345/789789
Austrian Airlines	1-800/843 0002	0207/439-0741
British Airways	1-800/247 9297	0345/222111
Continental Airlines	1-800/231-0856	0800/776464
Delta Air Lines	1-800/221-1212	0800/414767
KLM	1-800/225-2525	0208/750-9000
Lufthansa	1-800/645-3880	0345/737747
Northwest Airlines	1-800/225-2525	01293/561000
Quantas	1-800/227-4500	0345/747767
SAS	1-800/221-2350	0207/734-4020
Southwest Airlines	1-800/435-9792	---------
Swissair	1-866/245-6654	---------
United Airlines	1-800/241-6522	0800/888555
US Airways	1-800/428-4322	0800/777333
Virgin Atlantic	1-800/862-8621	01293/747747

Packages vs. Tours

When it comes to travel lingo, most people confuse packages and tours. In the industry, a tour usually refers to a group that travels together, follows a flag-toting leader, and is herded on and off buses. Obviously, we seldom recommend this kind of mindlessness.

A package, on the other hand, is a travel deal in which several components of a trip — transportation, accommodation, airport transfers and the like— are bundled together for sale to independent, unescorted travelers. Many independent travelers purchase complete vacations from travel agents without ever knowing that they are buying a package. That's OK — packages can offer great values. Package companies buy in bulk, and are often able to sell complete vacations for less than you'd pay when buying each component individually.

TAXI

339

Cars & Driving

Don't bring a car into New York City. It's stupid to drive around the city if you don't have to. Traffic is horrendous and during business hours it's usually much faster to take the subway. Street parking is difficult to find; garage parking is super expensive (from $20 to $40 a day), and the fines for illegal parking are steep. Worse yet, you may return to your vehicle's parking spot only to find it has been towed—an expensive and stressful experience not worth risking.

Rentals

Rent a car only if you're ▮▮▮▮▮ to travel extensively outside ▮▮▮. Be aware that prices for car rentals from Manhattan and the three area airports are the highest in the nation—by far. And the big international car-rental firms are the most expensive. Rates do vary, but expect to pay about $80 a day and $450 a week including unlimited mileage for a two-door tin can. Compare Avis (tel. 800/331-1212), Budget (tel. 800/527-0700), Hertz (tel. 800/654-3131), and National (tel. 800/227-7368). Note that visitors from overseas can secure better deals if they book and prepay before leaving for the United States.

Local rental firms are cheaper, but their cars are decidedly w▮▮e. Try Aamcar, 303 West 96th S▮ btw. West End Ave/Riverside Drive; tel. 1-212/222-8500).

The best way to cut costs is to take a train to the sticks to pick up your rental. Ramp Ford, 4869 Nesconset Hwy, Port Jefferson (tel. 631/473-1550) rents compact cars for about $40 a day.

THE MAJOR CAR RENTAL COMPANIES

Alamo	800/327-9633	702/263-8411	www.freeways.com
Avis	800/331-1212	702/261-5595	www.avis.com
Budget	800/527-0700	702/736-1212	www.budgetrentacar.com
Dollar	800/800-3665	702/739-8408	www.dollarcar.com
Enterprise	800/736-8222	702/795-8842	www.pickenterprise.com
Hertz	800/654-3131	702/736-4900	www.hertz.com
National	800/227-7368	702/261-5391	www.nationalcar.com
Rent-A-Wreck	800/535-1391	702/474-0037	www.rentawreck.com
Thrifty	800/367-2277	702/896-7600	www.thrifty.com

Document Regulations

Brits, Kiwis, South Africans and, most Euros don't need a visa to enter the US for less than 90 days. A passport with an expiration date at least six months later than the scheduled end of your visit to the United States and a round-trip (return) ticket are usually required for entry, along with proof of sufficient funds.

Citizens of most other countries, including those of Australia, must also obtain a tourist visa, available from US embassies and consulates.

Canadians can enter the US without passports or visas, and need only proof of residence.

Medical Requirements

Inoculations are not normally required to enter the United States.

Customs Requirements

Each adult visitor may bring into the US free of duty: one liter of wine or hard liquor; 200 cigarettes or 100 cigars or three pounds of smoking tobacco; and $100 worth of gifts. Stupidly, no goods are allowed in from Cuba, North Korea, Libya, and other enemies of the US. It's also *verboten* to bring foodstuffs (particularly cheese, fruit, cooked meats, and canned goods) and plants (including vegetables and seeds). Foreign visitors may import up to $10,000 in US or foreign currency with no formalities; you're allowed to move larger sums, but they must be declared to Customs upon entering.

Insurance

Because there is no national health system in the United States and medical care is extremely expensive, we strongly advise you to wait until you return home before you fall ill. Failing that, you might wish to take out a travel-insurance policy that covers sickness or injury costs. Travel insurance is often available through automobile clubs and travel agencies.

Dollars & Dont's

The almighty dollar is the coin of the realm, and is divided into 100 cents. Greenbacks come in $1, $5, $10, $20, $50, and $100 denominations. If you encounter a $2 bill, think about keeping it as a souvenir—everyone else does.

Coins are minted in 1¢ (one cent or "penny"), 5¢ (five cents or "nickel"), 10¢ (10 cents or "dime") and 25¢ (25 cents or "quarter") denominations. Although they exist, you will rarely encounter 50¢ (50 cents or "half dollar") or $1 ("buck") coins.

"Foreign-exchange bureaus" that are common in Europe and Asia are rare in the US—they don't even exist at many airports in the United States. Don't even think of trying to exchange foreign currency outside most major US cities.

Travelers New Yorkese

New Yorkese	Translation
The City	Manhattan
The Met	Both the Metropolitan Opera and the Metropolitan Museum of Art
The Garden	Madison Square Garden
The Village	Greenwich Village
MoMA	Museum of Modern Art
The Island	Long Island
Hero	Sub sandwich
Pie	A whole pizza
Slice	A single piece of cheese pizza
Regular coffee	Cream, no sugar
A schmeer	Cream cheese
Egg cream	Seltzer, milk, and chocolate syrup
Mayo	Mayonnaise
Stand *on* line	Stand *in* line
Sneakers	Tennis shoes
Water fountain	Drinking fountain
Washda closendaws	What you do on the subway

Traveler's Cheques

Traveler's cheques denominated in US dollars are accepted at most hotels and restaurants, as well as in larger stores. Do not bring traveler's cheques denominated in other currencies as nobody will know what to do with them.

You'll find the best exchange rates at **American Express** (tel. 800/528-4800 for the nearest location), where checks from all issuers are exchanged commission-free. Some restaurants and many hotels will exchange traveler's cheques, but their rates are always much worse than banks'.

Credit & Charge Cards

The US practically runs on credit. The federal government is overextended, and so are most of the country's citizens. Yes, credit cards are accepted virtually everywhere. MasterCard (EuroCard in Europe, Access in Britain, Chargex in Canada), Visa (Barclaycard in Britain), American Express, Diners Club, Discover, and Carte Blanche are not only accepted in most hotels, restaurants, and retail stores, but are increasingly the payment of choice in food and liquor stores as well. Most ATMs accept credit cards for cash advances (be sure to have a Personal Identification Number).

Essentials for Foreigners

Business Hours Most offices are open Monday through Friday from 9am to 5pm. Stores are usually open daily, including Sunday. Banks are usually open Monday through Friday from 9am to 3 or 4pm; 24-hour automated-teller machines (ATMs) are installed at most banks and many other places as well.

Climate Average monthly temperatures are listed above. Check avantguide.com. for this week's weather conditions.

Computers/Internet If you have trouble jacking in, visit EasyEverything, 234 West 42nd St (btw Seventh/Eighth Aves) a cyber spot with 648 PCs that's the choice of NYs digerati.

Currency Exchange In New York, visit American Express (tel. 1-800/528-4800 for the nearest location). They exchange foreign currency commission-free, and offer competitive rates.

Drinking Laws In the US you can be drafted into the military at age 18, but you must be 21 to legally purchase alcohol. Go figure. Beware that New York City enforces an open-container law, which prohibits drinking alcohol in parks and other public places. That's why you see all those folks in summer walking around with brown bags.

Electricity 110-120 volts AC, 60 cycles. European appliances need to be plugged into converters.

Embassies/Consulates In addition to embassies, all of which are located in Washington, DC, many countries maintain consulates in major US cities. In addition, most countries staff a mission to the United Nations in New York City.

The embassy of **Canada** is at 501 Pennsylvania Ave. NW, Washington, DC 20001 (tel. 1-202/682-1740). There are Canadian consulates in New York, Los Angeles, Atlanta, Buffalo (NY), Chicago, Dallas, Detroit, Miami, Minneapolis, and Seattle. The embassy of the **United Kingdom** is at 3100 Massachusetts Ave. NW, Washington, DC 20008 (tel. 1-202/462-1340). British consulates are located in New York, Los Angeles, Atlanta, Boston, Chicago, Houston, Miami, and San Francisco. There are also consular offices in many other secondary cities. The embassy of the **Republic of Ireland** is at 2234 Massachusetts Ave. NW, Washington, DC 20008 (tel. 1-202/462-3939). There are Irish consulates in New York, San Francisco, Boston, and Chicago. The embassy of **Australia** is at 1601 Massachusetts Ave. NW, Washington, DC 20036 (tel. 1-202/797-3000). Australian consulates are located in New York, Los Angeles, Atlanta, Honolulu, Houston, Miami, and San Francisco. The embassy of **New Zealand** is at 37 Observatory Circle NW, Washington, DC 20008

TAXI

343

(tel. 1-202/328-4848). There is a New Zealand consulate in Los Angeles.

Emergencies 911 is the number to call to report a fire, to call the police, or get an ambulance. From public telephones no coins are required for a 911 call.

Gasoline (Petrol) One US gallon equals 3.8 liters or .85 Imperial gallons. Most gas stations offer lower-priced "self-service" gas pumps and several grades of gas; fill your rental with the cheapest, usually 87 octane, which is referred to as "regular."

Holidays Banks, government offices, post offices, and many stores, restaurants, and museums are closed on the following legal national holidays: January 1 (New Year's Day), the third Monday in January (Martin Luther King Day), the third Monday in February (Presidents' Day, Washington's Birthday), the last Monday in May (Memorial Day), July 4 (Independence Day), the first Monday in September (Labor Day), the second Monday in October (Columbus Day), November 11 (Veterans Day/Armistice Day), the last Thursday in November (Thanksgiving Day), and December 25 (Christmas). Also, the Tuesday following the first Monday in November is Election Day, and is a legal holiday in presidential-election years.

Information (see Chapter 2/Information).

Taxes There is no VAT or any other national sales tax in the US. Instead, each state and municipality is entitled to levy its own tariff on purchases, and these range from nothing to about 8.5%. Hotel "bed" taxes can be 15% or more. Taxes are already figured in to some services, including transportation, telephone calls, and gasoline, otherwise they are tacked on at the register.

In New York, the combined city and state sales taxes amount to 8.25%. The local hotel-occupancy tax is 13.25%.

Telephone/Fax The cost of a phone call varies widely in the US, depending on which private carrier you are using. Local calls made from public pay phones cost between 20¢ and 35¢. In New York City they cost 25¢ for the first three minutes.

Long-distance and international calls can be dialed directly from almost any phone. Because most American pay phones don't accept "smart" cards, it can be both expensive and unwieldy to call long distance on a roll of quarters. Pre-paid phone cards are the cheapest way to go.

= Public Holidays =

January 1	New Year's Day
January (3rd Monday)	Martin Luther King's Birthday (observed)
February (3rd Monday)	Presidents' Day
May (last Monday)	Memorial Day (observed)
July 4	Independence Day
September (1st Monday)	Labor Day
October (2nd Monday)	Columbus Day
November 11	Veterans Day
November (4th Thursday)	Thanksgiving
December 25	Christmas Day

These are usually sold in denominations of $10 and $20, and are available at newsstands and drug stores throughout New York City.

When calling from the US to other parts of the United States or to Canada, dial 1 followed by the area code and the seven-digit number. For international calls, dial 011 followed by the country code (Australia, 61; Republic of Ireland, 353; New Zealand, 64; United Kingdom, 44), the city code, and the telephone number of the person you wish to call.

Be forewarned that hotel surcharges on both long-distance and local calls can be astronomical. Think about using a public pay phone in the lobby.

For local directory assistance (a.k.a. "information" or "directory inquiries"), dial 411; for long-distance information, dial 1, then the appropriate area code and 555-1212.

Time > The contiguous United States is divided into four time zones. From west to east, these are: Pacific Standard Time (PST), Mountain Standard Time (MST), Central Standard Time (CST) and Eastern Standard Time (EST).

New York is usually five hours behind Greenwich Mean Time. Daylight-saving time, which moves the clock one hour ahead of standard time, is in effect from the last Sunday in April through the last Saturday in October.

Tipping > Hourly wages in the service industry are very low as waiters, bartenders, and the like are expected to make the bulk of their money from tips. That's the reason why service in America is so good compared to Europe. Here are the rules of thumb: Restaurants, bars, and nightclubs: 15% of the check to waiters; $1 per drink to bartenders; $1 per garment to check-room attendants; $1 to parking valets, when they retrieve your car. Cab drivers: 15% of the fare. Hotel personnel: $1 per piece to bellhops; $10 per service to the concierge, especially if you plan on staying there again. Airports: $1 per piece to redcaps. Hairdressers: 15 to 20 percent, provided they didn't scalp you.

VideoSystem > NTSC

TAXI
345

Planning — *International Systems of Measurements*

Length

1 inch (in.)	= 2.54 cm		
1 foot (ft.)	= 12 in.	= 30.48 cm	= .305 m
1 yard	= 3 ft.	= .915 m	
1 mile (mi.)	= 5,280 ft.	= 1.609 km	

miles to kilometers
multiply the number of miles by 1.61
(100 miles x 1.61 = 161 km).

kilometers to miles
multiply the number of kilometers by .62
(100 km x .62 = 62 miles).

Liquid Volume

1 fluid ounce (fl. oz.)	= .03 liter		
1 pint	= 16 fl. oz.	= .47 liter	
1 quart	= 2 pints	= .94 liter	
1 gallon (gal.)	= 4 quarts	= 3.79 liter	
	= .83 Imperial gal.		

US gallons to liters
multiply the number of gallons by 3.79
(10 gal. x 3.79 = 37.9 liters).
US gallons to Imperial gallons
multiply the number of US gallons by .83
(10 US gal. x .83 = 8.3 Imperial gal.).
liters to US gallons
multiply the number of liters by .26
(10 liters x .26 = 2.6 US gal.).
Imperial gallons to US gallons
multiply the number of Imperial gallons by 1.2
(10 Imperial gal. x 1.2 = 12 US gal.).

Temperature

degrees Fahrenheit to degrees Celsius
subtract 32 from °F, multiply by 5, then
    divide by 9 (85 °F - 32 x 5 ÷ 9 = 29.4 °C).
degrees Celsius to degrees Fahrenheit
multiply °C by 9, divide by 5, and add 32
(20 °C x 9 ÷ 5 + 32 = 68 °F).

Area

1 acre = .41 hectare
1 square mile (sq. mi.) = 640 acres
    2.59 hectares = 2.6 km²

acres to hectares
multiply the number of acres by .41
(10 acres x .41 = 4.1ha).
square miles to square kilometers
multiply the number of square miles by 2.6
(10 sq. mi. x 2.6 = 26 km²)
hectares to acres
multiply the number of hectares by 2.47
(10 ha x 2.47 = 24.7 acres).
square kilometers to square miles
multiply the number of square kilometers by .39
(100 km² x .39 = 39 sq. mi.).

Weight

1 ounce (oz.) = 28.35 grams
1 pound (lb.) = 16 oz. = 453.6 grams = .45 kilograms
1 ton = 2,000 lb. = 907 kilograms = .91 metric ton

pounds to kilograms
multiply the number of pounds by .45
(10 lb. x .45 = 4.5 kg).
kilograms to pounds
multiply the number of kilograms by 2.2
(10 kg x 2.2 = 22 lb.).

#11
Indexes

TAXI

355

index #11

TAXI

353

TAXI

35'

#.11 index

Book Index